MIMICS – THE OTHERS AMONG US

Dedicated to Our Friend Timothy Green Beckley
(Mr. UFO)

God Speed with Your Journey on the Mothership.

MIMICS – THE OTHERS AMONG US

ZONTAR PRESS

Mimics – The Others Among Us

By Sean Casteel & Tim R. Swartz

Contributors: Timothy Green Beckley, Scott Corrales, Paul Eno, Chris Holly, Hercules Invictus, Philip Kinsella, Brent Raynes, Paul Dale Roberts, Gene Steinberg, Lon Strickler, Nigel Watson, John Weigle

Foreword by Brian Young

Copyright © 2023 by Sean Casteel, Tim R. Swartz
dba Zontar Press

ISBN: 979-8-9866449-2-9

Published in the United States of America
By Zontar Press

www.conspiracyjournal.com

FOREWORD

When Tim Swartz contacted me to ask if I would write a foreword to the book he and Sean Casteel had just finished two thoughts went through my head. First thought, why would Tim ask his most skeptical friend to write it? My second thought was, "YES, Hell Yes!" Being a fan of Tim's work as a writer and researcher I was honored to be asked. I just couldn't pass up the opportunity.

So, let's address the elephant in the room. I said it, I am a skeptic. That simply means I want convincing evidence before I believe something. I am NOT a blanket denier. Sadly, too many "skeptics" seem to be. One must have an open mind if they want to find the truth when possible.

As a historian, I am aware that mimics, in one shape or another (pun intended), seem to be a part of every culture, civilization and religion. Wherever there were people there were legends, myths, stories, and folklore. Call it what you will. However, mimics, by one name or another, have always seemed to be with us.

The prophets, seers and sages passed along tales of angels, daemons, witches, shapeshifters, and creatures both benevolent and malevolent. These tales were often meant to be allegorical. Morality tales used to educate, or in extreme cases, indoctrinate the public. At times, mimics are nothing more than mythological in nature, often used to explain the unexplainable. As humankind's understanding of their world grew, some of these creatures vanished. They were relegated to folklore and fantasy. Only to be replaced by newer, more creative proxies.

Mimics are also a crucial part of our pop culture. For example, Superman is a mimic, an alien who walks among us. Clark Kent is a true mimic hiding in plain sight. Science fiction is littered with aliens, alien/human hybrids, and men in black. The newest darlings of mimics come in the forms of clones and Artificial Intelligence. The Horror film genre, of which I am a self-admitted addict, gives us just about every kind of mimic. Vampires, Monsters, ghosts, the undead, demons, and shadow people are omnipresent. Perhaps this is because these legends are ingrained in our unconscious minds. Are we wired to acknowledge and fear these entities? If so, why?

It isn't just in popular fiction. Depending on which poll you choose to believe, somewhere between 44-80% of Americans believes in angels and 39-85% believes in aliens. Interesting side note, the belief in angels continues to drop every year, where just the opposite is true for aliens.

So, what are these beings? I have no shame in admitting, "I don't know!" Whether you are a believer or a skeptic, the fact remains that the world we share is complex. There are things that we may never understand. However, that shouldn't stop us from asking questions.

I would like to finish by saying the authors have done incredible research into both historical and contemporary mimics. The finished product is a truly fascinating study into the topic. As a result, the book may pose more questions than it answers, which I enjoy.

Oh, I finally realized why Tim Swartz asked me to write this foreword. He knew if I were asked, "Are mimics real?" I would be honest enough to respond, "I don't know!"

-Brian Young

CONTENTS

There are beings that lurk in the shadows, hiding their true forms from human eyes. These are the hidden ones, the masters of disguise, the creatures that walk among us.

INTRODUCTION

THE OTHERS AMONG US

Tim R. Swartz

It's not a new idea...that we're not alone...that the Earth is also home to "others"; others who look like us...others who act like us...others who secretly live among us. Ghosts, angels, demons, extraterrestrials, interdimensional travelers, etc. We have tried throughout the centuries to put names to that which tries to remain hidden and unnamable. Nevertheless, despite their efforts to keep to the threshold of human awareness, it's clear the others have been with us since the beginning, taking on the roles of teachers, messengers, protectors, tricksters and adversaries.

There are countless science fiction novels and movies whose plot involves "the others" in one form or another. John Carpenter's film "They Live" is probably the best known example of a world that has been infiltrated and controlled by an extraterrestrial race.

Modern UFO lore, from the very beginning of the 1950s contactee era, referenced how the Venusians, along with other visitors from nearby planets, looked so much like us that they managed to clandestinely secure jobs in major corporations and even high-ranking political positions. This paranoid viewpoint was a good reflection of the world politics of the 1950s and 60s.

Comic books and television illustrated how the possibility of extraterrestrial visitors reflected some of the anxieties of that time.

11

One good example comes from the comic "There are Martians Among Us," from *Amazing Fantasy #15 (1962)*. In the comic, a search party gathers around a landed alien craft, but they can find no sign of alien beings. Radio announcers warn those nearby to stay indoors. The action shifts to a husband and wife as he prepares to ignore the warning and leave their home. As he waves goodbye he reminds his wife to stay inside. The wife, however, decides to slip out to the store and is attacked and dragged off. The husband returns home and, finding it empty, runs towards the telephone in a panic. In a twist, the anxious husband reveals that he and his wife are the Martians.

The fear that there might be alien enemies in our midst resonates with fears of Soviets and communists from the McCarthy era. Ultimately, in this story, the humans are the ones who accost and capture the alien woman. The shift in perspective puts the humans in the position of the monsters.

WALK LIKE A MAN

Age-old mythologies and religious texts throughout history brim with tales of beings that resemble humans in appearance or character. According to Wikipedia, these humanoids can pass unnoticed in human society. Often it is their oddly shaped eyes that give them away, but the differences are usually small enough as to not attract attention. Sometimes they live separated from society, live in alternative realities, or appear at night or under specific circumstances. This category includes witches, elves, fairies, nymphs, and house spirits.

The deities of pagan religions were often said to disguise themselves as humans. The Greek god Zeus was said to be particularly fond of taking on the form of a human in order to discretely conduct his business on Earth. According to the Torah, angels always appeared in human disguises. Philosophy professor Peter Kreeft, in his book "*Angels and Demons: What Do We Really Know About*

Them?" - 1995, Ignatius Press, asserted that when an angel wears its human disguise, mortal beings cannot penetrate the disguise due to the superior abilities angels possess.

Religions such as Hinduism, Buddhism, and Native American beliefs have traditions where gods and spirits descend to Earth in human form to help or hinder humanity. In Native American myths "the sun, moon, and morning star seem free to take human form and roam the Earth, seeking love and other adventures." ("*American Indian Myths And Legends*" - 1984, Random House).

Throughout Europe, faeries, leprechauns, elves and other elemental-type creatures were known in folklore to have the ability to use "glamour" to make them appear to be human...so much so that they could fall in love with a person, marry and have children. It wasn't until they had to return to the "fairy kingdom" that their true identity was revealed. There are also the "Changelings," faeries who had been left in place of a human child or baby who had been stolen by the faeries.

Supernatural creatures like vampires and werewolves were said to have the ability to take human form when needed. These were different, though from the "shapeshifters"... creatures that may temporarily disguise or transform into a human shape, but their true forms are entirely different.

The shapeshifting alien is especially popular among those who think that mankind is controlled by a race of reptiles that either evolved on planet Earth, then left to explore the cosmos only to return and find the planet now controlled by talking apes, or the other theory, which contends that the reptilians are visitors from some other star system who came to Earth and infiltrated ancient civilizations in order to control all humans.

It's thought the reptilians, over the centuries, bred with humans to form crossbreeds so they can control us by making us dumber, slower, weaker and easier to control. They are believed to be able to take on human forms by creating vibrations that give us the illusion that they are human. These reptiles control us by creating wars and mindless entertainment to keep us distracted. Some parts of the political cult Qanon, a well known right-wing conspiracy group, have embraced the reptilian idea to help demonize their political opponents.

LUIS ELIZONDO RESPONDS TO QUESTION ABOUT MIMICRY

Former Pentagon Director of the Advanced Aerospace Threat Identification Program (AATIP) Luis Elizondo, in an interview on "Theories of Everything with Curt Jaimungal," was asked "Is there any evidence that these X (aliens, creatures, future humans) can shapeshift, can look like other humans or other creatures?"

Elizondo answered: "You know, I don't know, but I'll tell you, mimicry is something that is common in nature, and it's even common in what we do. There are species who use mimicry to defend themselves in the animal kingdom. Let's take a coral snake versus a king snake. The coral snake is very deadly, while the king snake has the same colors except that the color arrangements are in opposite order. These animals mimic other animals, for example, for protection.

"So if there is a species that is far more advanced than human beings, it's not inconceivable – look, we can go to the panda exhibit in the zoo in China and see that zookeepers will often wear these – and it appears quite ridiculous to us, but not so ridiculous to the pandas – the zookeepers are required to wear a panda suit, big furry teddy bear suits.

"They do that, so that when they go into the enclosure to clean up the enclosure and whatnot, provide food, they don't disrupt the panda population, or at least as little as possible. Of course it's entertaining to us as humans to see a bunch of people walking in furry suits, but at the end of the day it's effective.

"So I don't think it's inconceivable. The problem is that, when we start going down the road, when you say 'shapeshifting' and things like that, immediately we start going into the world of 'woo' and the paranormal, and there is nothing wrong with that.

"You know, I've written articles on the paranormal, and everything in science, by definition, is paranormal until it becomes normal, frankly. So the problem is that we don't have hard evidence. We have a lot of anecdotal evidence, a lot of people report seeing things, that these UAP can look like an aircraft, that sometimes they disguise themselves as a 747 or that the occupants can make themselves look like human beings.

"I don't really know. During our time in AATIP we were focused primarily on the nuts- and-bolts of these UAPs, and what our military witnesses and collection capabilities were telling us at the time was that we didn't have any reports of 'shapeshifting.'"

THE HUMAN ALIEN

Since I brought up aliens in the previous sections of this introduction, I can note that the "human-looking" alien (HLA) associated with the UFO phenomena is a subject that will be discussed throughout this book. It can't be avoided, as it is one of the more controversial parts of the UFO phenomena. This is because if one considers that UFOs (at least some UFOs) are physical spaceships from other planets, the occupants 99% of the time are described by witnesses as humanoid in appearance.

This is just speculation of course, but it appears unlikely that the universe is filled with intelligent life that evolved the human-type shape. Namely, one head, two arms, and two legs for bipedal motion. There could be all kinds of explanations, and these will be discussed by our team of investigators and writers who contributed to this book.

The website newanimals.org, which deals more with cryptozoology than aliens, lists five possible explanations for the HLA phenomena that should be of interest to readers.

#1: HLA are not real (i.e. hoaxes, misidentification or hallucination).

#2: HLA are from another planet.

#3: HLA are actually advanced technology secretly created by modern governments.

#4: HLA are from some other dimension of reality (usually explained as paranormal, sometimes explained with weird physics).

HLA #5: Aliens are actually a species of human, a species that developed high technology ages ago and then retreated to a secluded life in underground or underwater bases or on other planets.

If HLA are real and idea #5 is true, then aliens would be the opposite of Bigfoot. Instead of being more primitive humanoids, they could be more advanced, or at least our intellectual equals. They could be our hominid cousins that decided sometime in the past that humans were too dangerous and withdrew to hiding places all over the planet.

It is an interesting concept that was suggested, in a fashion, by John Keel in his book "*Our Haunted Planet.*"

"One basic fact should be obvious from the foregoing: these entities and things are not necessarily from some other planet. They are actually closely tied to the human race, are a part of our immediate environment in some unfathomable fashion, and to a very large extent are primarily concerned with misleading us, misinforming us, and playing games with us. These mysterious members of H.G. Wells

'Wings Over the World' are our benefactors and our enemies. They educate us and they torment us. They have given us hope, guided our religions and philosophies, and watched us crawl out of the caves and build rockets to the moon."

These creatures push the limits of what it means to be human. What do we do with something that is so similar to us but at the same time so completely different? What does it say about us as humans if these creatures make us question our own humanity?

"Living among us undetected may be creatures (not necessarily alien) with all the outward appearances of human beings," Ufologist Alex Saunders wrote in "Quest Magazine," October 1969. "The mimic would of necessity be a 'lone wolf,' likely living in a large, bustling city where the eccentric and the odd may flourish unhindered. For it is a curious fact of nature that that which is in plain view is often best hidden."

STRANGE GIRL DRESSED LIKE A BALLERINA

On a pleasant Saturday afternoon in 2004, Winchester councilor Adrian Hicks encountered someone so odd it made him think that he had seen a real live extraterrestrial. At the time, Hicks was a Lib Dem councilor for the city of Winchester, located in Hampshire, England.

In either January or February 2004, Hicks was strolling down the city's busy High Street. He said: "I was near The Works bookshop when I saw this strange woman, a humanoid walking with a penguin-like gait. She was dressed somewhat like a ballerina, with very large prominent eyes and was twirling her hands in a circular motion.

"She seemed friendly and totally at ease with us. She wasn't scared; she was smiling, and seemed to be enjoying herself among us. She walked very slowly up the High Street. I remember she was very interested in the clock over Lloyds Bank. She was taking it all in.

"She was human enough to get away with it. Everybody's heads were turning."

Councilor Hicks, an orthopedic technician in the A&E department at the Royal Hampshire County Hospital for some 35 years, said he saw the creature at about 1:30 PM and urged others who witnessed the strange girl to come forward. He is certain that at least one woman took photos. He added: "This was definitely a close encounter of the first kind.

Drawing of the strange "alien" girl seen by Winchester councilor
Adrian Hicks in 2004.

"I was very confused and shocked. I was going to say 'excuse me, you're not from around here?' but I thought at the time it was best to leave her alone. However, now I regret not plucking up the courage to speak to her."

Our friend the "alien ballerina" is a perfect example of the mysterious beings that may be living among us...secretly, quietly. They may have been with us since the beginning of our own days on planet Earth. Or they may be recent arrivals, slowly infiltrating humankind for purposes that are known only to them. It should be pointed out that in nature, mimicry is used for one of two reasons:

1. As a disguise in order not to be eaten by a sneaky predator. 2. As a disguise so a sneaky predator can catch and eat something.

Whatever the reasons, it does bring into question what it is to be human, and to consider that we need to look beyond surface appearances before any judgments are made.

Such creatures tap into deep, unconscious fears. Things that are familiar to us can elicit the darkest terrors. When any person we meet might be a shapeshifter, or when our friends might be extraterrestrials, or when our newborns seem strange and somehow different, everything changes for us.

Who are the mysterious "others"? Beings who look like us and try to pass themselves off as human, but clearly aren't. These mimics of man apparently have been with us throughout history, but the question remains: Who, or what, are they?

SHADOWS OF A PARALLEL HUMANITY

Scott Corrales

Trying to find the right quote to kick off a chapter is often elusive, but not so in this case. What are we to make of the possibility – nay, the likelihood – that a "shadow humanity" lives among us? Nearly perfect doppelgängers who walk our streets, travel our roads and perhaps even sail our oceans without attracting the least bit of attention until something slips, much like a CGI creation (a "synthespian" in industry parlance) given away by too perfect dental work, a much too perfect jaw line or eye color bordering on the unreal. Paul Eluard, the French surrealist, is best remembered by his dictum that "There are other worlds, but they are in this one." Without too much effrontery, one could rework his saying into "There is another humanity, and it lurks among us."

Those of us who grew up on the steady diet of science fiction that John Keel cautioned us about in *"The Mothman Prophecies"* have no problem grasping the concept. "Lost in Space" introduced us to protagonist John Robinson's anti-matter double in 1967s "The Anti-Matter Man" – an identical version of the hero, but cruel and calculating, supplanting the professor among his loved ones. Perhaps more to the point are the aliens in "The Invaders"— creatures able to produce perfect simulacra of human beings, but with a creepy internal structure and, of course, the trademark little finger. One of the most poignant moments in the series is when one such creation, portrayed by Susan Strasberg, decides to flee her alien originators to live a normal human existence. "My life is valuable to me," she declares at one point. It doesn't get much more human than that.

THE MAN WHO CAME FROM NOWHERE

Spanish researcher Salvador Freixedo described a singular case, which revolved around the love affair between a well-to-do Venezuelan woman named Lula and a thoroughly unusual man known only as Jorge, in his book *"La Granja Humana."* After a courtship laden with supernatural events, the couple married, and the strange man proved to be a wonderful husband, although he remained particularly adamant about not discussing his origins, relatives or livelihood. Lula jokingly accused him of not being human – a charge which Jorge never really denied. For her peace of mind and that of her relatives, he said that he was the son of Argentinean immigrants and the owner of a small printing shop that never seemed to transact any business.

The couple's friends testified to Jorge's astounding powers of precognition – he could accurately foretell the future to the extent of adjusting his behavior beforehand. He possessed superhuman physical prowess, doing things that would have proven lethal for a normal person. Jorge would go to the beach on the worst possible days, challenging the waves and swimming miles away from the shore to the distress of lifeguards. Upon emerging from the water hours later, he would gallop at full speed up and down the length of the beach, to the amazement of onlookers. People driving along the road opposite the shore would stop their cars to witness the spectacular display of locomotion.

In spite of his prowess, Jorge's health was far from good. He would complain to Lula that the "atmosphere" was killing him, and would often lapse into catatonia, recovering enough to take a whiff from a small crystal vial that he always kept close at hand, recovering completely in seconds. Lula was warned many times to resist the temptation to look into the vial or try to sniff it. On one occasion, she weakened while her husband was in one of his trances. Suddenly, she heard him say, "Lula, quit fooling around with it."

The respiratory problems continued until Jorge lapsed into a coma from which he did not emerge. A medical technician took a few X-rays of Jorge's lungs, and was stunned to discover that the patient had no lungs whatsoever. The attending physician berated the technician for his carelessness, and ordered that a new set of X-rays be produced. The result was the same. Not only did Lula's mystery husband not have a pulmonary apparatus, he had some bizarre organs that were foreign to human anatomy.

Before dying, Jorge instructed a servant to buy several yards of bandages, stating that his corpse was to be swathed in bandages like a mummy and silver coins were to be placed between his fingers. No autopsy, he said, was to be performed. Lula insisted on complying with her husband's wishes and allowed no autopsy. Eight years later, she informed Freixedo that the time limit imposed by law for exhuming a body would be up soon, and she would like him and other friends to be present at the exhumation.

Freixedo travelled to Caracas, only to learn that Lula's whereabouts were unknown to her mother and friends. This, he states, is where interaction between non-humans and humans acquires a negative cast. Lula had allegedly experienced terrible bad luck after following the orders given by a nocturnal apparition that claimed to be Jorge's spirit. Apparently, she was told that she "had a mission to perform" (a message given to many contactees, from Moses on down). As of 1989, Lula was still missing.

In the year 2022, the knee-jerk reaction is to say that "Jorge" was a human facsimile cleverly crafted by a shrewd extraterrestrial presence, observing human behavior to ascertain whether Earth is ready for admission to some galactic polity or another, as the ETH cargo cult owns ufology lock stock and spaceship. But it is more intriguing to suppose that he was a member of this 'cryptohumanity' which has been with us forever, perhaps even predating us, given names that vary from culture to culture (Sidhe, Djinn, etc.).

Furthermore, at no point did Lula think that her unusual husband was in any way extraterrestrial – those hoping for a Hispanic Mork from Ork will have to look elsewhere. She described him to Freixedo as an outstanding spouse and a loving father to her children from a first marriage. His psychic abilities, on the other hand, could be disturbing, particularly the gift of precognition. "He used precognition as something quite ordinary. In many cases he foresaw and predicted the future and adjusted his behavior accordingly, either refraining from embarking on a course of action or else engaging in activities that the future would keep him from doing," writes Freixedo, who goes on to describe an incident on a Venezuelan highway while the couple drove along in their car. Jorge suddenly became alarmed, telling Lula that a truck some distance away was about to crash. To her astonishment, a passenger car merged too quickly from the right and hit the vehicle, causing it to overturn.

The couple had no offspring, so prurient thoughts of a "hybridization operation" by unseen forces can be set aside. The relationship brings to mind legends of sylphs and undines and their relationships with humans, such as the story of a 19th century Parisian bookseller who was able to locate any printed work for his clients, supposedly thanks to the assistance of an undine with whom he had dealings. We can even go back to the early days of Rome, before the trappings of republic or empire, when king Numa Pompilius ruled the city, guided by the wise counsel of the nymph Egeria. Skeptics snort and dismiss all these entities as figments of ancient imagination, the stuff of mythology and Renaissance statuary.

Jorge's breathtaking prowess as a swimmer, the affection of the undines toward humans, could lead one to believe that of all the non-human, para-human, crypto-human orders, these have the greatest affinity toward our own species. But the water elementals have a darker aspect in both Mesoamerican and European tradition, so a closer look at the "chaneques" is in order.

Tradition holds that the "chaneques" are the spirits of either dead, unbaptized children or adult humans who died by drowning. A researcher who spent some time in Mexico spoke to a number of shy peasant girls, who described how the creatures would have a good time playing in the water basin behind their homes; the elusive beings would cause the crockery left to soak in the basin to rattle. In their tradition," chaneques" were aquatic beings, swimming in and out of the basin through its drainpipe. Another man explained that he had witnessed the apparition of his grandfather, a fisherman who had drowned at sea, now converted into one of these beings. He explained that when these creatures appear at night, the purpose is to drown humans and add them to their ranks; apparitions by day are to impart wisdom.

While some may find this folklore charming and having nothing to do with serious matters like ufology, there is a strong point of contact that should not be overlooked: the disappearance at sea of Dominican celebrity Freddy Miller, who supposedly reappeared as a changed being.

On May 5, 1959, a boat sailed out of the Dominican Republic carrying 45-year-old television producer and director Freddy Miller and his passengers (two women and two children) and disappeared without a trace. Fourteen years later, on September 22, 1973, insurance salesman Virgilio Gómez was driving along the highway to service a new account when he saw a person waving him down by the roadside.

According to Gómez, a man in a green outfit informed him that he was Freddy Miller, adding that he had "supposedly" drowned along with some other people, but that he had in fact been rescued by a modern device, "a module known to people as a UFO."

The witness remarked that his alien interlocutor had a disgusting grayish-yellow skin tone that he found repulsive, spoke in a thick, deliberate voice and was virtually hairless. The entity's body was covered by a form-fitting green coverall without zippers or pockets.

In 1980, Luis Ramirez Reyes, one of Mexico's foremost UFO writers, had an experience of this nature during a stay at his friend Dr. Paco Medina's country house in Moyotepec, Morelos state. He had originally accepted the invitation to the country retreat to investigate a tree on the property which had allegedly been zapped by a passing UFO for no apparent reason. Upon reaching the site, Ramírez was able to confirm the unusual damage to the tree. Since the hour was late, both he and his host turned in for the night. It was to prove one of the most frightening nights in the ufologist's life.

As he drifted off to sleep, a heavy weight dropped beside him in the guest room bed. Ramírez awoke with a start, thinking a snake may have dropped onto the bed from the rafters. Frozen in place, he managed to extend a hand to feel what it was that had fallen into the bed. To his complete astonishment, the bed was empty. The following day, he had the opportunity to speak with the children who performed housekeeping duties for his host, and was startled when they calmly told him that he had been visited by dwarves. "They are like children, but we call them 'chaneques' here," he was informed. "They play with us when we sweep and mop the house."

Unwilling to be the victim of childish pranks, the investigator subjected the youngsters to a cross-examination in Dr. Medina's. They indicated that the entities would chase the children around whenever they arrived; allegedly out of fear of being harmed by adult humans, the entities remained invisible, but could be clearly seen by young humans, who described them as being large-headed, bald, slender, and for modesty's sake, clad in "cloth shorts."

Ramírez's host later informed him that both he and his family had been subjected to the nocturnal antics of these "chaneques" more than once, to the extent that his wife refused to return to the country house. The creatures could be persuaded to desist by asking them to do so "using kind words."

This experience convinced Ramírez of the interdimensional origin of these and other similar entities, which in spite of their playfulness can be outright frightening.

The chaneque were known to lead people astray, making the victims wander around the jungle for days. Later it was believed that to escape the chaneque one must wear his shirt inside-out.

STRANGERS FROM SOMEWHERE

In the late '60s, two enigmatic individuals checked into a Miami hotel for an extended stay and befriended the chambermaid in the process. When the woman asked them where they were from, the men replied that they hailed from "the north of the continent," stressing that they did not mean the lands north of the United States. The chambermaid and her husband detailed their experiences to paranormal researcher Salvador Freixedo: one of the men was tall and blond, with a command of many languages and possessing telepathic abilities. His sidekick was short in stature, Asian-looking and wore an orange-colored uniform, and gave the impression of being a retainer or bodyguard to the other man.

According to the chambermaid, the blond produced what appeared to be a ball and stuck it to the wall in defiance of gravity. He then asked the woman to address it, which she did, noticing swirling waves of light within the device, which would follow her in the air every time she made a move. The chambermaid and her husband witnessed the activities of the tall blond and his companion on the beach during stormy weather, pointing what appeared to be cameras and other devices at the rough seas. While cleaning their rooms (the pair refused to leave their rooms while she cleaned), the chambermaid noticed a suitcase filled with "billiard balls" pulsating with light, as if filled with electricity. The two strangers disappeared as suddenly as they had come.

MANIFESTATIONS OF THE DAMNED

Leafing through old bestiaries and almanacs can be an interesting experience, a journey into the mindset of cartographers, scholars and naturalists of a bygone age. Populating unknown or unexplored parts of the world with drawings of headless people, beings who used a single giant foot as shelter against the rain or the sun, and animal-headed entities were no different from our drawings of putative extraterrestrials, although current academic thinking would probably declare something along the lines of "a xenophobic vision of non-Europeans by Eurocentric thinkers."

However, what can we say when similar images appear in the Aztec codices, those ancient drawings in black and red ink, that told the history of a civilization?

Two of these compendiums - "*The Codex Florentinus*" and "*The History of Tlaxcala*" - provide readers with the strange story of the omens which foretold the destruction of the Aztec Empire and the arrival of the Spanish conquistadores. The earliest of these events took place a full ten years before the invasion, and included a tsunami in the Inland Sea of Texcoco, the burning of temples by bolts from the blue, the first recorded apparition of La Llorona (the goddess Cihuacoatl) and other disasters. The last of these portents was truly hideous: the appearance of the two-headed crypto-humans dubbed "Tlacanzolli" (literally "split men") in the vicinity of Tenochtitlán, the Aztec capital. "The History of Tlaxcala" records the event thus:

"The eighth prodigy and signal for Mexico was that often would be seen two men joined in a single body, known to the natives as Tlacantzolli. Others would see bodies with two heads emerging from a single body, taken to Great Montezuma's Black Hall. Upon arrival, they would disappear, and all of these portents, and others, would become invisible. They foretold the end of the natives, as the end was upon them, and the whole world would end and be consumed."

The fact that these monsters already had a name indicates that they were known to the Aztecs, and that they would vanish into the waters of the lake, making them a kind of Mesoamerican "nixie," or water spirit. One can visualize the sorcerers of the Aztec court in their "black chamber" concealing their astonishment and possible fright at having these entities brought to them, only to inexplicably vanish.

UNDER THE TUTELAGE OF NONHUMANS

Salvador Freixedo's *"La Granja Humana"* (Posada, 1989) presents the high-strangeness story of a young Mexican named Jose Luis and his bizarre friendship with a small child/man known only as "Fair" due to his blond hair.

Jose Luis told Freixedo that he had first encountered his odd friend during a camping trip: a group of schoolboys had pitched their tents in the woods and encountered another boy their age (or so they thought) who led them to his own "tent" -- a rectangular, shiny affair resembling an excursion bus. From that moment on, "Fair" became a fixture in the lives of Jose Luis and his friends, visiting them at school to fill their heads with tales of space travel and the future, and making a point of visiting Jose Luis at home on his birthday year after year. The strange little visitor earned the affection of Jose Luis' parents "because of the good advice he always imparted" to their son and his companions. In a manner worthy of an "Outer Limits" episode, people noticed that "Fair" never seemed to age with each subsequent birthday visit, but said nothing either out of fear or due to a belief that the small figure may be suffering from a glandular disorder. But his enigmatic visitor's apparent lack of development was the least of Jose Luis's problems.

"Fair's role in the Mexican youngster's life seemed to be, suggests Freixedo, to groom him for future greatness (whether this greatness has been achieved remains unclear) by clearing any and all obstacles. When Jose Luis took a humble job in an important corporation, a number of managers supposedly died of a variety of symptoms until Jose Luis found himself in a powerful position--all of this after consultation with "Fair." Something similar occurred when Jose Luis remarked that he was in love with a married woman:

The fact is that one day, when Jose Luis was feeling particularly depressed, "Fair" told him: "You're sad and I know why."

Jose Luis tried to deny that he was particularly sad about anything...but "Fair" insisted: "You're in love with a young woman who can't return your affections because she's married. You're saddened to see that achieving your wishes seems impossible [...] Don't worry. Within a year, when I come back to visit you, you'll not only be married to the young lady, but you'll also have a child by her - no matter how impossible it may seem." (Freixedo, p.210)

And so it was. The method used to remove Jose Luis' "rival" from the picture isn't mentioned. It also brings to mind the scene in John Boorman's "Excalibur" (1981) in which the wizard Merlin assures Uther Pendragon that he will have his way with the lovely Igraine and have a child - the future King Arthur. One wonders if Jose Luis's offspring - now an adult - is also under the tutelage of "Fair."

Freixedo elaborates further about the experiences of Jose Luis and his mysterious friend, but the above will suffice for our purposes. Did the diminutive and ageless "Fair" belong, as the author suggests, to the order of intermediary beings between humans and angels known in the Islamic world as the Djinn? Citing Gordon Creighton's work on this order of nonhumans, whose reality is accepted in religious courts throughout the Middle East and North Africa, Freixedo discusses their capricious behavior toward humans, often selecting one of us as a protégé or even as a pet, and manifesting a fascination for human reproduction and human affairs (much like the abducting "Greys" our own time).

How far does this interest extend on the part of these powerful yet far from divine order of beings? Anthony Roberts suggests that the large-eyed, black-haired and pointed-faced Mesopotamian love goddess Ishtar was of their number (said physical traits being common to ultraterrestrials, in his opinion) along with other similar entities. Ancient myth had it that no mortal - understandably - was immune to the goddess of love. But what about today?

A curious little book entitled *"UFO Encounters of the Fourth Kind"* (Zebra Books, 1978) explored the carnal obsessions evinced throughout history by these beings who appear to us now as "space people." Author Art Gatti made reference to a 1969 epidemic in Morocco having to do with "Aycha Kenaycha," described as a "dark demoness" or succubus who appeared to drug users undergoing astral experiences by summoning each of them in their mother's voice. The drugged-out astral traveler would find himself facing an astral form capable of stealing their souls, not just their astral selves. Gatti states that the nationwide epidemic which filled insane asylums and jails to capacity ended in the 1970's, and that its end was brought about by the Islamic equivalent of exorcism rites...or a drastic reduction in hashish consumption.

SHADOWY BEINGS OF THE CANARY ISLANDS

Perhaps one of the most unusual stories involving the actions of diminutive creatures in our times involves the series of bizarre events taking place in the ever-mysterious Canary Islands, off the western coast of Africa. It was here, on the island of Tenerife, in a town with the ominous name of La Matanza ("the slaying") that diminutive, dark olive-green colored beings were reported on many occasions by visitors to the area, with the added riddle of the seeming complicity among local humans to "keep the lid" on such stories.

Nonetheless, locals and visitors alike agree that the dwarves are very real, and are known as "los diablillos" (the imps). Appearing after dark at a beautiful country retreat known as Finca del Duque, it was at first believed that the short-statured creatures were attracted by the activities of couples using this remote area as a lovers' lane. Further cases have shown that any human presence after sundown produces the appearance of the "diablillos."

In November 1992, an anonymous resident of Tenerife drove to the lovers' lane one evening with his girlfriend. From within the car they were able to hear the sound of branches rustling as if being parted by someone. The driver looked out the window and allegedly saw a creature some three feet tall and covered in grayish or black fur all over. The entity carried a staff or rod of some sort in its hand, and was described as having "cat-like eyes." The couple left the area in a hurry, refusing to return even by daylight.

Alberto Dieppa, a young man from the island of Gran Canaria, discussed his 1993 encounter with the beings during an interview with journalist Carmen Machado. According to the story, Dieppa and his friends drove to the remote Finca del Duque simply to enjoy the ride. The group remained within the car with the dome light on, chatting late into the evening, when they suddenly became aware of six or seven presences outside their vehicle, staring at them intently. Dieppa turned on the headlights, and was in for the surprise of his life. "They were like little children with adult faces," he explained. "They appeared to be naked, at least from the waist up. What I did notice was their dark, olive green skin color and their intense red eyes."

The car's occupants remained in stunned, paralyzed silence until one of them began screaming hysterically, causing the driver to set the car in motion and abandon the area as quickly as possible. Dieppa added that at no point did the "diablillos" try to block their way. In fact, they seemed to vanish as soon as he touched the ignition key.

Badly shaken, the friends agreed not to discuss what had occurred at Finca del Duque, not even among themselves. Intrigued by the incredible experience, Dieppa returned alone two weeks later. Although he was unable to see anything on this occasion, he claims to have felt the presence of the creatures surrounding him. The experiencer told the journalist that he believes the imps to be an integral part of the island rather than creatures from another planet, suggesting that there may well be a "portal" of some sort to a dimension producing these creatures.

The "los diablillos" are drawn to any human activity taking place after the sun goes down. Even though they are thought to be supernatural creatures, they are eerily human-like in appearance.

TOWARD A CONCLUSION

A scientist would look at all this evidence with a measure of condescension and dismiss it as unscientific. If you want alternate humanities, little man, busy yourself with the different hominid species that we know so little about - the procession of Denisovans, Floriensis, Luzonensis and Naledi that have interested pop science in recent years. Some may be satisfied with this grudging handout, but not others. What are we to make, for instance of the "golluts" that were found up to not so long ago in the valleys of the Spanish Pyrenees? This mountain range even has its own Sasquatch population, but discussing it here would be a digression.

The "golluts" - called such on account of their propensity to develop huge goiters around their necks - were considered a damned or excluded population, completely different from Catalonian stock or even the seed of prior invaders (Celts, Romans, Goths). They were also called "nans" (dwarves) due to their height, standing just a little over four feet tall. One can imagine how these characteristics would merit an unwarranted inclusion in medieval bestiaries.

Despite having lived there for centuries, the "golluts" were not acknowledged until the 1880s through the work of the anthropologist Miguel Moratillo. Marginalized as they were, the mystery about them only increased. It was later said that they were a linked to a Central Asian population that had been swept into Western Europe during the great wanderings of the 5th century AD.

If parallel humanity does not have a paranormal origin, perhaps it hails from a neighboring reality. We can allow ourselves to entertain thoughts of the Green Children of Banjos, the man from the netherworldly "Republic of Tuared" and similar situations that have filled paranormal chronicles for decades. Perhaps they come to live among us to secure vital necessities that only Homo sapiens can offer - a train of thought that leads us to the belief in changelings, for example. Or could members of this parallel humanity come to dwell among us as teachers and guides, much like JRR Tolkien's order of wizards? The "Red Man" who appeared to Napoleon Bonaparte on critical occasions, the "Grey Man" who visited Swedish King Charles XII, or even the entity that supposedly showed George Washington a vision of the destiny of America?

Looking at the state of the world today, it is not unreasonable to fear that a new, parallel humanity may supplant our own.

The Watchers were angelic beings who were assigned by God to watch over humanity. Instead, they found human women so beautiful that they abandoned their roles to become consorts to the women of Earth.

SUPERNATURAL BUT HUMAN-LOOKING ENTITIES IN THE BIBLE

Sean Casteel

The Bible abounds with references to supernatural but human-looking entities. The stories range from an invasion of sexual predators from the skies to sharing a simple meal with a stranger who keeps his holiness hidden from his hospitable host.

FORMERLY RIGHTEOUS SEXUAL PREDATORS

The story of the lustful angels appears in Genesis chapter 6 in the Biblical text and is also referred to in the apocryphal Book of Enoch. The Book of Genesis only briefly mentions Enoch, saying he was righteous enough in the eyes of God to not be forced to endure death but to be taken immediately to heaven instead. In the Book of Hebrews, the Apostle Paul uses the word "translate," intended to mean that Enoch became an ascended being like unto an angel, most likely a human-looking angel. His name was then changed to "Metatron."

According to an online article called "Enoch and the Watchers," from the website "Timeless Myths" and written by Jimmy Joe (aka Blademaster), it was during the time of Jared, the father of Enoch, that the angels, known as the Watchers, came down to Earth to take mortal women as wives and mate with them, begetting monstrous children. Some of the details can be found in a collection of Rabbinic legends, called the Haggada, while other information comes from a non-canonical book called the Book of Watchers.

The leader of the Watchers was an angel called Shemhazai, who was amenable to taking earthly women as wives, but only if his fellow Watchers swore a pact to follow through and not turn back before the deed was accomplished. Two hundred angels then descended to Earth divided into groups of ten under the leadership of their respective captains.

Another legend from the Haggada reveals that the angel Shemhazai lusted after a maiden named Istehar, but she tricked him into revealing the Ineffable Name of God, which she used to ascend to the heavens, thereby escaping violation by Shemhazai. God rewarded Istehar for her piety and her chastity by commemorating her as the seven-star constellation Pleiades.

In a manner completely the opposite of Istehar, a woman idol worshipper named Naamah first deceived and seduced the angels, not the other way around.

"They were victims of her beauty," Joe writes. "She became mother of an unknown number of demons."

It was also said of Naamah that she would wander through the night and have relations with any man sleeping alone in the house during the waning of the moon, thus taking away his strength, much like a succubus.

THE JUDGMENT OF THE UNNATURAL OFFSPRING

When Enoch reached adulthood, he lived alone in a cave to avoid the wicked children fathered by the Watchers. One day he heard a voice appointing him as the Scribe of Justice. The voice told him to go to the Watchers and announce their fates and punishments for their wickedness in cohabiting with mortal women. The children of the

Watchers would suffer for the sins of their fathers, and the Watchers themselves would be forbidden to return to heaven or even to apologize and plead their case before God.

Meanwhile, when the offspring giants had consumed most of the food from men, they began devouring ordinary people and sucking their blood, like vampires.

Among the other sins of the fallen Watchers was teaching their mortal children the forbidden arts and the lore of enchantment and divination. They also taught them sorcery and astrology and how to make weapons for war.

Not all the Watchers who looked down from heaven were evil, however. There were holy Watchers, archangels like Michael and Gabriel, Uriel and Raphael. They heard the cries of men as they perished under the hungry giants. God sent the righteous angels to do battle with the Watchers before ultimately deciding to send a flood to destroy the evil from the face of the Earth, sparing only Noah and the occupants of his ark.

In any case, although the Bible and other sources never flatly declare that the Watchers were human-looking in appearance, they must have been sufficiently human anatomically in order to mate with mortal women at all. When their offspring died the death that comes to all mortals, it is said their souls began to roam the Earth as evil spirits, a circumstance that continues to this day.

THE ATTEMPT TO RAPE HUMAN-LOOKING ANGELS

In another familiar story from the Book of Genesis, two angels appear to the Lord's servant Lot just prior to the destruction of Sodom and Gomorrah. The story is told in the 19th chapter.

"The two angels came to Sodom in the evening; and Lot was sitting in the gate of Sodom," the scriptural account begins. "When Lot saw them, he rose to meet them, and bowed himself with his face to the earth, and said, 'My lords, turn aside, I pray you, to your servant's house, and spend the night and wash your feet; then you may rise up early and be on your way.' They said, 'No, we will spend the night in the street.'"

After further strong entreaties from Lot, the angels agreed to spend the night in his house. Lot then made a feast that included unleavened bread and the angels ate with him. Here we obviously have entities that are human enough to consume bread yet inspire awe and fear from within their human-looking bodies. As the visitors made ready to retire for the night, the men of Sodom, both young and old, surrounded the house and called out to Lot: "Where are the men who came to you tonight? Bring them out to us, that we may know them."

They use the word "know" in the sense of "carnal knowledge," and, again, the angels must look human enough to inspire homosexual lust in the men of Sodom. Lot begs the crowd not to act so wickedly and offers his two virgin daughters to them instead. The crowd then denounces Lot as a newcomer with no right to pass judgment on them. They proceed to attack Lot and attempt to break down the door of his house.

At that point, the two angels "put forth their hands" and brought Lot back into the house and shut the door.

"And they struck with blindness the men who were at the door of the house," Genesis continues, "both small and great, so that they wearied themselves groping for the door."

A WARNING TO TAKE IT ON THE RUN

The two angels next questioned Lot about who was in his household, warning him to take his people and flee, "for we are about to destroy this place, because the outcry against its people has become great before the Lord, and the Lord has sent us to destroy it."

When morning came, the angels again urged Lot to take his wife and two daughters away from the coming destruction, "lest you be consumed in the punishment of the city." Still Lot lingered, so the angels seized Lot and his family bodily and set them outside the city. Then the Lord rained on Sodom and Gomorrah brimstone and fire out of heaven. When the prophet Abraham visited the area shortly thereafter, he saw that "the smoke of the land went up like the smoke of a furnace."

Avenging angels in human form are primary elements of this familiar story, creatures able to move freely among both the righteous and the wicked without being seen as "alien" at all.

Lot's decision to be hospitable when he first encounters the two angels is echoed in the New Testament Book of Hebrews, chapter 13: "Do not neglect to show hospitality to strangers, for thereby some have entertained angels unaware."

This is yet another reference to angels whose appearance is human enough to be mistaken for simple casual travelers who are able to share a meal with the people they encounter.

What do angels look like? According to some Biblical accounts, they might look like you or me.

Belief in "the good people" has been prevalent throughout history. Neither angels, nor demons, it is thought that they are a people who live invisibly among us humans.

GLAMOUR OF THE SHAPESHIFTERS

Tim R. Swartz

At one time it was common knowledge that humans were not the only intelligent creatures on this planet. It was thought that we shared this world with a myriad of other beings that have gone by such names as "The Good People," "The Fae," "Faeries," "Elves," etc. Every country, every region, have their own beliefs, names and descriptions of the "others" whose societies are parallel to our own.

There's no shared consensus on how these elemental beings exist. Some think they are spiritual creatures that never lived as humans and remain invisible to our eyes unless they want to be observed. Others say they are physical creatures who live, love and grow old just like we do.

Whatever their existence, to those who truly believe, there is no question about their reality.

ILLUSION OR GLAMOUR

It's important to remember that despite modern renditions of the Fae as being tiny, gentle winged creatures that live on flowers and consort with butterflies, the real faerie folk were nothing like that. It was thought that "the others" had the ability to shape-shift, using "glamour" to trick us foolish mortals into letting our guard down.

It was thought that glamour was a sort of powerful magic with the capability to make a person see, hear, feel, taste, and even touch something that is different in nature than what they normally perceive. Sometimes glamour included actual shapeshifting to a form that wasn't the person's own. Or it was used in hiding and disguising or making things and persons invisible to human eyes. They were said to be able to change their size and make themselves appear very small or very large. The difference between illusion and glamour is that glamour is more subtle; in some cases it includes not only false sensory input, but false emotional input, such as fear, love, or compulsion.

Of course, not all elementals were thought to be able to take on different forms, but many could, and were all too willing to do so when they interacted with people.

THEY BECKON

The problem with "the good people" is that humans can never tell exactly what they are dealing with. Some of these beings can occasionally be friendly and helpful, while others are downright dangerous and malicious. It is often impossible for humans to predict which mood one of these creatures will be in when we meet them.

The Irish Púca could be the bringer of either good or bad fortune. They were known to either help or hinder travelers and rural communities. The Púcaí (plural) can have dark green/black or white fur or hair, similar to a cat or dog. In Irish faerie and folk tales, the creatures are shapeshifters and could take the form of horses, goats, cats, dogs, roosters, or hares. They may also appear in human form, sometimes including various animal features, such as a tail or long ears.

In Germanic lore there are Kobolds, dwarf-like beings that tend to attach themselves to an estate or property. They're considered a household faerie and are known to aid the family with undone chores and tasks around the home. They're also known to be shapeshifters, disguising themselves as rocks, branches, and other manner of inanimate objects in an attempt to "hitch a ride" with someone in order to take up residence in their home.

Another aspect of shapeshifting creatures is their ability to use their sexuality to attract unsuspecting humans for seduction and/or other dangerous doings. Maureen Duffy, in her extensive study of fairies in literature, "*The Erotic World of Faery*" (Cardinal, 1989), describes how fairies are an embodiment of repressed desires. Folk culture favored greater sexual freedom than the church could sanction, and faerie tales allowed writers to deal with taboo subjects and taboo desires in an indirect way. Duffy notes that malignant spirits are more common than benevolent ones and she links the latter to a cheerful and open sexuality.

The Irish glanconer, or Love-Talker, appears in the form of a charming young man – but woe to the woman who walks with him, for she will pine for this faerie's touch and lose all will to live. The leanan-sidhe is the faerie muse who inspires poets and artists with her touch, causing them to burn so brightly that they die long before their time. The woodwives of Scandinavia are earthy, wild, and sensuous – yet their feminine allure is illusory and from the back their bodies are hollow.

It seems fairly obvious that both faeries and humans found each other attractive. Throughout the centuries, scores of humans succumbed to the romantic allure of faeries. One of those unions can be witnessed in the history of the faerie flag of the Scottish MacLeod clan, a gift to their chieftain from his departing faerie lover, the mother of his half-faerie son. Today the flag can be seen in Dunvegan Castle, and it is said to increase the chances of fertility as well as provide protection in battle.

It was thought that faeries were sexual beings who often initiated relationships with humans...most of which ended tragically.

THE SPAWN OF THE FAERIES

As to be expected, the union between human and faerie often produced children. Renowned faerie expert Katharine Briggs observed in her book, *"The Fairies in Tradition and Literature,"* that faeries "are apparently near enough in kind to mate with humans – closer in fact than a horse is to an ass, for many human families to claim faerie ancestry."

In 1616, Katherine Jones Dochter of Shetland was tried for witchcraft. During the proceedings, she confessed to a forty-year affair with a faerie man whom she called "the bowman." He first came to her when she was a teenager (a "young lass" as she described herself) and they had a child together. A relative recalled that she had seen "ane little creatour in hir awin hus amongst hir awin bairns quhom she callit the bowmanes bairn." In this case the child stayed with the (human) mother and the (faerie) father was seen once or twice a year- at Halloween and on Holy Cross Day (September 14th) - when he visited her for sex.

However, not all human/faerie affairs end up happily in the boudoir. One type of elemental shapeshifter, called a nixie, used glamour and the promise of a romantic tryst which usually resulted in a not-so-happy ending. This not-so-friendly creature is able to shapeshift into beautiful young women, handsome men, a crying child, all in order to lure in unsuspecting victims. With men she appears as an enchanting woman, her voice filling them with lust and hypnotic desires. With unbaptized women, the nixie appears to be a strong, handsome man who promises marriage and a privileged life.

The ultimate fate of those unlucky enough to encounter a nixie is not sensual or material pleasures; instead they find themselves lured into a cold lake, or deep, dark river where their horrific fate awaits them.

SELKIES

Another water-related elemental is the Selkie, which is one of the most notable mythical tales in Irish and Scottish myths and legends. Also called Seal Folk, the Selkie is similar to mermaids, sirens and swan maidens in other cultures. It is a creature that takes the form of a seal in the water, but is able to take off the seal skin on land and emerge as an irresistible human to land dwellers.

While the Selkie is certainly a manipulative creature – as all faeries are said to be – it is not malicious, at least not for the most part. Not only do Selkies have a deep affinity for the human race, they are also attracted to us – physically, emotionally and sexually. Should one of these magical things develop a lusting for a human, they will take off and carefully hide their sealskin in order to come ashore in human guise. A twist on this aspect of the legend maintains that if the person in question can locate the hidden hide, then the Selkie will remain with that same person and the Selkie's love will last as long as their human companion lives.

However, even if the Selkie truly loves its human companion, the time eventually comes when the yearning to return to the sea becomes overpowering and, finally, irresistible. It was said that the Selkie – which, in typical faerie style, has an extremely long lifespan – will only return to the sea when its human partner has passed. When the grieving process is over, the Selkie will then seek out the sealskin that it discarded and hid years earlier, take on its original seal form, and return to the seas.

As for the children of a human/Selkie relationship, they are usually abandoned when their Selkie mother returns to the sea. One version of the legend of the Selkies states that although the Selkie wife was never seen again in human form, her children would sometimes witness a large seal approaching and gazing at them wistfully. The children of such unions may be born with webbed hands or feet, a trait that can be passed down to their descendants.

Although most stories revolve around female Selkies, there are also tales of male Selkies who are said to have very handsome human forms, as well as seductive powers that are irresistible to human women. The male Selkies usually seek those who are dissatisfied with their lives, such as married women waiting for their fishermen husbands. If these women wish to contact the male Selkies, they would shed seven tears into the sea.

The number seven shows up in Selkie mythology once again as some say that the Selkie could only assume human form once every seven years because they are bodies that house condemned souls. They are also thought by some to be either humans who had committed sinful wrongdoing or fallen angels.

KITSUNE

Asia has its fair share of shapeshifting elemental beings as well. Known throughout the Far East is the Kitsune (Fox-Spirit), also known as the Kumiho in Korea and the Huli Jing in China. The fox is a curious mythological figure, almost universally representing sexual desire, cunning and trickery, and, while relations between the fox-spirit and humans ranges from benign to malevolent, Asian myths of the fox-spirit are peculiarly tinged with eroticism.

The Japanese fox-spirit called Kitsune is more clearly deified, and its stance towards humans is more ambivalent (although fox erotic seduction of humans still figures prominently). Kitsune are adept at shape-shifting from male to female, from animal to human, and back again. The kitsune is a prankster, a disrupter, a trouble-maker, a master of illusion, a challenger of accepted notions, a wild card.

Kitsune are alternately cunning and playful, mysterious and malevolent, untrustworthy and loyal – supernatural beings that, not unlike the gods of ancient Greece, are capable of mating with humans and producing offspring. Shapeshifting is a primary kitsune skill. They often confused their victims with visions or seduction, and would commonly attack in retaliation for a perceived slight.

Their victims were usually male, as the Kitsune were believed to either be female, or human women possessed by it. Typically, a young man unknowingly marries a fox wife (kitsune nyobo) that has taken on a human guise. When the husband eventually – inevitably – discovers his partner's true nature, the Kitsune – who may, in fact, have proven to be a devoted spouse, and whose half-human children inherit supernatural qualities – is forced to leave her family behind.

In some cases, a husband is seduced by a Kitsune into abandoning his wife and children to start a second family, only to wake, as if from a dream, emaciated, filthy, disoriented, and far from home. He must then return to face his abandoned family in shame. Kitsune have the ability to bend time and space. What had seemed many years enjoying a new, fulfilling life in opulent surroundings turns out to have been merely days or weeks living in squalor – a Kitsune alternate reality. Even the duped husband's newborn son turns out to be an illusion.

In many legends, a Kitsune would pose as a distressed female traveler or monk on a pilgrimage and would convince a villager to take them in for the night. The next morning, they would find that their food and valuables had been stolen. Alternatively, the Kitsune would seduce and deceive its victim into going to a desolate place where they would likely be killed.

STILL AMONG US

Even though these stories may seem quaint and old-fashioned, remnants of a less-enlightened, superstitious time – in some parts of the world, the belief in faeries remains as strong as ever.

Hallgerður Hallgrímsdóttir, a photographer from Reykjavík, Iceland, wrote in her book *"Please YoursELF – Sex with the Icelandic Invisibles,"* that "sex with humans is rather mundane compared to making love to an elf."

Hallgerður claims many Icelanders have been lovers with elves in secret for centuries. "Elf sex is possibly the safest sex on earth. They don't carry sexually transmitted diseases and you can't get pregnant or make an Elverine pregnant unless you both want to, which is not unheard of. And YES there are female elves, elverines. And they're HOT, HOT, HOT, even to girls. That reminds me: All elves are bisexual, but guys and girls not ready for some same sex action don't worry, no elf will do anything you don't want to. They can sense your longings and not-longings."

According to a 2007 study by the University of Iceland, an estimated 62% of the nation believes that the existence of these beings is more than a fairy tale. However, this statistic covers both sincere believers and agnostics who lean toward the "why not" end of the spectrum.

Whether one is a believer or not, it matters little to the "others." They obviously have their own agenda when it comes to interacting with humankind. At times they may look and act like us, but if you ever suspect that you are in the company of one, be careful not to look too deeply into its eyes. If you do, you may find yourself forever entwined in its delicious embrace.

Hallgerður Hallgrímsdóttir, a photographer from Reykjavík, Iceland, says elves are very flexible so they can use sexual positions which would not be possible for humans.

It was thought that humans were essential to faeries for a healthy bloodline. This is a belief that has reoccurred in modern UFO abduction cases.

CHILDREN OF THE SUPERIMPOSED REALITY

Tim R. Swartz

One of the things that I enjoy when researching something is finding similarities spread out over time and distance. As it has been previously suggested by such notables as Jacques Vallée and John Keel, "out-of-the-ordinary" events have been occurring since the beginning of human existence. A high-percentage of these experiences are often repeated decade after decade, usually in a vacuum of information concerning past events.

The certainty that humans are not the only intelligent creatures on this planet is almost universal. Whatever the names they are said to go by, the "others" apparently live alongside us, never being seen unless they desire it. They can interact with us because they either look like us or can easily do so.

Whatever their origins, the "others" must be closely related to Homo sapiens as stories from all over the planet tell of sexual activity (even love and marriage) between people and the others. These unions, not surprisingly, have also produced children, half human, half-others. World mythologies overflow with tales of the children of these otherworldly affairs. The Greek divine hero Heracles, for example, was the son of Jupiter and the mortal Alcmena.

Modern UFO-related stories have incorporated the tales of hybrid children, giving the phenomenon a veneer of technology with extraterrestrials using science (rather than glamour or magic) to breed with humans and save their failing species. With the exception that the modern "extraterrestrials" are said to be without emotions (so no love affairs), if you were to replace the word "extraterrestrial" with "faerie," the similarities between these tales are impressive.

CHANGELINGS

The faeries of old had a predilection for not only spiriting children away but also leaving one of their own behind to be raised by unsuspecting humans. Think along the lines of a paranormal cuckoo. These faerie babies, known as "changelings," were said to be weak, sickly, and often mischievous.

The belief in changelings was widespread in medieval Europe, and it was thought that faeries, elves, and other supernatural creatures were responsible for the theft of human babies. Many parents believed that their sickly or disabled child was a changeling left by the faeries and that their real baby had been taken away.

Changelings were sometimes described as looking old, with wrinkled dark skin and sunken eyes. Other times they were said to have odd features, such as overly large, blue eyes or small heads with slightly pointed ears. If they do have hair, it is said to look like spun gold, or thin and straw-colored.

Changelings were often used to explain the birth of children with physical or mental disabilities, as it was thought that these children were not of human origin. In some cultures, people would try to "exchange" the changeling back with the faeries by leaving the child alone in a wooded area or by mistreating it to the point that the faeries would fear for its health.

However, the changeling legend was also used to explain other phenomena, such as sudden changes in behavior or personality. In some cases, it was thought that a person who had suddenly become ill-tempered or prone to mischief had been replaced by a changeling.

Sir Walter Scott wrote about a Manx changeling in *"On the Fairies of Popular Superstition."*

"I [Scott's source] was prevailed upon myself to go and see a child, who, they told me, was one of these changelings, and, indeed, must own, was not a little surprised, as well as shocked, at the sight. Nothing under heaven could have a more beautiful face; but, though between five and six years old, and seemingly healthy, he was so far from being able to walk or stand that he could not so much as move any one joint; his limbs were vastly long for his age, but smaller than any infant's of six months; his complexion was perfectly delicate, and he had the finest hair in the world. He never spoke nor cried, ate scarcely anything, and was very seldom seen to smile; but if anyone called him a fairy-elf, he would frown, and fix his eyes so earnestly on those who said it that it was as if he would look them through.

"His mother, or at least his supposed mother, being very poor, frequently went out a charring, and left him a whole day together. The neighbors, out of curiosity, have often looked in at the window, to see how he behaved while alone; which, whenever they did, they were sure to find him laughing, and in the utmost delight. This made them judge that he was not without company, more pleasing to him than any mortals could be; and what made this conjecture seem the more reasonable, was that, if he were left ever so dirty, the woman, at her return, saw him with a clean face, and his hair combed with the utmost exactness and nicety."

THE EXTRATERRESTRIAL CHANGELING

There are both men and women who claim to have produced their own versions of the changeling, but rather than being from the faerie world, these changelings are said to be the product of extraterrestrial intervention.

New Jersey artist David Huggins has claimed a lifetime of extraterrestrial sexual interaction. He says he has fathered many half-human, half-alien children, and has shown off paintings with weird hybrid babies he claims are his. The 78-year-old Huggins lives in Hoboken, New Jersey, and claims to have fathered 60 alien children. He knew that this was necessary to help create hybrids of humans and aliens.

The January 20, 2016, issue of the "Irish Mirror" told the story of two women who claimed to "to have had sex with aliens and gave birth to hybrid babies." Former marketing executive Bridget Nielson and video game designer Aluna Verse claim that between them, they have had 13 children with aliens.

David Huggins shows off a painting of his "extraterrestrial" lover whom he named Crescent.

Nielson, at 27, said the sex was the "best ever" and that thousands of women around the world are missing out on such experiences because they have actually had hybrid children with aliens – but don't realize it.

Although she lives with her father in Sedona, Arizona, she claims to have had regular contact with aliens and now has 10 hybrid children – four boys and six girls. She said: "They are not just taking our children - they are creating a hybrid race to better humanity."

Video game designer Aluna Verse, from Los Angeles, says she was taken on board a landed space ship in a "dream state" and described the sex she had as one of her most "vivid" memories. She says the result was that she has had at least one hybrid daughter and possibly more.

These people all claim to have sired hybrid babies of some kind. Yet the proof of such otherworldly progeny has always been lacking. Nevertheless, there have been reports of babies with unusual physical characteristics that sound suspiciously like the descriptions of hybrids by their human parents.

The following two stories come to us courtesy of Lon Strickler, who produces the excellent blog "Phantoms and Monsters."

I received the following anecdote from a young woman in May 2012:

The Kansas Babies

Hello - something happened last summer that has left me with many questions and few answers. I was employed at an appliance and furniture rental & sales business in Great Bend, Kansas. One morning a co-worker and I opened the store. When we arrived we noticed that the backdoor was open and when we entered the backroom all the lights in the store had been turned on. It didn't look like a break-in because the security latch was intact. The security system had been disabled–there was no power indicator on the code box. We immediately called the police and the store manager to report the situation. We were told not to open the store and to remain in the back office until someone arrived.

A few minutes later, after hanging up the phone with the store manager, a police officer was knocking on the back door. I let him in and told him what we had found when we arrived. The officer started to walk through the back room and into the showroom when we started to hear a baby cry. I thought that a customer may have somehow entered the store and that they had a baby with them. My co-worker and I followed the officer in the direction of the crying – well, I didn't believe what I saw. There were two babies lying on a twin size bed display. The officer told us to stay there while he checked the rest of the store. He had also radioed for another police officer to come to the location.

I looked down at the babies, who were both tightly wrapped in dark green cloth. Both babies were quiet, very still, and looking at me and my co-worker. I was taken aback by their odd eyes – both babies had large pupils that were black. There were no irises and neither of the babies blinked. The police officer was soon back with us – he commented on the babies' eyes as well. In fact, he was totally freaked out – so much so that he looked scared.

The store manager soon arrived as well as a senior police officer. We all stood around the bed looking at these strange babies who laid there quietly watching us. The store manager pulled my co-worker and I to the side and told us to go ahead and leave. He was not opening the store until he found out what was going on. We quickly headed toward the back door and left.

I wasn't scheduled to work until a couple days later but I had talked to a few co-workers who said that the atmosphere in the store was very strange. They had been receiving weird telephone calls and that the security system alarm would trip on several times during the day.

I got to work a little early for my next scheduled shift. When I arrived the store manager was sitting in the office, so I asked him what had happened after we had left. He said that two young women, who said they were from the municipal court, eventually showed up and took the babies. The senior police officer told him later that he had no idea who the women were but that he was told by his superior not to impede. He thought they were probably from McConnell AFB in Wichita. He also said that the babies were very quiet and seemed relaxed the entire period that they were there.

I stopped working there not long after. Things were just never the same and it got tougher each day – especially when odd-looking people would come into the store and just walk around. I didn't feel comfortable being there.

They Are Among Us

A few days ago, a Memphis, Tennessee, woman called into TN MUFON to report that she was sure she had just had an encounter with an alien/human hybrid baby at Coscos in Cordova, Tennessee. She and her granddaughter had gone there to pick up a birthday cake. As soon as they walked through the entrance, a tall Asian-looking man, who was apparently in a big hurry, walked directly across their path, almost running into them. He was dressed casually in all black clothing and had a Caucasian-looking infant in a carrier basket strapped in front of him. He seemed to take no notice whatsoever of her and her granddaughter as he marched on past them without one word of apology for his near collision with them. My correspondent, who has asked to remain anonymous, told me that seeing a man of Asian descent who was over six feet tall was in itself unusual, but she had to confess that the racial contradiction between himself and his infant companion startled her more than anything else.

She didn't get a good look at the baby at that time. If she had, she might have stopped in her tracks right then and there and asked her granddaughter, "Did you see that?" But neither she nor her granddaughter commented at that moment about this sudden "close encounter." They just proceeded on back to the bakery as if nothing had happened. After they purchased the cake, they started heading towards the entrance to leave. As they did so, the lady told me she spotted this Asian fellow moving rapidly down some aisles and taking a quick, sharp right-angle turn to cross over to another aisle. He didn't have a shopping cart and hadn't picked up one item from the shelves. Maybe he was just anxiously looking for one thing for some emergency need, possibly to do with the baby.

Just as the lady and her granddaughter were approaching the front of the store to leave, the second "close encounter" occurred. The Asian man suddenly appeared again and walked by them. My witness then got a good look at the baby. This woman swears to me that this infant had intensely bright blue eyes with no white area surrounding them! I talked to other researchers like Linda Howe about this report and was assured that these all blue-eyed people are being seen all over now in different parts of the country, adults as well as children. The Native American Medicine woman Three-Spirit Wolf who spoke in Memphis last June told us after hearing this recent story from Memphis that she had met some of the hybrids out in New Mexico last year. They were wearing dark sunglasses. One of them removed his glasses to reveal his utterly eerie-looking all-blue eyes without the white. He asked her if people had commented to her about seeing him or some of his other hybrid companions. Apparently they are trying to be as inconspicuous as possible in public.

Top alien abduction researcher Dr. David Jacobs of Temple University is convinced that the alien hybridization program is alarmingly evident in our society now. I know this lady who reported seeing the all blue-eyed baby in Memphis just the other day. I can vouch for her credibility. She saw what she saw. Maybe this can be explained as some weird new mutation showing up in the human eye at this time...or maybe it is true that "they" now walk among us.

(Postscript: The lady told me that when they got back home, she asked her granddaughter what she thought about seeing the strange Asian man and his all blue-eyed baby in the carrier. The lady had thought it a little curious in fact that her granddaughter, who usually comments on seeing cute babies in public, had not said one word about this. The granddaughter said she hadn't noticed this man or the baby!)

Source: Phantoms & Monsters

phantomsandmonsters.com/2012/11/black-eyed-children-encounters.html

HIGH STRANGENESS AT THE MALL

The next story is courtesy of Denise Stoner who, along with researcher Kathleen Marden, authored the book "*The Alien Abduction Files.*"

"My Mom and I had gone to the mall on Christmas Eve for a couple of last minute stocking stuffer type gifts. We actually knew what we wanted so we parked outside J.C. Penney's on the side where those goods were. We went in and immediately noticed that, even though it was late afternoon, there were only a few shoppers. We picked out our gifts and got in line at the cashier in back of two other people. We could easily see the exit door and the sun in the parking lot since we were facing that way. The glass doors opened and two very tall, thin women entered. They had long, almost waist length, blond hair parted in the middle on top and it was thin in texture. Their skin was also pale and I did not notice any makeup, but they each had huge piercing blue eyes. Their gait was odd, like they were too tall (approximately 6'1) to walk smoothly. I was already an investigator for MUFON so I was aware of oddities in people and had done background searches for the federal government, so I was trained to be observant.

"They were pushing one of those umbrella-style strollers with no fancy attachments – just the hammock-type bed, wheels, and handles. I noticed they had no purses or accessories, such as a diaper bag to carry diapers or bottles, etc. The women moved slowly it seemed and drew my attention to the stroller. There was a baby blanket in the bottom portion and on top the head of a baby no bigger than a small grapefruit, pasty colored skin, no noticeable nose, a line for a mouth and huge dark eyes taking up most of the rest of this head. I wondered if the baby was deformed but knew this was not the case somehow. The baby appeared alert and was staring up at me. My Mom bumped me with her arm to get my attention and said 'What is wrong with that baby?' I felt I needed to tell the person in front of me because we had been talking with her about being slow in finishing up our shopping. When I tapped her on the shoulder I then was shocked to see not only her but the lady in front of her and the cashier were kind of frozen in place. Everything seemed to be moving in extremely slow motion around us.

"The blond women seemed to pass the thought to me that I needed to take another good look at the baby and study it. Then as if a film was put back in to normal speed they walked past me and the cash register began to work, people - the only three in the area – were moving again as if nothing had happened. I told my Mom to hold our places and I ran after the women. Just next to us was the infants' clothing department. The women had turned in to that aisle. I followed and, when I turned in to the aisle, they disappeared. Just gone like they had never been there. I ran back the short distance to my Mom and told her they were gone. We checked out and my Mom kept saying, 'What was going on with that baby?' I told her no one goes shopping with a baby that tiny without taking needed supplies, bottles, diapers, clothes, etc.

"I remember asking her if she thought we had seen something alien such as a hybrid and she just shook her head as if there was no answer. We stepped out the door and that's when the experience with the men took place. When we exited the mall and my Mom had already stepped off the curb to locate my car, I was stopped by three men who were leaning on the brick wall by the door. Wearing black suits, black hats, white shirts, sun glasses. Short in stature. The only difference from your reports was the fact that one had a briefcase - black also. I don't recall their mouths moving but it could be I was just nervous.

"One of them said, 'You will not discuss what happened inside that store. Do not talk about it to anyone – do you understand?' I did not answer, then I stepped off the curb as I felt I was in danger and called after my Mom. Just after I stepped off the curb I turned back to discover these men were gone and there was nowhere for them to go other than into the parking lot or further down the sidewalk as there was a brick wall where they had been that continued down the length of the building to the only door, which we had come out. We had been shown something in the store we both feel wasn't normal and were talking about it as we left to see if we were imagining things when I met these men. Does this sound typical of these types? I am too old to be abducted and used for breeding and have had a hysterectomy so that could not have been the purpose – to show me a child of mine – and I felt nothing like that was going on."

The changeling phenomenon appears to have comfortably adapted to the 21st century, rewriting its history away from faeries and pucas, and instead towards extraterrestrials and spaceships. We can speculate endlessly about what we are dealing with...aliens, angels, demons, faeries, interdimensional tricksters? The list could go on and on.

"What we have here is a complete theory of contact between our race and another race, nonhuman, different in physical nature, but biologically compatible with us. Angels, demons, fairies, creatures from heaven, hell, or Magonia: they inspire our strangest dreams, shape our destinies, steal our desires... But who are they? "

- Jacques Vallée, Passport to Magonia (p.129)

HAUNTED ST. LUCIA: Ti Bolom

Paul Dale Roberts, HPI's Esoteric Detective

When my half-brother Joseph (Joe) Anthony Soyo went on vacation to St. Lucia, I asked him to dig up some information on The Ti Bolom. The Ti Bolom is also referred to as the "little devil." The island has sightings of these little beings and some families on the island have been terrorized by these creatures. Legend has it that children who were not properly baptized and face an unexpected death become Ti Boloms. These Ti Boloms hide in bushes and try and lure locals and tourists into the bushes and steal their souls.

According to my brother, a local heard a baby crying and followed the sounds into a secluded part of the island, only to come face-to-face with a Ti Bolom. The Ti Bolom jumped on the local and sat on his chest and sucked out his soul from his forehead. Another local heard the screaming of the man and ran over to him. The victim of this Ti Bolom explained to the man about what happened and then went into convulsions and died on the spot. Some locals are known to summon Ti Boloms by placing a raw egg under their pillow. They will then sleep on the pillow with the raw egg for three days and, on the third day, a Ti Bolom will appear. Then the Ti Bolom will become a servant to the local that summoned him, doing the evil bidding of the summoner.

Now, I know that this myth sounds like a fantasy, but there have been news reports as recently as 2014 describing Ti Bolom encounters. Below are two reports that I discovered:

St. Lucia News Online

May 29, 2014

Evil spirit forces family out of Castries home, but haunting continues. Apparitions of a black male figure, scratching and tapping sounds, a croaking frog, doors opening and closing, whispers, and knocking, all sound like scenes from a Hollywood horror movie, but this is currently happening right here in St. Lucia. About three weeks ago, a Guyanese family was forced to flee their unfinished three-bedroom house in Bisee, Castries, by what they describe as an "evil spirit" which has not only possessed their 16-year-old son but has no intentions of leaving until all members of the family are killed.

Dominica News Online

March 12, 1998

When a man in the small community of Sarrot in Bexon, St. Lucia, decided to take a photo of himself, little did he know it would turn into a sensation. According to HTS News, when the photo was viewed something in the background "turned out to be a shocking revelation." The daughter of the man said only three individuals were in the room when the photo was taken but somehow something else appeared in it. And she said it does not look like any of the other people present. Soon news of the photo began spreading and residents of the community became convinced that the image in the picture is not human. Many said it is in fact what is well known by folks in St. Lucia as a Ti Bolom. According to St. Lucian folklore, a Ti Bolom is a two or two-and-a-half-foot boy or girl that is brought into the world on Good Friday by someone with evil intent. After it is brought into existence, the Ti Bolom carries out its master's evil bidding with great relish. The stories go on to say that the Ti Bolom survives on raw meat, which the master must supply in great quantities or be eaten himself. Family members of the man in Bexon are now convinced that there are unwanted guests in the house and some supernatural being has taken over.

● ● ●

My brother Joe says that the girl he was dating made the claim that her uncle was terrorized by a Ti Bolom. The story goes that her uncle got into a physical altercation with a man at a bar over a woman that both were courting. Her uncle got the best of the man he was fighting. As her uncle was leaving the bar, the man that he fought with cursed him and said within the week he will be visited by a Ti Bolom. This prediction came true.

In one week, her uncle came face-to-face with a Ti Bolom. The Ti Bolom that the uncle came in contact with was an evil little boy that had black eyes. The white of the eyes or the sclera was all black. The uncle, while looking at the Ti Bolom, heard a voice in his head telling him to kill himself. The uncle then started praying out loud and finally the voice in his head stopped and the Ti Bolom vanished. The next day, the uncle went to his local church and had the priest pray over and bless him. After the blessing from his priest, he was no longer bothered by the Ti Bolom.

Out of all the Carribbean islands, it would seem that St. Lucia is the main focus of the little devils known as Ti Bolom.

In the summer of 1692, a uniquely strange occurrence began on the outskirts of Gloucester, Massachusetts, with a bizarre, almost alien, force laying siege to the entire town.

THE DEVIL'S RAGE UNLEASHED IN GLOUCESTER, MASSACHUSETTS?

Sean Casteel

An incident said to have taken place in Gloucester, Massachusetts, in 1692, in the midst of the infamous New England witch trials, has continued to be told more than 300 years later, standing the tests of both time and believability.

According to an Internet posting on a site called "Historic Ipswich," "A new and unique outburst of Satanic rage revealed itself. Gloucester was invaded by a spectral company of Indians and French."

When the spectral figures fired their weapons, the bullets had no effect. However, real bullets were dug out of the trees they had hit with their rifles, indicating that the figures had a real-world physical presence. Their speech was in an unknown tongue.

"The alarm became so great," the website continues, "that Major Samuel Appleton of Ipswich sent about sixty men on the 18th of July 'for the town's assistance under these inexplicable alarms, which they had suffered night and day for about a Fortnight together.'"

A TIME OF WITCHES AND PHANTOMS

Another posting, this one by writer Brant Swancer, provides more background.

"It was in this era that superstitions still pervaded the local populace," Swancer writes, "when witches and devils were believed to prowl the wilderness to send people cowering in their homes in fear, the idea of magic and witchcraft very much alive. Townsfolk began coming forth with accounts of the sounds of the disembodied marching of men through the streets, complete with the clomping of horse hooves and sometimes even the sound of cannon fire and the roll of drums, but there was never any sign of an actual source for these anomalous sounds."

There began to be reports of the apparitions of mysterious figures that would appear to raid the settlement and seemed to be Indians or French troops but who could not be captured or injured. It was at first thought that the figures were just the typical raiding parties, but it soon was rumored that they could not be killed and could vanish at will. The local troops would battle with the interlopers, only for the figures to melt away and leave no bodies or blood behind. Talk was soon going around that these were not real men at all, but rather devils or demons taking the form of men to work towards some nefarious means to sow chaos in the colonies.

A local minster named John Emerson was asked by historically renowned Puritan clergyman and writer Cotton Mather to write a brief account of the spectral appearances.

"I hope the substance of what is written will be enough," Emerson writes, "to satisfy all rational persons that Gloucester was not alarmed last summer for above a fortnight together by real French and Indians, but that the devil and his agents were the cause of all the molestation which at this time befell the town, in the name of whose inhabitants I would take upon me to entreat your earnest prayers to the Father of Mercies, that these apparitions may not prove the sad omens of some future and more horrible molestations to them."

THE BRAVE STRUGGLE OF EBENEZER BABSON

The Historic Ipswich website recounts a frequently told anecdote about the strange period.

"In the midsummer time," it begins, "in the year 1692, Ebenezer Babson, a sturdy yeoman, with the rest of his family, almost every night heard noises as if some persons were walking or running hither and thither around the house. He being out late one night, when returning home saw two men come out of his own door, and then at sight of him run swiftly from the end of the house into the adjoining cornfield. Going in, he immediately questioned his family concerning these strange visitors. They promptly replied that no one at all had been there during his absence."

Staggered by this denial, Babson grabbed his gun and went out to confront the intruders. He soon saw the two men running into a nearby swamp. He then overheard one say to the other, "The man of the house is now come, else we might have taken the house." Then Babson lost sight of them.

Expecting an immediate attack, Babson and the whole family rose in consternation and rushed to the nearest garrison, which was located close by. Upon entering the fortification, they heard heavy footfalls, as if a number of men were trampling on the ground around it. Babson again took up his rifle and ran out, whereupon he saw the same two men running down the hill into the swamp.

SHOOTING AND MISSING AND SHOOTING AGAIN

For the next several nights, these men, or devils in the form of men, continued to appear in the same mysterious way, presumably to draw the local men into a wild goose chase after them. On July 14, Babson and his companions saw a half dozen men whom they supposed to be trying to lead them into an ambush. Babson fired at two of the skulking vagabonds but his gun misfired and the targets got away and hid themselves in the bushes.

Babson's comrades called out to him, "Here they are!" Babson saw three men stealing out of the swamp side by side. With sure aim, Babson fired his weapon and all three fell as if shot. He called out to his companions that he had killed three. But as he approached the supposedly dead men, they all rose up and ran away, apparently without hurt or wound of any kind. One of the spectral soldiers shot at Babson. The bullet narrowly missed him and buried itself in a tree. It was afterward dug out and preserved as a trophy of the combat.

After reloading and regrouping with his fellow combatants, Babson again shot at one of the specters, who dropped before their eyes. Upon searching for the intruder's dead body, they discovered he had disappeared. They next heard loud talking in an outlandish jargon they could not understand a word of. Crestfallen and exhausted, they returned to the garrison to report their failure to subdue the enemy. As soon as they arrived, they saw more men skulking among the bushes, men who prudently stayed out of gunshot. A few days later, they saw eleven men emerge from the orchard who seemed to be performing some strange incantations.

The colonists fired into the throng and had the same lack of success, managing only to make them scatter. It was now clear that the strange visitors bore a charmed life, and that the village was in great peril from this diabolical invasion, the end of which remained unknown. A reinforcement of sixty men from Ipswich, led by the aforementioned Captain Appleton, came promptly to the rescue and gave the garrison much encouragement, surrounded as they were by the Powers of Darkness, against which lead and steel were of no effect.

WERE THEY ONLY MERRY PRANKSTERS?

For two weeks, the village was kept in a state of continual crisis, night and day. The infernal visitors showed themselves first in one place and then in another, until an enemy soldier seemed to be lurking in every bush. Though repeatedly shot at, none could be killed. The invading devils threw stones, beat upon barns with clubs and otherwise acted more in the spirit of diabolical revelry than as if driven by some deadlier purpose. They moved about the swamps without leaving any tracks, such as an ordinary person would.

"In short," the Historic Ipswich site writes, "it was evident that such adversaries as these were must be fought with other weapons besides matchlocks and broadsword. Consequently a strange fear fell upon the area."

Finally, the ghostly enemies became even more insolently bold, refusing to run when chased and treating their pursuers with open contempt. It was understood that these insults proceeded from specters, and not from beings who were vulnerable to manmade weapons. And so the colonists ceased their efforts in the unequal contest. At that point, the demons disappeared.

None of the local clergymen doubted that the unaccountable molestations were caused by the Devil and his agents who took human form for the better execution of their dark design. However, it is not very clear what that design was. The specters appear to have been a harmless sort; they did no injury either to the persons or the property of the inhabitants.

The above accounts consist of the sworn testimony of men who actually fought with and drove the invading phantom troops before them into dark swamps and thickets. These witnesses are all persons of character and credibility, and their testimony remains unshaken by any subsequent revelations to this day.

The creatures were said by all the witnesses to be human in appearance. Whether the invaders' true form originated from somewhere demonic or extraterrestrial is anybody's guess.

Above: Dolores Barrios, who was seen at George Adamski's UFO Congress in 1954, was suspected by the crowd of being a visiting Venusian. Below: Photo taken by August C. Roberts at the New Jersey home of Howard Menger in 1959 allegedly showing three Venusians - (R to L) Valiant Thor and his companions Dunn and Jill.

ALIENS AMONGST US

Nigel Watson

Aliens have never shown themselves to the public and proved for certain that they exist. There has yet to be the proverbial landing of flying saucers on the White House lawn.

Instead of an outright public visitation or invasion of Earth, the aliens prefer to infiltrate humanity through more subtle means. The contactees of the 1950s were the first to tell us that many aliens look just like us and can go about their business undetected. Some aliens are humanoid or they are shapeshifters who can appear humanlike when desired. Other aliens can take over human bodies or share our minds to guide our behaviour. And then there are people who realize they have alien origins and abilities.

U.S. author Brad Steiger formulated a simple questionnaire in 1967 to help him interview paranormally talented individuals. After using it for two years, people began spontaneously saying that they had dreams and memories of having arrived on Earth as part of an expeditionary unit thousands of years ago; others regarded themselves as survivors of an interplanetary war or as beings of light that have now become contained in a physical body.

Over the years, with the help of his wife Sherry Hansen, he developed the "Steiger Questionnaire of UFO, Paranormal, and Mystical Experiences." After interviewing 40,000 people he found that a high proportion had dreams or memories of viewing Earth from space, being a member of a UFO crew, visiting Earth as a Being of

Light, seeing Earth in prehistoric times, viewing crystal cities and receiving knowledge from aliens onboard a UFO.

Brad noted the case of a thirty-two-year-old man, living in Ontario, Canada, who said:

"On my native planet, I was a dream interpreter. I was sent to Earth to help prepare Earthlings for the coming UFO contact on a global basis.

"I lived in a city of light, of crystal buildings, where everything was peace and harmony. I used dreams to interpret any forthcoming health problems and to help people better understand themselves. We had conquered pain and suffering by our mental abilities-and these are gifts that we will one day be able to give to Earthlings."

Another respondent was a Cherokee physicist, who remembered living in the Pleiades constellation. He said:

"We lived in domed cities with translucent walls. We could fly, communicate with animals, and transport ourselves instantly to other parts of our world.

"I remember our city as a golden color - a place of great beauty and calm.

"I came with others from my planet to help Earth through its birth pains into an intergalactic community and oneness. We were members of the priest-craft in ancient Egypt; we were alchemists in the Middle Ages; we are scientists and clergy in the modern world."

Abduction researcher John Mack noted in his book "*Abducted*" the case of thirty-four-year-old Joe, who claimed he had weird dreams and alien experiences from childhood onwards. As an adolescent he recalled looking in a mirror when he suddenly saw an alien looking at him. It had green or grey warty and bumpy skin with a small round head on a thin neck.

Under hypnosis he told of his struggle between being human and alien. In his abduction memories, he recalled that he had an alien identity, "Orion." In this humanoid manifestation he was nearly eight feet tall, but he thought he could shorten himself if he wanted to. In this state he had sexual intercourse with an alien woman called Adriana.

Doreen Virtue, in her book *"Earth Angels: A Pocket Guide for Incarnated Angels, Elementals, Starpeople, Walk-Ins, and Wizards"* noted the case of Mary Kay:

"Through guided visualization, I was taken on a trip to find my home. Jesus came forth as my guide. We went deep into the earth, and then all of a sudden, we were up in the sky. We ended up at a really bright star, so bright that I couldn't see anyone. There, I felt the love I'd been searching for my entire life. When I asked where I was, I immediately heard the word Sirius... and I had never heard that word, or of that star, before."

The day after witnessing a UFO near Jacksonville, USA, Lydia Stalnaker suddenly became psychic. Under hypnotic regression she recalled being inside a UFO where she was strapped head-to-head with another woman on an operating table. As this was spun round, her mind was merged with the other person's mind. This turned out to be the mind of a female alien called Antron.

Antron is thousands of years old and lives in a glass tube onboard a spacecraft that is close to Earth. She came from a green planet that has two suns in another galaxy from ours. Through Lydia she explained that:

"Man was here originally, in the beginning, as we are. He was built to live forever, but he failed and now we have come to take the people that have chosen of their own free will to live correctly. They will be recolonized to live as in the original beginning. We are sent to do this job."

COMMANDER SANNI CETO

Cari Barlow's alien experiences are exceptional by anyone's standards. She says:

"I have known I was from elsewhere since I was born. It was confirmed to me when my ex saw me 'shapeshift' in bed while sleeping at about 3 AM. I was visited by my ET family when I was five or six-years-old. Their visits occurred every night it seemed for about two months. Their last visit consisted of letting me watch them place implants behind both of my eyes.

"That was the only visit where they let me remember what happened and I remember it like it just happened. I have been left alone pretty much when it comes to sightings. However, since I have met Sanni, I have had many sightings with her and recently one experience aboard her people's ship!"

Cari Barlow and Sanni at the Grand Canyon.

Sanni's full name is Commander Sanni Ceto. Sanni is a hybrid and can receive transmissions from her people at all times, similar to channelling, but not the same. When she was four-years -old lightening hit the front porch of her home and she began having movie-like flashbacks. She said the flashbacks featured her in "an aircraft that resembled a flying wing-type airframe along with four others who were my crewmates as we were seated in swivel-chairs around consoles in a cockpit with a huge u-shaped window or view-screen.

"I turned my head away from my screen, which was as thin as your present laptops and came out from the wall as a flat panel. The force fields linking my vehicle to the three others in our squadron went down suddenly. It was my task as Lt. to monitor force fields and defences of my vehicle along with the three others which were discs (ships). At the time of the hit by the bolt of electricity there was a loud 'boom!' and then we went down.

"The first flew downwards and impacted the desert while mine went on a-ways to hit a mountain side. I was ejected from my aircraft and hit a big rock and my side was badly burned. In this present incarnation that same side hurts every year since usually around end of June into your month of July."

She remembers that she and her crew were labelled and put into zippered bags and flown to the eastern USA, where she was kept as a test subject on "level 2 and 1."

This is no more or less than a memory of being onboard one of the flying saucers that crashed in Roswell, New Mexico, in 1947! It is her view that the severe storms combined with weather-modification technology using special research balloons caused their aircraft to crash.

Now, with the help of Cari, Sanni helps to awaken people to their own ET identities.

AVRIL

This is not just an American phenomenon. In Britain, Avril Jenson has always been aware she is different from other people and she finds it significant she was born in 1947, the year of the Roswell crash and when the term flying saucer was coined.

As a precocious child Avril built towers and geometric shapes with old bike wheels and wood. She said she would often hide inside her creations because: "It is like being back inside your seed case, your atom." Her creations enabled her to hide from people whilst still being able to observe them. Later, she thought these were early attempts at building a time machine.

When aged three she saw an alien family with the mother holding what she thought was a handbag. In adulthood she identified her as an Anunnaki deity depicted on a Sumerian tablet. The Anunnaki are claimed by author Zacharia Sitchin to be giant humanoids who arrived from the 12th Planet and bred with humanity.

Avril confesses that "I reached my peak at five." This was when she began to intuitively understand the patterns of life people followed and she saw: "Nature as a protective cover, and childhood like a kind of nakedness." She also found she was able to create aerial mind views of the landscape and used her mental mapping ability to go on long walks and nature rambles.

Throughout her life she has been fascinated by reversals of all types from right to left, up and down, and mirror images. She imagined rooms being tilted upside down, and enjoyed dressing up as other people and identifying with their personalities.

Another major theme of her life has been to try escaping from the restrictions of normal life and existence. When she was six-years-old she was fascinated by fairies and magic carpets, to the extent that she would make wings from bamboo canes and bed sheets.

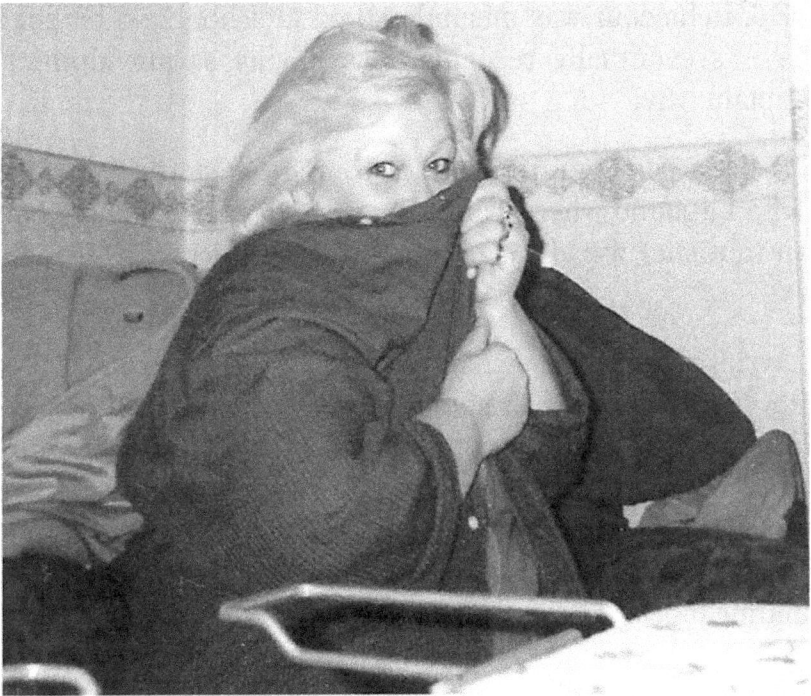

Avril Jenson

In 1969, Avril, along with her mother, saw a UFO outside their home in Washingborough, Lincolnshire. At first they thought it was no more than car headlights coming over the hill, but then a huge grey conical object completely blocked their view of the sky. Her mother said "It's a spaceship" and they both ran into the house. The local RAF base at Waddington is claimed to have tracked a UFO on radar on the same night.

Like many UFO experiencers, she is averse to meat products and is allergic to certain food types. She is prone to getting and quickly recovering from mystery illnesses and has many obsessions. These obsessions include collecting period clothing, leather books, miniature wooden boxes and ladies' hats. Avril is also fascinated by turbine engines and has an empathy with machinery, science and mathematical formulas.

Her behaviour was misunderstood at school and by her family but she was eventually recognized as having savant abilities. This helps explain why:

"I felt as if I had dropped in from another world, desperate to know who I am and where I am from. I always feel I can get back into my own (autistic) world by getting 'into' the mirror. It is 'me' in the mirror."

Avril experienced what she called a "neurological circuit quantum leap" when she was 33 years old. She said: "I moved into a new form of investigation. Previously, I had considered universal structures designed by nature. Now I moved into human structures, discovering that manmade geometric structures can make you ill, and identifying strains of illnesses from their constructs, or foundations and building blocks."

It is her view that there is a common language, non-verbal, amongst the highest functioning of autistic species. They have brains that are neurologically wired differently and in the late 1940s signals from outer space told them to reveal their existence to the world. Avril states that the Holy Lamas thousands of years ago used meditations and mantras that linked them to deep space, and that people like herself are now evolving to again bring about our awareness of the alien presence.

ASHTAR IS IN COMMAND

Commander Ashtar Sheran told channeller Blossom Goodchild that he would be coming to Earth in a giant UFO on the 14 October 2008. The prediction got world-wide publicity but he never turned up.

Ashtar has had a long history of communicating with us. Contactee George Van Tassel got psychic messages from starship commanders, starting from 18 July 1952. One of his contacts was a commander called Ashtar, who claimed that humans were created when his fellow Venusians visited Earth thousands of years ago and bred with apes.

He linked the Space People with events described in the Bible, for example that Mary was an alien and that the Ten Commandants were delivered to Moses by the aliens. He claimed that if we continued with our nuclear testing there would be a polar tilt and only those who abided by the 'Golden Rule' would be saved by the Space People.

In the late 1990s ufologist Dr. Bruce Maccabee got some messages from Ashtar Command. The first message threatened that if he did not cooperate with them, he would be ruined. This was received via meditation by a woman who said she had never heard of Ashtar. When they asked how he could cooperate, he was reprimanded for asking such an impudent question. This Ashtar was quite a spiky character. Later, Dr. Maccabee used another medium who contacted an Ashtar who was much friendlier towards him.

On an even more sinister and deadly note, Radar 1, led by Guillermo Romeu, was a group that broke away from a contactee cult called ASHTAR. Based in the village of Boulougne, Buenos Aires province, Argentina, they gathered followers and stocked up with an arsenal of weaponry to protect themselves from the "grey" aliens.

These activities prompted the authorities to raid their headquarters on 12 January 1998, and Romeu apparently killed himself. This story is quite confusing and might even be part of an Internet myth or rumour.

According to the Ashtar Command website:

'The Ashtar Command is an etheric group of extraterrestrials, angels and light beings and millions of 'starships' working as coordinators of the activities of the space fleet over the western hemisphere. Under the spiritual guidance of Sananda (the Most Radiant One), the ascended master who walked the Earth incarnated as Jesus the Christ, Ashtar, the commander of the galactic fleet and representative for the Universal Council of the Confederation of Planets, is currently engaged in Earth's ascension-process."

Their website links to many other related sites and channelled messages from Ashtar:

http://ashtar.galactic2.net/

IMPLANTS

Steven Munday is married with two children and manages a shop in Rugby. No one would suspect that his life has been shadowed by UFO sightings and paranormal experiences. As proof of his special relation with the aliens he has a pill-shaped implant in his left forearm.

His extraordinary experiences began when he saw a golden orb in the sky at age eleven. Then two years later he said he was tagged by the aliens:

"It was one evening in the summer of 1974. I was riding my bike to a friend's house near Northampton.

"The journey should have taken me 15 minutes, 20 minutes at the most. Yet, I seemed to blank out sometime during this trip. All I can remember is one minute I was riding along in bright sunshine, and then I found myself a mile further down the road wrestling with a wobbling bike, going downhill. Time had obviously moved on, as it was now dark. When I got to my friend's home it was 2 hours after I first set off, so I 'lost' about 1 hour and 45 minutes of time.

"Although it was a very disorientating experience I didn't really take much notice of it. I didn't have any flashbacks or nightmares. It was only when I was taking a shower a few days later that I felt a stinging pain in my left arm.

"It was then that I found a small object underneath my skin.

There was no sign of a scar or entry point, just a red mark. It's about 1 centimeter long by 3 or 4 millimeters wide. Since then the object has never changed shape or moved. You can roll my skin over it, so it seems to be an object independent of my body."

The implant goes through periods of being active and inactive. It can trigger scanners in supermarkets and it causes digital watches to break down. He speculates that it is being used to monitor his movements and enables them to contact him.

In adulthood, UFOs have kept appearing in his life. In 1979 he was riding a motorbike with his girlfriend when they saw a lozenge-shaped object. No time loss was experienced, but as they viewed the object they seemed to be trapped in a timeless vacuum.

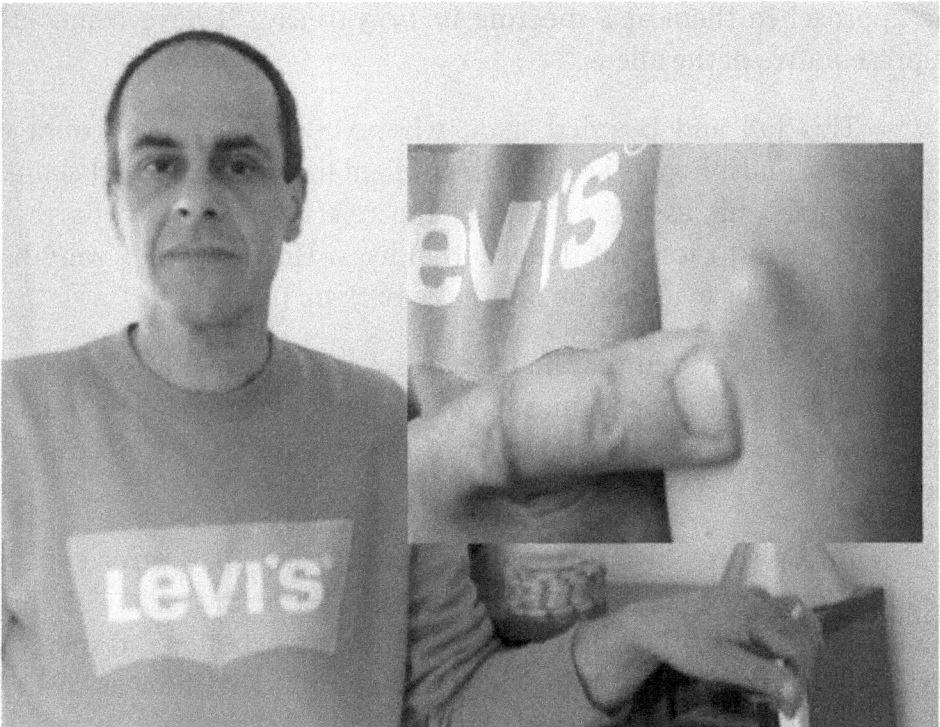

Steven Munday, along with a close-up of a pill-shaped implant in his left forearm.

The implant seems to have also given him clairvoyant and paranormal abilities. He has been able to leave his body to remotely view other places, and a month before the Twin Towers were destroyed in 2001 he had nightmares about explosions, buildings collapsing and people falling from great heights.

His two brothers have also had UFO contacts and paranormal experiences throughout their lives. They all share a rare blood type, and Steven wonders if "through our DNA and genetics we are specially chosen by these forces."

GARY

Gary claims he is an alien trapped in the body of a human being. He startled UFO researchers Jenny Randles and Peter Warrington when he approached them at a meeting in 1975 to say: "I have come as a representative of the aliens."

This tall and bearded man, who exuded a powerful aura of authority, almost hypnotically inclined them to believe his wild claims. This included his assertion that all the rejects are sent to Earth in order for them to sort out their eternal lives. However, they were not impressed by the evidence he offered to back up his claims.

They discovered that he lived a generally normal life. He had a responsible job as a mechanical research and development technician and his wife accepted his claims even though she did not necessarily believe them.

In the spirit of open-minded investigation they agreed to his request for them to arrange a meeting with the scientist Eric Laithwaite. They had no hopes for this encounter, but as it transpired Eric had a long conversation with Gary and felt that he was of help with his research into electro-magnetic propulsion systems.

Gary claims to be an alien trapped in a human body.

As they kept in contact with Gary, Peter and Jenny experienced a lot of coincidences connected with their lives and UFO research. For example, a UFO witness called Mr. L said he met an alien who told him: "A thousand of your years are but a day to us." Not long before Gary had said the very same thing to Jenny over the phone. Even stranger Joyce Bowles, who had a UFO encounter in November 1976, drew a picture of the alien she saw that looked just like Gary.

Terry Shotton was another UFO investigator who came into contact with Gary in the late 1970s. Not long after meeting him, Terry started having numerous UFO sightings and mediums started getting into contact with him. A fellow investigator lost one hour of time, and on another occasion was compelled to move away from a bus stop seconds before a car skidded into it.

Gary said that as a child he was surrounded by a light from above when playing in his garden in Northamptonshire. Looking up he saw an ovoid shaped cloud that was covered with scintillating colours, ranging from mauve through to magenta and turquoise. Since then he has never seen colours of such purity and beauty. When it flew away he had a great feeling of loss. This is when he thinks his alien self took over the boy's body. Terry got him to recall this event under hypnosis. As he recalled seeing the multi-coloured cloud he repeatedly said "I understand" without being able to elaborate what this meant. At the same session Terry was also going to undergo hypnosis but after seeing what happened to Gary he chickened out of it.

Over time Gary started contradicting himself and going on flights of fantasy. Jenny and Peter were worried that he was becoming mentally ill. They accepted that he did seem to have psychic powers and thought that at one stage "some type of phenomenon" used him to fulfil a specific purpose.

Gary explains that: "This was the time they started not to be able to keep up with me. Anyway, as we parted company back then, I went on to do other things for a later date. The paranormal events still keep on popping up, so that side of things has not changed at all…"

Today, Gary says:

"I am not alone in what I have said, and although I was the one to 'come out of the closet' first as you might say….there are still thousands still in there. They chose to come here to help humanity out at this time; humanity is about to go through a very difficult time with change and things happening to the planet. Although I made this statement a very long time ago, you are now able to see in your weather patterns that things are 'different' to what they used to be……This difference had not started back then! There is far more to come and your scientists know this now but don't know in what way."

He asserts that otherworldly powers exist and one of them is hostile. This hostile power is encouraging us to destroy our own planet for its own amusement.

ALIEN EXAMINATION

"I am not from this planet, but don't be nervous," said a stranger who asked Dr Leopoldo Diaz Martinez to carry out a thorough medical examination of him because he "travelled a lot."

The man who came to his office at the Hospital del Ferrocarril del Pacifico, Guadalajara, Mexico, in 1976, seemed at first glance to be like any other person. The main exceptional features of the man, who was 5ft 2in tall, was that his skin was very white and his eyes were violet colored. He had no hair except for some black hair around his eyes and temples. Otherwise he seemed like a healthy 40 to 50 year old, so Dr. Martinez was shocked when the man told him he was 84 years old.

The stranger told him that many aliens lived on our planet and they wanted us to find alternative sources of energy, as we are polluting our planet and are coming close to destroying ourselves. He said that they tried speaking to scientists and governments but they were arrogant and did not want to listen. This attitude was confirmed when Dr. Martinez made a special trip to the United Nations in New York to tell a delegation about his encounter. They listened to him but they decided they could do nothing about the matter.

Reference: *"Alien Liason."* Timothy Good, Arrow Books, 1992, 74-76.

HOW TO DISCOVER IF YOU ARE A STAR PERSON

Commander Sanni Ceto says you can identify a Star Person mostly by the way they look at life. Usually ETs are not able to understand negativity of any kind. They respect life of all types, do not focus so much on greed, control, ego and power, but tend to be gentle, loving, compassionate souls. Some Star Seeds, called "hybrids," can even shapeshift into their true ET form.

Here are some of the signs that indicate that you might be a Star Person:

A history of UFO and paranormal experiences.

Strange memories and dreams, especially of flying and visiting strange planets.

Psychic abilities and being highly intuitive.

Sensitivity to light, sound, electricity and electro-magnetic fields.

Subject to chronic sinus trouble, subnormal blood pressure and insomnia.

You have an extra vertebrae and have a rare blood group.

Awareness of an alien implant inside your body.

An affinity with nature and the distant past of humanity.

Doreen Virtue, a clairvoyant and spiritual counsellor, has worked with several people who are either knowingly or unknowingly Star People. She has identified several features of Star People:

1. They have crescent shaped eyes.

2. Are always helpful.

3. Are unable to cope with such common human behaviour as violence and cheating.

4. Are often out of synch with human customs like marriage.

5. Know deep down that they are not of this Earth. They feel abandoned or lost on Earth.

To confirm if you are a Star Person, Doreen suggests that you write a note asking that you receive a lucid dream about your origins and that you will remember it when you wake up. Slip this note under your pillow before you go to sleep and in the morning you might have your answer.

Catherine Adams provides more information about how to discover your alien identity and links to literature on this subject at:

http://litespirit.com/star.html

SUMMARY

The aliens amongst us are of many different types and origins. These range from aliens that look like us to those that deliberately take on our form to fool us.

Then there are the people who believe they are genetically related to aliens, or that they are sharing their body with an alien presence, or that in essence they have an alien soul or spirit at the core of their being.

Looking over the stories of Star People, it does seem that most of them have a childhood UFO experience followed by a lifetime of UFO related dreams, memories and encounters. They are also prone to having psychic abilities and paranormal experiences. Their beliefs shape their view of life on Earth and they try to live in harmony with their fellow man and the environment. Many believe they are here for the purpose of helping humanity to evolve to a higher level of spirituality and to warn us that the Earth is on the brink of destruction if we do not mend our ways. Only the future can tell......

References:

'*Gods of Aquarius: UFOs and the Transformation of Man,*' Brad Steiger, New York, Harcourt, Brace, Jovanovich, 1976.

'*The Star People,*' Brad Steiger and F. Steiger (Paschal), New York, Berkley, 1981.

'*Starborn,*' Brad Steiger and Sherry Hansen Steiger, New York: Berkley, 1992.
'Brad and Sherry Steiger's Mysteries and Miracles' website:
http://www.bradandsherry.com/

Doreen Virtue's 'Angel Therapy' website:
www.angeltherapy.com/

A two-disc DVD 'Cmdr. Sanni Ceto talks about her past life experience as commander of the UFO that crashed in Roswell NM, in 1947' is available at:
www.ufoshows.com/special.htm

Sanni Ceto's 'Commander Star Base' website:
members.tripod.com/~sanniceto/index.html

'*UFOs: A British Viewpoint,*' Jenny Randles and Peter Warrington, London, Robert Hale, 1979.

'Star People and Wanderers' website:
www.v-j-enterprises.com/starpeop.html#index

Katharina Wilson's 'Alien Jigsaw' website:
www.alienjigsaw.com

STRANGE VISITORS IN ST. LOUIS
St. Louis, USA, 1970

In a suburb of St. Louis, Missouri on May 15, 1970, Dorothy Simson was doing her work at her motel desk, as usual, examining billing documents, when she heard what she described as a "whistling sigh."

She looked up and saw that four people were standing in front of her desk. They were not normal people. They were tiny, and looked strikingly alike, as if they were members of the same family. There was a man, a woman, a boy, and a girl. They all looked young, and the "children" were almost as tall as the "parents." But they were all so tiny that they just reached the desk.

Dorothy saw that they all looked expensively dressed. The males were in tailored suits, the females in pastel peach dresses. Their hair did not look real, to the point that Dorothy thought that they were wearing wigs.

In a high pitched voice, the man said:

"Do you have a room to stay? Do you have a room to stay?"

Dorothy said yes, and told him the price, but the man did not seem to understand what she had said, and he turned to the female as if she could help him understand, but she said nothing. There was an uncomfortable period of silence, and finally the man reached into his pocket and took out a pile of banknotes, some of large value, and handed them to Dorothy.

She noticed that the banknotes were very crisp, to the point that she suspected that they were counterfeit, but a quick informal testing suggested they were authentic.

So, she took two twenty-dollar bills, covering a stay for the strange family, and gave back the rest. She asked the man to sign the room reservation form, but the man was so small that he could not reach the form on the desk, so Dorothy did it for him. The man declared that his name was "A. Bell."

He stepped forward, so Dorothy had a better look at his face and realized how strange it was.

Dorothy asked "Where are you from?"

The little man's answer was odd. He shot an arm upward, pointing at the sky, and said:

"We come from up there. Up there."

But the woman pushed his arm down, and spoke for the first time, saying that they were from Hammond, Indiana. She gave a street address.

The man then signed the register, but so awkwardly that Dorothy thought that he did not seem to know how to use a pen.

Then the woman asked where they could eat, so Dorothy indicated the direction of the motel's restaurant and the little family went there.

In the course of events, several members of the motel personnel became aware of the weirdness of the tiny "family." The motel manager insisted to Dorothy that she check the Indiana address the woman gave, and it appeared that both the name and the address were bogus.

While the weird four were at the motel's restaurant, the bellhop came over to store their luggage. He checked the parking lot to find a car with an Indiana license plate, but there was none.

The hostess who led the strange family to a restaurant table noticed that the chin of even the adults just reached the top of the table.

The little man read the menu aloud and kept asking odd questions about where milk, vegetables, and other common food come from.

The woman ordered peas and milk for herself and the children, and peas, a small steak, and water for the man. Their manner of eating was weird: each picked up a single pea with a knife, brought it to his or her tiny mouth, and inhaled it with a sucking sound. The father was unable to get even a small piece of steak through his mouth that was just a slit. They stopped eating all at the same time, and the man gave a 20$ bill to the waitress, who went to get change. But when she returned, they were all gone.

They were then found by the bellhop, who retrieved their luggage and stepped into the elevator to lead them to their room. But when the elevator door opened, the small family stepped back, showing fright and confusion. The bellhop had to reassure them that there was no danger in stepping in an elevator.

After letting them into the room, he turned on the lights, and the man suddenly began shouting at him that the light would hurt the children's eyes. The bellhop himself was now frightened by the small people and fled without waiting for a tip.

The bellhop, the manager, and Dorothy agreed that they would watch for the little people's departure next morning, but they could not see them again, although the front door was the only door they could pass through without setting off a security alarm. The alarms were checked and were in good order.

John E. Schroeder, working with the UFO Study Group of Greater St. Louis, interviewed the five motel employees who had dealt with the strange people. Schroeder found the witnesses to be credible and all were sincerely bewildered by the weirdness of the events.

Schroeder noted the description the motel personnel gave: the little people's heads seemed somewhat larger than normal, with their faces thinning abruptly to their chins. The eyes were large, dark and slightly slanted. The noses had practically no bridges; two slits for nostrils, and the mouths were tiny and lipless, no wider than their nostrils. All were pale skinned, with color descriptions varying from pearl to pale pink to light grey.

Sources: "The Strangers Among Us," report by Schroeder, John E, in "The UFO Enigma" #7, June 1987.

ENTITIES THAT MIMIC PEOPLE

Paul Dale Roberts

DEMONS & GHOSTS WHO MIMIC

As a paranormal investigator and investigating over 2,500 cases, I have discovered that either ghosts or demons seem to enjoy mimicking people. On some of my cases, especially my demonic cases, I will get EVPs in which the entity will sound like one of the occupants in the house. Case example: A case in Yuba City, CA, the patriarch of the household will hear his son talking in the bedroom. When the father opens the bedroom door, his son is not in the room, in fact his son is outside playing with his sister.

Another case that occurred in San Jose, California, the mother of the household hears her daughter chanting and she runs into the hallway to see her daughter walking down the hallway and then vanishes. The mother opens up her daughter's bedroom door and her daughter is sound asleep.

Is it possible that these children are astral projecting and that is why family members see them as ghostly figures? Or is it a ghost or demon mimicking the children of these households?

One EVP that I captured, it sounded like the couple's daughter. The EVP said..."it's time to leave now!" The daughter was in the bedroom sleeping, so we knew it wasn't actually the daughter talking into the recorder. The mother listening to the EVP exclaims..."That's my daughter's voice!!" The mother and I, ran into the daughter's bedroom and yes, she was in a deep sleep.

CROCOTTA - A CRYPTIC THAT MIMICS

My uncle Jose "Joe" Causing was a Merchant Marine and when he made a stop in India, he heard about a cryptid called the Crocotta. The Crocotta is a mythical dog wolf and is seen in India and Ethiopia. Its appearance is of a large dog, head of a hyena, has a horse like main, and a tail of a lion.

A local saw a Crocotta that was orange yellow with spots. The local told my uncle that the Crocotta can mimic human speech and will sound like it's in distress. The local said the Crocotta that he encountered cried like a small child and was yelling "Amake sahayya kara" (which means "help me" in Bengali). The local ran over to where he heard the voice and encountered the Crocotta. The Crocotta chased the local and when the local reached 3 people on a trail, the Crocotta vanished. The local told my uncle to be wary of where he walks and the Crocotta is known to be deadly.

DOPPLEGÄNGERS

When I was stationed in Germany with the U.S. Army, I took some R&R with my Sergeant Major to Slovenia and Croatia. While visiting these countries, I would ask the locals about various paranormal legends, and I was told about two legendary doppelgänger stories.

The first story is about a woman waiting for a bus and across the street she sees a bus passing by and in the last window of the bus, she sees herself staring back at her. One week later, her father died. She believes by seeing her doppelgänger, that she was cursed. The other story I heard about is that a popular teacher was teaching her class to her 5th grade students. The students looked out the window and saw their teacher outside tending to her roses and she was also in the classroom teaching a history lesson to her students. When the children told the teacher that she was also outside tending to her roses, the teacher looks outside and her doppelgänger had already vanished.

BLACK EYED BOYS

Jihanna is a paranormal experiencer and she contacted me on the paranormal hotline. She had a very interesting story to tell. This is her story. Jihanna tells me that last year in her home in downtown Sacramento; she encountered the paranormal phenomenon the Black-Eyed Boys.

She remembers that in June 2009, she saw a tall skinny kid with a baseball cap on, dirty white t-shirt, blue jeans and tennis shoes standing with a short stocky boy wearing a flannel red shirt, blue jeans and tennis shoes standing out on her driveway. They kept looking towards her kitchen window and she thought it was quite odd, because their faces seemed to be blurry. No matter how hard she tried, she could not recognize their faces. Every part of their bodies was crystal clear, but when she looked at their faces, their faces were completely indistinguishable.

The boys stood on her driveway for up to two hours and still looking towards the kitchen window. Finally, she had enough and went outside to confront the boys. When she confronted the boys, she noticed that they had no white in their eyes. Their eyes were completely black. Cold chills ran down the back of her spine. Somehow, she mustered up enough courage to ask them why they were standing in her driveway. The boys simply said... "We are sorry, we are just hungry, can we come in for a bite to eat?" She told them no. They kept asking if they could come in, Jihanna ran back to the house and locked the door, she was terrified.

Jihanna says in her own words:

"Beware strangers in the dark and lonely places where despair clings to the air and the past becomes eternal." - Benedict P. Elliot, 1887

"For a period of three days straight, they kept showing up on my driveway. Enough was enough and I called the police. When the police came they were nowhere in sight." After that, they never showed up on her driveway, but every once in a while, she would see them in the downtown area, like they were following her. Jihanna says: "They will be behind a tree, I will drive to another section of Sacramento and I would see them again or I will see them on the side of the road as I am driving by and they will just stare at me. What is amazing is that they can be in two different locations miles apart as quickly as I can drive from one point of town to another point of town.

"They always wear the same clothes. This year, I haven't been pestered by these black-eyed boys and I hope they will never come back again."

UPDATE: In 2014, Jihanna had some new neighbors that moved in next door. The neighbors were a couple (husband and wife) and their two boys. The two boys resembled the black-eyed boys! The only difference is that she can make out their faces, one boy was skinny with the same baseball cap on and a dirty white t-shirt and the brother was a short stocky boy wearing a flannel red shirt. It was uncanny, how they resembled the black-eyed boys that once terrorized her. The brothers when wearing other type of clothes helped Jihanna forget about the black-eyed boys, but she wonders if the black-eyed boys were somehow connected to these 2 brothers or they were mimicking a future event?

If the mysterious Black Eyed Children come knocking at your door...don't ever let them in!

WHEN THE BLACK-EYED CHILDREN COME KNOCKING

Sean Casteel and John Weigle

Just what or who are the black-eyed children? The phenomenon has been the subject of books and generated a great deal of interest on the Internet. But, as is the case with most paranormal entities and events, a final answer still eludes investigators.

Researcher and author Jack Kirby offers the following online summation of the black-eyed children.

"In general, the encounters are as follows," Kirby writes. "Kids, between the ages of six and 16, with pale skin, solid black eyes, and working in groups of two or more, arrive at someone's home or vehicle, knock on the door, and then insist upon being let inside. Anyone who encounters them reports immediately being overwhelmed with a sense of dread and foreboding. Besides blacked-out eyes, these children typically appear normal, although sometimes their clothing or language is reported to be outdated. Overall, though, they look like normal kids. In a way, their innocence is what makes them truly terrifying."

THE PRICE OF MOVIE TICKETS

"While it may not be the earliest sighting of all time," Kirby continues, "the earliest widely reported sighting was in 1996, by Brian Bethel, a journalist from Abilene, Texas. In Bethel's report, he describes being in his vehicle late one evening. He had pulled into a parking lot near a movie theater to write a check. He was so absorbed in this that he didn't notice two young boys approach his car and tap on his driver's side window. Bethel rolled down his window and noted immediately a 'soul-wracking fear,' though he couldn't understand why.

"The older of the two boys said that he and his brother wanted to catch a movie but had forgotten their money at home – and asked Bethel to give them a ride. They assured him that it wouldn't take long, they were just two kids, and that they didn't have a gun. Bethel found the assurances unnerving and noted that the last showing of the film they wanted to see had already started and would be nearly over by the time he could drive them anywhere and get back. In his account of the incident, he stated that when he broke eye contact with them, his fear became all-encompassing, and it wasn't until he broke eye-contact that their eyes became completely blacked out. The older boy began to get frustrated when Bethel made excuses for not giving them a ride and said that they couldn't get into the car unless Bethel said it was okay. After that, Bethel tore out of the parking lot. To this day, he still stands by his story.

"It's easy to disbelieve Bethel's story," Kirby concedes. "Particularly with the Internet's ability to grow new legends with relative ease. A subgenre of the paranormal known as Creepypasta has taken this type of experience and run with it. Creepypastas are horror-related legends that have been copied and pasted around the Internet. In fact, the name Creepypasta is a blending of the words 'creepy' and the action 'copy and paste.' These Internet-circulated stories are often brief, user-generated, paranormal stories intended to scare readers. They include gruesome tales of murder, suicide, and otherworldly occurrences and, by their nature, most are inherently fictitious.

"Is Bethel's story nothing more than Creepypasta?" Kirby asks. "Perhaps, but not entirely, as his story predates the genre and the websites that dive it. There is no doubt, however, that as Bethel's story became more widely known, particularly on the Internet, it encouraged a lot of people to come forward with their own Black Eyed Kid encounters."

DAVID WEATHERLY PRESENTS ADDITIONAL CASES

How long have BEK reports been around?

Investigator and author David Weatherly said in a lecture presented to the Close Encounter Research Organization International that he wanted to determine whether the stories were urban legends or the result of media influence. He found that the solid black eyes are common on TV now, to include "The X-Files," which featured the "black oil alien" that entered into people and turned their eyes black. There's even a BEK pictured in a scene in the 1977 film classic "Close Encounters of the Third Kind." The image is found in a painting behind actress Teri Garr, who played the wife of the character who was the main witness in the film. A clear view of the painting and information about the artist can be seen at:

http://twocrowsparanormal.blogspot.com/2013_11_01_archive.html

While there are a great many contemporary accounts of BEK from the U.S., Australia, South Africa and the U.K., Weatherly still wanted to learn whether the BEK are just a modern description of something that has been with us for much longer. He needed to look at things that fit the pattern but might have been described differently.

"I had to look through the cultural lens," he said, "of the people in the time period to discover more accounts."

One of those earlier accounts Weatherly unearthed took place in 1950, in rural Virginia. In a story passed down through the years by his family, a 16-year-old identified only as "Harold" was walking home one day and saw a kid leaning against the fence. Harold spoke to him but received no reply at first. Then the kid said, "I want to go to your house. You're going to walk me up to your house." The hair on the back of Harold's neck stood up; he saw the solid black eyes and his first thought was of how quickly he could get home. In what appeared to be mind-reading, the kid then said, "Now, don't you run away from me. You're going to walk me up to your house."

"Harold beat his personal track record making it home that day," Weatherly said.

As Harold ran up the driveway, he heard something that sounded like the scream of a bobcat. His parents believed his story, and his father took his shotgun and went out to search for the kid. His mother said, "Oh, Lord, Harold, you've met the devil. We're taking you to the preacher."

MANY POSSIBILITIES ABOUND

Weatherly went on to list some theories to explain the BEK: alien hybrids, the Men-In-Black, demonic entities, ghosts, vampires or the undead, and Djinn.

"This phenomenon really crosses over a lot of lines," he explained. "It has things in common with a wide range of different paranormal manifestations."

It's easy to understand how some of the theories could be offered. The typical gray aliens have pale skin and solid black eyes, and the resemblance is obvious. The "Selenites" in H.G. Wells' "The First Men in the Moon" (1901) also sound like grays. "This [image of the grays] is something that is somewhere in our collective consciousness at a deep level, has always been there and it just manifests in different ways."

Weatherly acknowledged that alien hybrids could explain the BEK, but he nevertheless doesn't think that is the answer. There is a small subset of people who are alien abductees and who have also encountered BEK. One should recall that abductees are often presented with a part human, part alien child they are told is "theirs," presumably so the aliens can study human nurturing responses to the hybrid children.

"That subset is the only group of people," Weatherly said, "that don't have terrifying experiences encountering these kids. They think that it's their child coming back to make contact with them."

The popularity of vampires in recent years makes some people make a connection between the undead and the BEK. Today's vampires are sexy, alluring creatures, but in the folklore and stories from which the legends originated, vampires had risen from the dead, were foul-smelling and basically disgusting to behold. In spite of how the media often portrays vampires with solid black eyes nowadays, they likely have little in common with the BEK.

There is one factor, however, that may tie the BEK phenomenon to other, better known paranormal manifestations. The vampires, the undead and demons seem to require an invitation before they can enter the space of a human target. This is one of the dangers posed by an Ouija board, in the sense that the user is issuing an invitation for spirits to enter, is in fact welcoming a negative entity into his body or mind and thus opening himself to a world of spiritual danger. Similarly, Weatherly said he has never heard of a case of the BEK forcing their way into a house or car. Every time, they try to get an invitation, and will ask for it again and again.

Weatherly told another BEK story to illustrate his point. This also took place in Texas, in the Dallas metro area. A man was coming home with groceries and found a kid standing next to the steps of his house. The kid asked, "Is it food time? I think it's food time, and you should invite me in." The witness next heard his 3-year-old pit bull start to bark. The dog charged to the front door, but suddenly put on the brakes and stumbled out onto the steps. The dog then jumped up, ran back into the house whining with its head down and its tail between its legs. The man went into the house, slammed the door and looked out the window. The kid was gone, but the dog was still terrified, even though it had killed rattlesnakes and driven off intruders in the past.

"This dog is a changed creature," Weatherly said. "It cowered under the bed in [the witness'] bedroom for days. He could only get it to go to the bathroom by dragging it out and taking it out the back door. He had to feed it under the bed. It finally recovered to where it will walk around the house, but it's a cowering, terrified animal. Something, something that these creatures are emitting, completely terrified this animal."

People suffer similar after-effects, including nightmares, repeated dreams of BEK, paranoia, the inability to return to the location of the encounter, disrupted sleep patterns, and various nervous conditions. They are, to put it simply, trauma victims. Something is happening, albeit sometimes at a very subtle level, that creates an intense level of fear in these people. But before the "flight response" kicks in, people often experience a brain fog that begins with the natural dutiful reaction that they should try to help the kid, which is quickly followed by a feeling that they are being eyed by a predator. There's confusion as the body senses the danger and fights off the desire to help, and not much is known about what could happen if the witness managed to overcome the impulse to flee.

ENCOUNTERING 'PURE EVIL'

In another case of a BEK encounter, a woman was driving home from work with her 10-year-old son, who was in the backseat of her SUV. She stopped at a convenience store and went in to pick up a couple of items. When she returned to her vehicle, there was a kid with black eyes sitting with her son, and they were touching. She grabbed her son and ran back into the store. The clerk went out to investigate, and there was no one there. He was ready to call the police but the mother told him not to. She called her husband, and he came. She didn't tell him what had happened. They changed vehicles, and she drove safely home, but the husband had an accident that totaled the car. He reported a foul odor in the car but remembered nothing else.

The son told his mother that he didn't know the BEK, but, "I asked him to get in, Mommy. I thought we could go play." The son became very ill, and his parents took him to a doctor. Every time the doctors thought they knew what was wrong with him, the symptoms changed. Their inability to diagnose the boy made it impossible to know how to treat him. The parents finally took the child home and held a vigil over him, although they were not a religious family. The boy eventually recovered.

His parents remain convinced that whatever they encountered that day was something of "pure evil," and that it was only through some kind of divine intervention that they didn't lose their son. This, too, is part of a recurring pattern. Most witnesses are not especially religious or spiritual when the encounter occurs, but often later come to feel that spiritual faith or belief offers some protection.

A NATIVE-AMERICAN LEGEND

"The most interesting theory," according to Kirby, "concerning the origins of Black Eyed Kids perhaps comes from an Iroquois Indian legend. According to this legend, the kids may be something called 'Otkon.'

"The Iroquois Indians believed in a dark power called the Otkon that could take over children and an 'Evil One' who would mate with human females to produce black-eyed, chalky-skinned, children. These children were killed by the tribe soon after birth and burned to stop them from resurrecting. Children wandering alone in the woods could also be taken over by Otkon and would re-emerge with black eyes and pale skin, acting nervously while repeating themselves over and over. Their goal was to destroy the tribe and infect all of the people with Otkon."

IRELAND'S EVIL FAIRIES

Another interesting theory is that these entities may be fairies. This story comes out of Ireland. A woman in Ireland had some odd encounters with black-eyed entities and consulted her grandmother about it.

As quoted by Kirby: "I phoned my gran," the woman writes. "Gran at this point is well into her nineties and doesn't understand the 'interwebs' as she calls them.

"I asked her a bit more about the limitations of faeries. She had some input that I shall share with you here. I'll do my best to use her words here.

"She said that the Fey are divided into two groups... Those that are evil and collect souls, specifically of children, to act as slaves to the Fey king, and those that are kind and who like and help humans.

"It is said that the evil Fey are in fact known to take the shape of a human child OR a beautiful woman, depending on the prey... As those are the two shapes that are most pleasing and will garner the most sympathy from humans. She did not have information regarding the eyes of the Fey, but she did say that the Fey cannot enter a person's home because that is protected by human energy. She did not know if they could enter if invited but she didn't see why not since that would lower the guard that surrounds the home.

"My gran has never heard of black-eyed children. However, she did say that when the Irish first came to America they brought relics and pieces of the faerie hills with them. She said another thing that I didn't even ask her about, but that she gave to me without prompt. She said that the Fey are attracted to thoughts of themselves. Meaning that if you spend a great deal of time thinking of or speaking of them that you are more likely to come across one. I thought that was interesting since I didn't ask her about that. But if I remember correctly all that is part of BEK lore."

POSSESSED OBJECTS?

In making some closing remarks in which he compared the BEK to the wicked spirits of Islamic mythology, called the Djinn, Weatherly recounted cases he has investigated of Western soldiers returning from the Middle East having purchased rings, necklaces and bracelets said to carry within them captured Djinn imprisoned there by sorcerers in the region. The sorcerers told the buyers how to release the Djinn, but not how to control them or bind them to the objects. These soldiers have since reported phenomena like poltergeists and unusual fires, and Weatherly believes the imported evil entities are having a field day, feeding off the resulting negative energy and thoroughly enjoying their own trickster antics.

"These beings," he said, "have their own agenda, and it's not a good one."

The complete text of Jack Kirby's article can be found at:

https://paranormalitymag.com/black-eyed-kids-a-new-phenomenon-or-old-world-demons/

David Weatherly has written two books, *"The Black-Eyed Children"* and *"Strange Intruders."* He has websites at:

http://twocrowsparanormal.blogspot.com

http://twocrowsparanormal.wordpress.com

http://leprechaunpress.com

Tulpas are imaginary companions who are said to have achieved full sentience, and possibly a corporeal form, after being conjured through "thought-form" meditative practice.

THOUGHTS MADE REAL

Tim R. Swartz

The human experience and our place in the universe are considered part of the great mysteries that define our existence. Are we nothing more than meaningless cosmic dust in an ever expanding and uncaring universe? Or, could we be an integral part of the universe to the extent that we have the ability to be creators ourselves? This process can be observed everyday with the physical things our minds first conceive, and then build... houses, cars, electronics, etc. But it's not just material things that are our creations; there's the possibility that our thoughts also give life, substance, to our world...our reality.

Part of our shared folklore that has been passed down over the centuries is that all of us possess the ability to create living thought-forms, or as they are known in occult literature, Tulpas. In contemporary paranormal discourse, a tulpa is a being that begins in the imagination but acquires a tangible reality and sentience. Tulpas are created either through a deliberate act of individual will or unintentionally from the thoughts of numerous people.

The term Tulpa began to be known in the West in 1929 following the publication of "*Magic and Mystery in Tibet*" by the Belgian-French explorer Alexandra David-Néel. She notes that some Tulpas are created on purpose either by a lengthy process resembling the visualization of Yidam, or, in the case of proficient adepts, instantaneously or almost instantaneously. In other cases, apparently the author of the phenomenon generates it unconsciously, and is not even in the least aware of the apparition being seen by others.

"A Tibetan painter, a fervent worshipper of the wrathful deities," David-Neel writes, "who took a peculiar delight in drawing their terrible forms, came one afternoon to pay me a visit. I noticed behind him the somewhat nebulous shape of one of the fantastic beings which often appeared in his paintings.

"I made a startled gesture and the astonished artist took a few steps towards me, asking what was wrong. I noticed that the phantom did not follow him, and quickly thrusting my visitor aside, I walked to the apparition with one arm stretched in front of me. My hand reached the foggy form. I felt as if touching a soft object whose substance gave way under the slight push, and the vision vanished.

"Even though the painter had not seen the phantom, he confessed that he had been performing a dubthab rite during the last few weeks, calling on the deity whose form I had dimly perceived, and that very day he had worked the whole morning on a painting of the same deity. In fact, the Tibetan's thoughts were entirely concentrated on the deity whose help he wished to secure for a rather mischievous undertaking."

THE YIDAM

A Yidam is a type of deity associated with tantric or Vajrayana Buddhism said to be manifestations of Buddhahood or enlightened mind. During personal meditation (sadhana) practice, the yogi identifies their own form, attributes and mind with those of a yidam for the purpose of transformation. Yidam is sometimes translated by the terms "meditational deity" or "tutelary deity."

Examples of yidams include the meditation deities Chakrasamvara, Kalachakra, Hevajra, Yamantaka, and Vajrayogini, all of whom have a distinctive iconography, mandala, mantra, rites of invocation and practice.

The creation of a phantom Yidam has two different objects. The higher one consists in teaching the disciples that there are no gods or demons other than those which his mind creates. The second aim, less enlightened, is to provide oneself with a powerful means of protection.

Reflecting on this, a Tulpa is a sentient being that becomes incarnate, or embodied through thought-form. A thought-form is a small packet of condensed psychic energy and, like all energy, the thought-form can be programmed to carry out specific tasks and/or directed to travel to a target area. They are more than just fleeting flights of subjectivity that pass through our minds and are gone...they are our creations.

Thought-forms are dependent on the people who generate the mental energy empowering them. A weak thought-form will quickly dissipate, accomplishing nothing. Good or bad, they are expressions of human creativity.

The practice of creating Tulpas is considered to be extremely dangerous for anyone who has not reached a high mental and spiritual degree of enlightenment and is not fully aware of the nature of the psychic forces at work in the process.

Powerful thought-forms, when neglected, can wreak havoc. Energy feeds on energy and a thought-form that is several weeks old will have absorbed all kinds of different influences, emotions and energies from its surroundings. This might appear amusing to some, but the mutated thought-form has often been known to reappear in the locale of its creator, only to wreak havoc, due to the outside energies it has accumulated.

If there is one thing that is important to know, it is that every thought, even the most insignificant, is a living reality. On the physical plane, a thought is invisible and intangible, but it is no less real. In its own region and with its own subtle matter, it is a living, active being.

Once the Tulpa is endowed with enough vitality to be capable of playing the part of a real being, it tends to free itself from its maker's control. This, say Tibetan occultists, happens nearly mechanically, just as the child, when his body is completed and able to live apart, leaves its mother's womb. Sometimes the phantom becomes a rebellious son and one hears of uncanny struggles that have taken place between magicians and their creatures, the former being severely hurt or even killed by the latter.

Tibetan magicians also relate cases in which the Tulpa is sent to fulfill a mission, but does not come back and pursues its peregrinations as a half-conscious, dangerously mischievous puppet. The same thing, it is said, may happen when the maker of the Tulpa dies before having dissolved it. Yet, as a rule, the phantom either disappears suddenly at the death of the magician or gradually vanishes like a body that perishes for want of food.

TULPAS STORM THE INTERNET

According to Nathan Thompson, whose September 3, 2014 article for *Vice* "Meet the 'Tulpamancers': The Internet's Newest Subculture Is Incredibly Weird," addressed the growing interest in Tulpas: "In 2009, the subject of Tulpas appeared on the discussion boards of 4chan. A few anonymous members started to experiment with creating Tulpas and fans of 'My Little Pony: Friendship is Magic' – known as 'bronies' – created a new forum on Reddit and crafted Tulpas based on their favorite characters from the show."

"The Reddit forum has 6000-plus members," writes Dr. Samuel Veissière, Visiting Professor of Transcultural Psychiatry, Cognitive Science and Anthropology at McGill University in Montreal. His study is the first academic literature about contemporary Tulpamancy. "The

Russian social networking site Vkontakte also boasts 6000+ members... [Although] actual numbers are difficult to estimate."

"The My Little Pony fandom was one of the first online communities to really grab hold of the Tulpa phenomenon," says Ele Cambria, a Tulpamancer from Warrensburg, Missouri. "Bronies are very accepting of weirdness; they have that mindset of, 'Wow, that's not normal; that's cool.' The [My Little Pony] characters evoke a simple goodness...what fan wouldn't want one for a friend?"

It wasn't long before Tulpamancy also started to attract manga and fantasy fans. "My Tulpa is called Jasmine," says Ele. "She's a human but from an alternative reality where she can do magic. I created her a dozen years ago for a fantasy series I write and then made her into a Tulpa."

From reading these descriptions it would seem that Tulpas are simply made-up characters, somewhat along the lines of the imaginary friends that many kids play with during their younger years. However, in Eastern traditions, Tulpas are more than imaginary friends. Tulpas are believed to be conscious beings with their own thoughts and desires and are not completely under their host's control. Practitioners report their Tulpas grow and develop, doing new and surprising things.

In October, 2022, Reddit poster dirtyslotmachine asked the Tulpa group if their tulpas have their own memories and can observe things you aren't paying attention to.

"I have a few weird experiences with my tulpa who is fully vocalized and I wanted to know if anyone else had similar things happen or how it's possible at all because years ago I wouldn't think it would be possible. For example, I'll be in the passenger seat of a car and I see someone in the corner of my eye and think to myself 'is that a girl?' and my tulpa responds that it is. I look at the person walking on the sidewalk and it's a girl.

"Tulpa jokes and says 'This guy should be paying more attention' then I end up drinking my water bottle with the lid still on it.

"Tulpa asks me 'What do you see?' As soon as she said that I see the letters 'EID' in my head and then it took me a minute to register that it said 'die' backwards. Just a harmless joke from her, though. She isn't malicious or anything like that. I don't understand how something of the mind could be aware of things that I am not consciously aware of."

"Tulpas are understood as mental constructs that have achieved sentience," Dr. Veissière says. Nearly 40 percent of his respondents reported that their Tulpas "felt as real as a physical person," while 50.6 percent described them as "somewhat real… distinct from [their] own thoughts."

In Dion Fortune's book, "*Psychic Self-Defense*," she mentions a wolf spirit that was tormenting her. This wolf it turned out was nothing more than a creation of her own will. It is also an incredible example of a Tulpa, with the exception that the wolf was never bound to her will.

A Tulpa can take on any idea, shape or purpose…the more complex the purpose, the more focus and energy required. A Tulpa created with a given purpose, such as protection, will be more effective than one whose purpose is to protect, warn, or even expedite services.

Some have asked if some thought-forms have a reality of their own, separate from the human mind, such as an elemental. Theosophists and clairvoyants Annie Besant and C. W. Leadbeater placed thought-forms in three classifications: (1) the image of the thinker; (2) an image of a material object associated with the thought; and (3) an independent image expressing the inherent qualities of the thought. Thoughts which are of a low nature, such as anger, hate, lust, greed, and so on, create thought-forms which are dense in color and form. Thoughts of a more spiritual nature tend to generate forms possessing a greater purity, clarity, and refinement.

Thought-forms then exist in either the mental or astral plane. Each entity is created from thought. Every thought is said to generate vibrations in the aura's mental body, which assumes a floating form and colors depending on the nature and intensity of the thought. These thought-forms are usually seen by clairvoyants and may be not only intuitively sensed by others, but actually seen as physical entities.

Taking all of this into consideration, it is not unreasonable to consider that all spiritual entities not considered to be human spirits may be constructs of the human mind...astral beings, elementals, angels, deities etc. Could this also explain other things? Such as cryptid c1reatures along the lines of Bigfoot, lake monsters, or even UFOs? Could all of these things be creations of the world's group mind?

Thought-forms sometimes occur spontaneously. "Group minds" can emerge whenever a group of people concentrate on the same thought, ideas, or goals, such as a team of employees or a crowd of demonstrators. To a certain extent, the group-mind possesses the group; such is seen in psychic bonding and power that coalesces in crowds, and in the synergy of a close-knit working group. Usually when the group disbands the power of the group-mind dissipates too.

If enough people believe in gods such as Zeus, or Odin, then those beings can take on a life of their own. There are old stories, mistakenly categorized as mythologies, where people actually had personal encounters with their deities, much like people today who say that under times of great personal difficulty they saw and spoke with angels or even Jesus.

We are not here to say that one's religious beliefs are wrong. Instead, we are suggesting that our combined personal beliefs may have a hand in creating spiritual beings that take on the role of ghosts, demons and even gods. The actual creative force in this and all other realities is far too complex for our minds to conceive. But perhaps we create our gods that are in OUR own image, not the other way around.

THE CREATION OF PHILIP

One famous attempt to create a Tulpa was conducted in 1973 by members of the Society of Psychical Research in Toronto. The objective of the group was to create a fictional character, which they named "Philip." Through a purposeful methodology, they attempted to contact the fictional entity and receive readily-apparent communications from it in return.

The group created a biography along with a sketch, to put a face on their fictional being. They then began formal weekly sittings in the "Philip Room," where they sat together and discussed Philip and his life, meditated on his being, and attempted to create a "collective hallucination" of his spirit. During the early sessions, the group sought to create a common mental picture of Philip and his surroundings, focusing on his appearance and day-to-day activities.

The group's sessions continued for several months with no results until it was suggested that the lights be turned off to create an atmosphere that was less academic and more conducive to the summoning of ghostly spirits. Just as if they were having a traditional séance, group members sat around the table, placing their fingers lightly on the surface, and called for Philip to appear.

Shortly afterwards, a loud rap echoed through the room. Members of the team noted later that the rap was distinctive, clear, and so violent that the table itself vibrated. This was followed by a number of distinctive knocks. After these first communications from "Philip," the group began querying the entity, agreeing on a "one rap for yes, two for no."

After this point the group began to experience a wide range of paranormal events that has never been explained scientifically. Philip began producing extraordinary visible physical manifestations. In response to questions, group members began to hear whispers in their ears. In one of the early sessions, the group was stunned when the table suddenly, and violently, jumped and slid across the floor. At one point the table began to "dance," tilting onto a single leg and spinning about with the group members frantically running in a circle in an attempt to keep their fingers in place.

Philip even seemed to display emotions of his own. He refused to answer certain questions, saying they were too personal. It even seemed that his feelings could be hurt. In one session a group member told him that he could be sent away and replaced. Afterwards, Philip's activity began to tail off.

In conclusion, the experimenters were never able to prove the "how" and the "why" behind Philip's manifestation. Did they conjure up an actual entity that simply latched onto the Philip story? Or, was Philip a direct result of the group's collective subconscious manifesting a thought-form...a Tulpa?

THE SLENDER MAN

A more recent example of how a thought-form might be created through "group-think" is the Slender Man phenomenon. The idea of the intentional creation of Slender Man as a Tulpa came as early as August of 2009, when the idea was first thrown around in the "Something Awful" forums where participants were invited to submit original scary stories and Photoshop images of paranormal phenomena. These submissions were the first creations of what would later be named The Slender Man.

The original fiction stories primarily had the Slender Man targeting children, though this quickly shifted to young adults – the most common online storytellers. The Slender Man stories often feature characters that fall down rabbit holes and discover an otherworldly presence is now stalking them, and whose very existence exudes malevolence.

While his presence sometimes encourages human violence (depending on the version of the story) it is the inhuman unknown that makes his story so terrifying. The basic premise is that the Slender Man is a non-human presence who stalks victims. He is faceless, thin, and grotesquely tall.

Depending on differing versions of the story, he may have arms that are tentacles; he is bald and almost always wears a suit. He is often hidden in or disguised by trees. He may be able to teleport and may cause physical illness and/or insanity in those he is around. He is the textbook definition of the uncanny – his similarities to human form yet otherworldly features and appendages make him almost human, but not quite. His blank face makes him both familiar and mutable.

The interesting thing about the whole Slender Man mythos is that it wasn't too long before people started reporting actual sightings of something that bore a striking resemblance to Slender Man. Some of these personal encounters happened long before the whole Slender Man meme began, so it is a question of is Slender Man a thought-form brought to life by the collective attention from the internet? Or is it a creature that was already real and superficially looks like collective ideal of the Slender Man? Or perhaps it is some supernatural entity with no true form that is able to "borrow" the form of the Slender Man to illicit as much fear as possible?

In 2014, two 12-year-old Waukesha, Wisconsin, girls lured a friend into the woods and stabbed her 19 times. Fortunately, their victim, Payton Leutner, who was intended as a "sacrifice" to Slender Man, survived the horrendous attack. The girls, Morgan Geyser and Anissa Weier, told authorities they believed that Slender Man could be found at his mansion, called Slender Mansion, in the Nicolet National Forest, and the attack was needed to appease him.

It appears that Slender Man may have been able to leap from the digital realm into the "real" world. Here are some other examples of encounters with the Slender Man.

"Years ago, before I had even heard of Slender Man, there was a story of him around my old neighborhood. We did not actually call him Slender Man, but some kids had reported seeing a tall, older man in a suit walking around the graveyard. There was a specific story that sticks out to me told by a girl that was in college at the time.

"This girl was my friend's older sister and she was telling me about how she was skateboarding home one night and she had to pass the cemetery, which was the block over from hers. She kept seeing tall, lingering shadows following her, but she thought nothing of it until she got home and saw a tall, older man wearing a black suit standing in her back yard. She ran inside and looked out the window to see him standing across the street under the trees. She said he didn't leave all night and that she would see him every now and then in the same spot.

"There were so many other stories almost identical to hers around my neighborhood. I never actually saw anything and I'm pretty glad that I didn't. I'd be worried that he was outside of my window right now, but I live across the country from my old home. I wonder if there are still stories of him there."

Another story is told.

"This happened at about the time I was four or five. Like any other little kid I would get scared of most things, but this one time scared me more than any other. After a normal day in the life of a kindergartner, I went to sleep at about ten o'clock or so. Half the time

I either forget my dreams or just don't dream at all. Tonight was not one of those nights.

"After drifting off to sleep I begin a very weird dream. I see myself walking down a long, narrow, dark corridor, light only coming from a door at the very end. I slowly walk through the hallway to the room, which is very bright, the entire room seeming to be covered in white. I walk into the room, but there's nothing to explore in there.

"As I'm about done looking at this room, I turn around back to the door to get in the corridor again, where this time there's a man standing there. I just see his long, black, business suit, and I start looking up closely. 'Okay, red tie...' I think to myself. I eventually look at his face.

"There is no face.

"I am looking at a white orb with a neck wearing a business suit, standing almost eight feet tall. Like any normal kid my age, I scream. The scream rips me away from the dream into real life. I'm sweating and my heart is racing. I look towards the clock to read 12:57 AM. My dad opens the door to my room, and when he comes in he asks what's wrong. Apparently, on my dad's recalling, he claims I said, 'Tall Stick Man.'"

Pastor Swope, who has the blog "The Paranormal Pastor," writes about a phone call he received in August of 2009, from a woman named "JoAnne":

"...from childhood I have seen this demonic figure. He is a tall shadow. He has no face, but he has long arms. Out of the corner of my eye on certain nights I see him and his arms seem to be reaching out to me, and when I turn to look at him, the thing is gone. I have the real feeling that if I don't turn around to look at him his arms will catch me up and I will die."

JoAnne then described some personal details of her life that accompanied the "Slender Man" appearance, which included child abuse and neglect at a young age. Close to the end of her letter she made the chilling announcement...

The Slender Man meme began in June 2009 when a competition on the web forum "Something Awful" asked for ideas for a modern myth under the topic: "Create Paranormal Images."

"I am afraid that he is stalking me, and that one day I will not be able to catch him trying to snatch me up. This fills me with such fear, words can't describe. Sometimes I think I am going nuts. I feel like he is going to get me when I don't expect it. Some nights I can't sleep. Noises outside make me jump. When the wind cranks up and things start to rattle, I am so scared. I need help!"

Swope responded to "JoAnne" and gave her some simple prayers and commands for the entity to leave her alone. He said that he soon started to receive other similar stories.

One anonymous comment was posted on his blog on January 12, 2010 that in part reads:

"My name is_____. I am being hunted by a shadow creature. It is tall and thin and tries to catch me in its long arms. I saw it in a dream, and now it is real. All I see in the face are two eyes, and when I look in them those arms try to get me."

Another was posted in July, 2011.

"...every night since the start of June, between 12 and 4 in the morning I get a phone call from my ex-girlfriend. She has been attacked or is being stalked by a ghost or something more. Let me tell you a bit about her before I go any further. She has severe depression, insomnia. She also has some mental trauma, what kind I will not say, because that is between me and her, but as far as I know, that could be the entire reason why this is happening. Anyways, since I've been dating her, a person she calls 'The Man' has been giving her distress. Apparently he's been around a lot longer then I've known her, but she says that it wasn't that bad when she was younger.

"Her first experience with 'The Man' happened when she was around seven or eight-years-old. She would see a man with no real face, just a body and a blank mass where a face was, in her backyard standing by the fence. Not really believing in ghosts, she freaked out and called her mom, saying there was a person outside. When her mom got there, she saw a glimpse of a person before he vanished behind the fence. How much of this is true, I don't really know. I was just told these stories by her family when I came over now and again.

"About a year ago, she called up around midnight complaining of 'The Man.' She said she could feel someone watching her through her windows, and she wouldn't get out from under her covers to turn on a light or do anything. But back then I was her boyfriend and had to fight the big bad monsters for her, so I had to coach her on what to do and when to do it so she wouldn't be scared. I would always tell her it's ok and that she will be fine. There were several instances where I believe either she was possessed or just the trauma of her past affected her to the point where she developed a split personality. It's also a reason why I think the trauma and 'The Man' are linked.

"I could immediately tell something was different because of her eyes. Normally they were a pretty blue, but then they were cold and grey. Finally, after we broke up, after three years, in January, the man seemed to disappear. Up until June she talked to me occasionally but never past midnight. But now she calls every night between 12 and 4 complaining of 'The Man.' I guess he's been watching her more and more. Every night he looks through her window or watches from the woods when she walks through her house..."

Swope wondered if this was all some sort of fiction become reality because of the overworking of imagination and psychosomatic power, like a Tulpa? Or is it a demonic entity that has taken on the guise of an internet mythos to feed on fear and destroy the minds of those that fall into its deception?

He was about to go with the latter until he heard a few stories that place the Slender Man in paranormal experiences before the mythos was ever created. The first came from a coworker of Swope's.

"Around 2002 she worked at another location and made friends with a woman who had paranormal encounters. One of the most chilling took place in the middle 1990s when in the middle of the might she woke up to see a tall, dark and thin humanoid figure at the end of her bed. It reached out its arms and its finger elongated to an inhuman length and reached toward her head.

"She was paralyzed, and. even though she tried to scream and move, she could not. As the tendril fingers wrapped around her head she lost consciousness. Soon after that she noticed she was sluggish. She became ill, had frequent headaches and nausea and could not sleep. So she sought medical help, and as a consequence had an X-Ray done of her head and upper torso.

"The doctors found that a small metallic object had been implanted into the base of her skull. When the doctors tried to remove the foreign object they found that it had become entangled into the central nervous system at the spinal cord, and it was too risky to remove. The woman even showed the operation scar to my coworker as proof. But my coworker still did not believe the story, which aggravated her friend very much. The friend then brought her X-ray to work and showed my coworker the proof. A small metallic object had been implanted at the base of her skull in such a location that made it inoperable."

Swope wondered whether this woman was an alien abduction and implant survivor. At first look that seems the conclusion, but the appearance and aftereffects of the encounter match the Slender Man mythos so closely it gives one pause.

"In fact, after telling my coworker of the Slender Man mythos," Swope writes, "she was shocked and a bit unnerved. It fit perfectly. But why the implant? Perhaps to follow you the rest of your life?"

CREATURES OF THOUGHT

Tim R. Swartz

One intriguing thought concerning the creation of Tulpas and thought-forms is the idea that much of the "High Strangeness" that people experience throughout the world might be a type of "Tulpa-Like" creation. By "High Strangeness," we are referring to aspects of already "strange" phenomena such as UFO sightings that go beyond someone seeing lights in the sky to those lights turning into a group of glowing humanoids who get inside a car and drive away into the dark.

You can also include strange creatures such as bigfoot, lake monsters, dogmen, lizardmen, giant birds, even things that look like prehistoric dinosaurs. We can certainly include ghosts, shadow people, fairies and elves, even Santa Claus. These creatures, for all intents and purposes, seem to have been dropped straight out of a fever dream and into our reality.

Some researchers have toyed with the idea that these modern cases of high strangeness demonstrates the existence of the mythological "Trickster" whose purpose is unknown, but who seems to be the guiding force in awakening the consciousness of humanity. This awakening is essential if mankind is ever going to shake itself free from the old gods, the old ways, and realize our true role in reality.

"The so-called civilized man has forgotten the trickster. He remembers him only figuratively and metaphorically, when, irritated by his own ineptitude, he speaks of fate playing tricks on him or of things being bewitched. He never suspects that his own

hidden and apparently harmless shadow has qualities whose dangerousness exceeds his wildest dreams." Carl Jung

The trickster figure is more than a mere story, more than a mere metaphor. It's an archetype of the collective unconscious. It is part of us, and our minds project it "out there" in symbolic, poetic, cryptic, semi-autonomous thought-forms that change from culture to culture, age to age, person to person, religion to religion.

In our modern space-age culture, it has taken the form of UFOs for many people. The archetype is projected "out there" in UFO form where it is seen by many people. A public dream that is solid enough for radar to bounce off of.

But how can that be, you ask? If UFOs are mere projections, then there shouldn't be any physical evidence, right? Radar can't bounce off a dream...you can't take a photograph of a psychic object, can you?

"Oh yes, this is an important point to make, which the flying saucer people are forever misunderstanding, and that is that saying the flying saucer is a psychic object does not mean it is not a physical object. Jung in "Mysterium Coniunctionis" is at great pains to say that the realm of the psychic and the realm of the physical meet in a strange kind of never-never land that we have yet to create the intellectual tools to explore. This is where the mystery of synchronicity is going to come to rest, the mystery of all kinds of paranormal activity on the part of human beings, and the mystery of the flying saucer." Terence McKenna

We are all psychic, and we are mostly ignorant of that fact. But our ignorance of that fact doesn't mean that our minds don't utilize that ability unconsciously. People who don't believe in psychic ability are still using it, unconsciously, even to protect their disbelief. It's called the sheep-goat effect. It was discovered by Gertrude Schmeidler.

"The data convinced me. Repeatedly, average ESP scores of subjects who rejected any possibility of ESP success (whom I called goats) were lower than average ESP scores of all other subjects (whom I called sheep). This was inexplicable by the physical laws we knew; it implied unexplored processes in the universe, an exciting new field for research. From then on, naturally, my primary research interest was parapsychology." Gertrude Schmeidler

Charles T. Tart, a psychologist and parapsychologist known for his psychological work on the nature of consciousness, agrees with Schmeidler's research.

"Goats," or test subjects who don't believe in psychic ability, unconsciously use their hidden psychic ability to suppress evidence that contradicts their conscious belief-system resulting in low scores. Sheep" are test subjects who believe in psychic ability and so they have nothing to fear from high scores. So their psychic ability comes forth to conscious awareness much easier.

"The sheep thought they could do it, they got 'good' scores, they were happy. The goats knew there was no ESP, nothing to get, they got poor scores, they were happy, that "proved" their belief. These were not people who were sophisticated enough about statistics to know that scoring below chance could be significant...Many other experimenters replicated this effect over the years. The only way I've ever been able to understand it is to think that the goats occasionally used ESP, but on an unconscious level, to know what the next card was and then their unconscious, acting in the service of their conscious belief system, influenced them to call anything but the correct one."

The same sort of thing is going on all the time, but on a much wider scale. We are sleepwalking through life, our minds are not really awake, and so we are unconsciously using our hidden (and sometimes not so hidden) psychic ability (including mind-over-matter) to project archetypes of the collective unconscious such as the trickster "out there" in psycho-physical form, where they can support and perhaps even guide our belief-systems.

The paranormal, psychic, mystical powers of our unenlightened, sleepwalking collective minds are creating tuplas, thought-forms, creatures of thought, and are projecting them out into reality in mythological forms. These forms are solid enough to bounce radar and leave physical traces because of our collective and unconscious mind-over-matter ability. The more we take the forms literally, as something separate from us and "out there," then the easier it is for the trickster archetype to remain on the threshold and string us along until we collectively awaken and realize that it has been us all along.

LIVING GHOSTS

Paul Dale Roberts

Every once in a while, I am a guest speaker here and there. I will find ghost hunters in my audience and one of the questions that I ask is...how many people here know what a "living ghost" is? It always seems like no one knows. In this chapter, I will explain what a living ghost is and tell you about a recent investigation that we had that dealt with a "living ghost."

PEOPLE WHO HAUNT

HPI (Halo Paranormal Investigations) received a call in which the occupants of a home in Sacramento kept seeing an old man using a walker falling down and hitting his head on a side table. The old man would then fade away. The occupants of this house saw the apparition of the old man three different times, usually around 5 PM. When I went to this home, I hung around and waited for 5 PM to come. When 5 PM came, there was no apparition of an old man with a walker. Nor was I able to obtain any kind of evidence, EVPs, etc.

So what do I think happened here? I discovered that the occupants had lived there for five years and the occupants before them were an old man with a walker and his wife. The old man with the walker is their uncle, who had given them the house and moved away to a rest home. Their uncle is very much alive. The occupants made the claim that the apparition that they saw did look like their uncle.

A living ghost is thought to be a disembodied spirit from
a still living person that haunts other people or places.

A GHOSTLY TWIN

This doppelgänger is an example of a living ghost. The residual energy
is so strong that every so often it repeats itself. It was a traumatic
event when their uncle fell and hit his head on the table. In fact, on
the day that he did that, they had to call an ambulance and he had a
mild concussion. The event itself released so much negative energy
into the atmosphere that the incident replays over and over again.
When the energy is at its peak, the new occupants are able to see the
event play out.

A similar incident happened in Chicago, Illinois. Year: 1974. A couple moved into a new neighborhood. The house they moved into seemed to be haunted, because at 2 am, they saw an apparition of a man walking over to the couch. Then an apparition of a woman appeared. The man, when confronting the woman, started slapping her. Then they both dissipated and vanished. The couple that moved into this home saw this incident four times.

On one particular day, they were invited to the neighborhood block party. The host of the party told them that they have a block party every Labor Day; it's a tradition. The host invited the couple to thumb through his photo albums of past events at this block party.

As the woman thumbed through one photo album, she was shocked and surprised to see the couple that had manifested in her home. She yelled out... "These are the ghosts in my house!" The host looked at the photo and said..."They are not ghosts. Both people are alive. They had domestic disputes, and the police have been to the house a few times. They got a divorce. The woman lives five blocks down the road and the husband moved out of state. They are very much alive."

This is an example of "living ghosts." The negative energy released into this home replays itself over and over again. Very strong negative residual energy. You do not have to be dead to be a ghost.

NERVOUS ENERGY

There is another example in which a politician was giving his first speech on a street corner in the 1800s. He was very nervous and did not like speaking in front of a large crowd. This nervous energy was released into the atmosphere and people to this day in Seattle, Washington, claim they see a man in a black suit, standing on a soap box and acting like he is talking to a crowd of people. Then he vanishes.

In Sacramento, another case of "living ghosts." At a costume shop called *Evangelines*, on the third floor, late at night, you can hear people laughing and talking, you can hear old 70s disco music, and you can hear the shuffling of feet. But when you go up to the third floor, there is no one there.

Back in the 70s, the third floor was a nightclub called D.O. Mills where people would have fun and dance. This is the strong positive residual energy that has impacted the atmosphere and replays itself over and over again. Another case of "living ghosts."

One of those living ghosts on the third floor could be me, because I was very heavy into the disco scene in the 70s and at times would party at D.O. Mills.

Special Note: In Japan, they also believe in "living ghosts," but there interpretation is somewhat different. Ikiryō (lit. "living ghost"), also known as shōryō, seirei, or ikisudama, is a disembodied spirit in Japanese popular belief and fiction that leaves the body of a living person and subsequently haunts other people or places, sometimes across great distances. The term(s) are used in contrast to shiryō, which refers to the spirit of those who are already deceased.

DOPPELGÄNGER STALKS HAUNTED SACRAMENTO HOME

The HPI team recently received a call for help from Rosey. Her family was experiencing severe and unexplained paranormal activity in their home in Sacramento, California, which was built in 1910.

The family was seeing lights going on and off on their own and shadow people in the house, and smelling a rotting meat-like odor. Rosey's husband and close friend had recently passed away.

Rosey's granddaughter was scratched on her back by an unseen entity, and a doppelgänger mimicked Rosey's appearance. Just recently, it made another appearance as Rosey's granddaughter.

SCOPING OUT THE HOME

Our team's psychic medium, Deanna Jaxine Stinson, and I went on a test run to view the exterior of the home. We had our dogs, Story and Champagne, with us.

I had not told Deanna the address of the home, but she was still able to point out the house immediately. She pointed at the house and said she felt strong negativity. At this point, the dogs started barking and howling.

Deanna then said that she sensed there was a curse placed on the house and the family.

As we parked by the home, Deanna began feeling nauseated. I immediately said that we should head home. As we were leaving the house, Deanna's nausea went away and the dogs stopped barking.

That night, I dreamed I was at a meat processing plant and there was meat hanging on hooks. As I approached the meat, it smelled foul. I wondered if the dream had anything to do with the home and the reports of the family smelling rotten meat.

When I told Rosey that Deanna felt the house was cursed, she agreed and believes it has to do with her downstairs renter, who practices Dark Arts, dark witchcraft, and does not like Rosey. In fact, this renter did not want me to cleanse the home and was very angry about it.

THE INVESTIGATION

When I arrived for the investigation, I gave Rosey a blessed care package created by Deanna that had assorted candles, Dragon Blood

Sage, and other items. Rosey briefed me about the torment she had felt in the home. Things had been so terrifying that she started crying during the interview.

Rosey recounted what sounded like doppelgänger activity. At one point, the entity presented itself to Rosey's granddaughter as an older version of the granddaughter. Rosey was also hearing whispering in the kitchen.

We captured an EVP of a woman saying, "Can you hear me?" in the kitchen, and, in one of the bedrooms, we captured an EVP that sounded like a woman and a man talking. The voices said, "They are trying to be quiet now." Our ghost-hunting teddy bear was beeping like crazy at the same time that we captured the EVPs.

At the end of the investigation, I conducted a Roman Catholic house blessing, with Rosey walking along with me. She was very emotional during the process, but both Rosey and her granddaughter were very appreciative that I showed up to conduct the investigation and cleansing.

Source: "Paranormal Underground" - October, 2020

PARASITE-MIMICS – DEVOURERS OF EMOTIONS

Paul Eno

Four times, various members of Lucy Cormier's family saw a female figure with long, blonde hair – looking just like the 15-year-old Lucy – leaning over the girl's bed while she was asleep. This took place not only at the family home in Glastonbury, Conn., but nearly 100 miles away, at their vacation home on Block Island, Rhode Island.

Minor poltergeist phenomena took place. Kitchen cabinets would rapidly open and close on their own, books and other objects in different rooms would move, and family members and guests heard occasional heavy footsteps in the attic and on the stairs. There were loud banging sounds on several occasions.

Interestingly, phenomena seemed to follow Lucy, not only at home but at the homes of friends. In the course of the case, I saw this myself.

Today, we might say that Lucy had an "attachment." But it was the mid-1970s, and I was very confused. A student for the priesthood, I had been involved in several exorcisms, as an assistant to the priest, and had been through the now-famous Lindley Street Poltergeist haunting in Bridgeport, Conn., with Ed & Lorraine Warren, in 1974.

I was confused because these entities just weren't playing the role they were supposed to, at least according to traditional paranormal ideas. The "demons" seemed to me more like provocateurs and cosmic mosquitoes than servants of Satan. In fact, they seemed to use our theology against us by exciting anger, fear, frustration and other negative emotions that they could "eat."

And there always seemed to be a trigger.

In Lucy's case, the trigger was the ubiquitous Ouija board, which she had received as a present the previous year. Merry Christmas.

In modern folk belief, using a Ouija board attracts demons, or at least negative human spirits. In my experience, the Ouija board and other sledgehammer divination techniques can smash through the membranes (physicists actually call them that) between parallel worlds, worlds that often have different laws of physics and very different inhabitants, and let in anything hungry and hostile that happens to be there.

THE OUIJA BOARD IS A DINNER BELL

Lucy and a friend had used the board often during the 1974 Christmas vacation. Both girls became fascinated by the "spirit world." Sure enough, here came – *ta da* – Arten the Spirit Guide! Arten communicated through the board, pretending to be the girls' friend but stirring up their emotions.

Lucy's older brother, Bill, her only sibling, became interested, too. I never met Bill because he had enlisted in the U.S. Navy, but was told later that he was a very happy and positive fellow, the sort of person whose lack of negativity hinders or even repels parasites.

Their ROCINO parents (Roman Catholic in Name Only) thought nothing of it.

In mid-1975, Bill left for basic training, perhaps removing a positive roadblock for "Arten" and, apparently, several associates.

Lucy and her parents were startled by certain phenomena that began late that year and continued into 1976.

In August that year, I was with Ed and Lorraine Warren when they happened to lecture in Glastonbury. I sat in the back of the hall. The young man who sat down next to me and started chatting, having no idea who I was, happened to be a concerned friend of Lucy's family who knew what was happening at the Cormier home. When Ed Warren asked me to stand up and be recognized, as an eyewitness to the still-being-talked-about Bridgeport poltergeist case, the young man's jaw hit the floor.

The next day, he put me in touch with the Cormiers, and, a few days after that, I interviewed Lucy for the first time. I felt, somehow, that Lucy and I weren't the only ones in the room. In fact, I felt three other presences.

"I'm not afraid at all," the girl told me. "I think it's fascinating, really. I have kind of a boring life, and I'm not very popular. I like the attention I get from Arten. In another life, I could have loved him."

This was the classic pattern, a parasite-mimic finding an "in" to make a girl, and perhaps her entire family, into a hot lunch. The Ouija board and the "Arten" persona were the ins. The resulting phenomena stirred up the fear and other negative emotions that fed the parasites. The skilful parasite makes its victims like it by feeding their egos. In Lucy's case, here was a teen with a "boring" life receiving attention from some dashing cosmic being.

I witnessed some of the phenomena for myself. And, at one point, I accompanied Lucy and her boyfriend to his sister's lovely 18th century farmhouse in nearby Coventry, Conn. We all saw an orange, glowing ball, what today would be known as an "orb," and something followed us around the house, turning on lights as we went.

The Ouija Board, while marketed as a game, is thought by many to be a dangerous conduit to unfriendly residents of the astral plane.

I turned around and followed it, more by feeling than sight. It led me into a bedroom and disappeared into what I was still calling a "portal." Today I would call it a "parallel world intersect point."

This case was, perhaps deceptively, easy to cure. My colleague Joseph Letendre, who later became an Eastern Orthodox priest, joined me in reading prayers with the Cormier family at their home. Then, in the absence of a priest, we took the liberty of sprinkling holy water around the house. Most importantly, we got Lucy to say that she didn't trust Arten, and would never engage in occult practices again. Hopefully, she meant it. She handed over the Ouija board and we destroyed it.

I was back to graduate theological studies at St. Vladimir's Seminary in New York that fall, so I admit that my follow-up with the Cormiers wasn't what it should have been. But as I left them, positive energy seemed to rule, phenomena had ceased, and Lucy seemed happy.

Also, hopefully, the parasites sought greener pastures.

The question arises: Was the Lucy-like figure the family members saw really a mimic, or was it an actual ghost, or perhaps another facet of Lucy (from a parallel life) looking in on her out of concern? We have seen overwhelming evidence that the latter is possible because, as I've said, parallel worlds often have very different laws of physics, and thus heightened layers of multiversal awareness and access.

In the ensuing decades, I have run into many more parasites who were mimics, and I will share a few more of these. But first, a look at parasites. Over the years, some nine different species of energy parasites have become evident, at least to me. Most can be responsible for mimic phenomena.

THE WISE

The most intelligent and resourceful parasite group is "The Wise," a term I use with the caveat that it means nothing good for the likes of us. These high-end parasites come across as very ancient and full of knowledge about the multiverse, their prey in general, and the inhabitants of our world in particular. They give the impression of knowing our species far better than we do. They are conversant in most, if not all, human languages, and have great telepathic power.

In my experience, they live and hunt alone. They will quietly park themselves in a place or time where they have access to a certain house or tract of land for centuries, picking up what knowledge they can and feeding on whomever comes along. I have found them to be arrogant, brilliant and extremely calculating. At the same time, once they know that you "have their number," they can become surprisingly willing to communicate in a smug and not-to-be trusted manner.

They can be brilliant mimics.

In a 1998 case in Pascoag, Rhode Island, a "Wise" parasite, which had probably been at the land for a very long time, decided to take up residence in the wall of a bedroom in a nearby house, whence it chose a temporary female resident as prey.

Through verbal and telepathic communication, it convinced this woman that it was her angry lover from a past life. The woman even wrote a love poem to the parasite, who was called Frank! "Frank" even convinced an experienced psychic that it was telling the truth.

There were physical phenomena. Most notably, the woman would wake up in the middle of the night, crying things like, "I died for you!" She would have red finger or claw marks around her neck. A scientist working with me at the time actually witnessed this.

On my advice, the woman moved out of the house and, in several years of my follow-up, had no more problems.

THE ELDERS

Like the Wise, the Elders seem to have great knowledge and experience, but they are more likely to be found working together and to be leaders among other kinds of parasites. They do not seem as interested in humans and human life as the Wise, except, of course, as food sources: snacks, as it were. I've seen some evidence that they also feed on animals.

One example of the latter took place on a farm in Maryland in 2002. The family contacted me through a mutual friend, noting that they were alarmed by banging sounds outdoors and in the farm outbuildings. Livestock seemed to "freak out" for no reason at all hours of the day and night. Hens were laying fewer eggs, and security cameras caught bizarre – almost lightning-like – streaks running around the property.

From the mimic standpoint, family members would hear livestock sounds coming from buildings and fields where there were no livestock at the time. On several occasions while outside the main barn, two of the sons heard chickens clucking all around them while there were no chickens.

What clinched this as a parasite (rather than just a common multiversal membrane overlap) for me was the admission that the whole family had been using – wait for it – a Ouija board for much of the previous year.

I advised dumping the Ouija board and weaponizing what my son and colleague, Ben Eno, and I refer to as the "Peter Pan Theory": Think happy thoughts. For a family, this includes reemphasizing their love for each other, reaffirming their faith in a positive way, enjoying positive humor and spending "quality time" together.

In this case, I also advised placing wind chimes around the property. Oddly enough, the sound seems to repel parasites. There are ancient folk beliefs about this, and they are the reason churches have bells.

I followed up for several years, and all remained calm at the Maryland farm, even the livestock.

THE FARMERS

These parasites seem to work quietly, in groups of four to eight, and will attach themselves to a human family, tribe or other community for long periods of time, cultivating situations and feeding off the results. Certain individuals of this species might concentrate on, or be in charge of, particular people in the human group. In many cases, the parasites are so unobtrusive that – except for occasional feelings of presences or negativity -- the humans have no idea they are being "farmed."

One characteristic of the Farmers is to mimic the voices of family members. Sometimes, these voices will hurl insults or obscenities to stir up one family member against another. Less obtrusive Farmers will cultivate psychic abilities among their prey family, sometimes for generations. This predisposes the family to accept mimicry.

I have run into these situations in a number of cases over the years.

THE PACK HUNTERS

This species is highly aggressive, highly provocative and usually will concentrate on one human at a time. Unlike most parasites, they seem highly mobile. Working in groups of up to six, they can and will follow a person from place to place. There is always a leader. If they get enough to eat, they can become poltergeists. Yes, my experience with poltergeists led me to believe early on that they are actually parasites. Pack Hunters also bond with their hosts, if the latter are willing enough, to cause the possession phenomenon.

They are particularly good mimics, and many hosts become convinced that they are being paid attention to not by parasites but by benevolent and protective spirits. In my opinion, Lucy (in the first case recounted in this chapter) with her Arten "spirit guide" might have been dealing with Pack Hunters.

I believe that Pack Hunters also were responsible for the two worst poltergeist cases I ever dealt with: the 1974 Lindley Street case in Bridgeport, Conn. (recounted in *Behind the Paranormal: Everything You Know is Wrong*, by Paul Eno and Ben Eno, Schiffer Books, 2016) and the 1979 "Baddest Poltergeist in New England" case (recounted in *Dancing Past the Graveyard: Poltergeists, Parasites, Parallel Worlds and God*, by Paul Eno, Schiffer Books, 2019).

THE ROGUES

These loners have many characteristics of pack hunters, but they operate on their own. They function freely through Ouija Boards and séances, and they too can be responsible for poltergeist phenomena or, if they get enough to eat, possession cases.

They are excellent mimics.

One interesting characteristic I've noticed with Rogues is that they are often confined to a certain geographic area, probably at points of multiversal intersect. They can travel short distances away from these spots, but are soon drawn or snapped back. Weird as it sounds, I actually had a Rogue in the car with me while I was on the way home from a case in 1998. As soon as we crossed the nearest river, it disappeared, snapped back to its base.

Rogues are very common, in my experience.

In a case in Burrillville, Rhode Island, that began in 1998 and went on for over 10 years, a Rogue that dominated a Passive (see below) preyed on a family in a house on a large patch of land to which it was attached. I actually saw this parasite with my own eyes and, later, photographed it.

Along with poltergeist activity in the house, family members would hear each other's voices when not present, childlike shadow figures would be seen around the house, and there were sightings of a little blonde girl with flowers in her hair.

What could be less threatening than that little girl? But I have found the little blonde girl among several archetypes that parasites mimic. More on archetypes later.

Among the actions I took in this Burrillville case was to advise the primary prey person (the mom) and the entire family to use the Peter Pan Theory. The positive energy this brought in had remarkable effects. The parents actually heard the Rogue stomping up and down outside their bedroom at night, apparently in frustration.

The daughter of the family appeared to be the next target. But by this time everyone in the family had become Peter Pan aces, and the Rogue and Passive left the house, the Rogue seeming to take up residence in a large tool shed at the far end of the yard, next to the woods.

There is an interesting sequel. Widowed a few years after the case began, the mom eventually married a full-blooded Aztec man, a genuine shaman, originally from Mexico, who was living in Rhode Island. He became a dear friend of ours and a mentor to Ben. Shortly after he moved into the house, the Rogue noticed the new energy, and tried to get to this new prey. Big mistake for the Rogue. The shaman knew all about what was happening and how to deal with it.

On one occasion – and I witnessed the whole incident – we were in the yard at night. The Rogue burst out of the shed and physically attacked the shaman, who was rolling on the ground. He threw it off, and the parasite then went after the man's teenage daughter, who began to shake uncontrollably. I hugged her to dissipate the energy, and the Rogue backed off. The shaman had claw marks all over his back.

The family eventually moved to North Carolina and has been living happily ever after, parasite-free.

THE PASSIVES

This interesting group seems to be satisfied filling the role of second-stringers, usually to the Elders but sometimes to other, brighter parasites. In paranormal cases, we often find the Passives in subservient positions, dominated, sometimes cruelly, by superior species. They seem to feed on, in a manner of speaking, whatever "crumbs" are left after the Elders or others are finished.

I have yet to find them acting as mimics.

THE LOST

There's a fascinating tendency among all parasites, especially the bargain models, to forget their own origins, and even their own identities, the longer they spend attached to their hosts or in worlds that are not their own.

That includes the Lost. They seem to operate alone, concentrating on one person even when there is little or no sustenance to be had from that person. Though I have rarely seen them as conscious mimics, The Lost often communicate verbally, and they will sometimes give the impression that they need sympathy. Rarely, they will even communicate remorse for their vampire-like lifestyle.

In one case, in the American Midwest in 2009, one of the Lost was constantly apologizing to its human host. The host could hear a human-like voice, but never saw the parasite. I find The Lost rather pathetic.

THE TRICKSTERS

The concept of the trickster is common in folklore and in all ancient religions. Indigenous peoples talk about trickster spirits, demons or gods who are very knowledgeable about humans, but who use this knowledge to play pranks, sometimes cruel ones, or otherwise flaunt accepted moral or social behavior. Often, they will use our own human failings and foibles against us.

When it comes to trickster parasites, they often come across as intellectual lightweights, but they are clever at the same time. They will get the energy flowing from their hosts through startling antics and unpleasant surprises. As with all parasites, their abilities to travel among parallel worlds will make it seem as though they can manipulate space and time, something that in itself, as the great 20th century horror writer H.P. Lovecraft pointed out, strikes terror into the human heart.

I believe that tricksters are often the "enlightened masters," "space brothers" or false spirit guides that have a field day among gullible psychics and mediums. And I have often found them as vocal mimics, sometimes pretending to be your dear departed Uncle Chuck or Aunt Belinda.

THE BRATS

Welcome to the bottom shelf of the parasite worlds: The Brats. These two-dimensional creatures act like spoiled, but sometimes frightened, children. In fact, they exhibit many of the same behaviors as maladjusted children.

Brats seem to live and feed alone on a specific human who is also alone. Often, an unhealthy bond will result. While Brats aren't very swift, they are very good at manipulating their hosts, and they're terrified of being separated from these hosts because they are among the most likely to forget who they are and where they came from.

While they would seem to be perfect candidates for mimics, I have never seen an example of that. Perhaps they have never worked out just how to do it.

LOST AND FRIGHTENED

Just as a point of interest, I have always found this tendency for parasites to forget their own origins completely enthralling, and it applies to all parasites to some degree, especially those in the lower ranks. Many are afraid, terrified, in fact, to separate from their hosts because they can't recall where or when they are from, or where or when to return.

THE ARCHETYPE MIMICS

Along with the little blonde girl with flowers in her hair, I have seen parasites mimic "The Man In The Checkered Shirt," which I have encountered twice but been unable to photograph – too quick for me.

My good friend and colleague Heidi Hollis has identified and coined names for still more of these archetypes, including Shadow People® and The Hat Man®. Heidi has trademarked these terms, apparently to no avail: They have been embraced by paranormal researchers everywhere and have joined the lexicon.

THE TULPA

From the tradition of Tibetan Buddhism comes the Tulpa, believed to be a thought-form created by someone as a spiritual exercise and that can take on a form, and even a life, of its own. There are stories of Tibetan monks over the centuries who created Tulpas, only to lose control over them. In some cases, the Tulpa took over the scene and made the monk's life a misery.

This raises more questions.

Could what I interpret as parasites, or at least some of them, be thought forms created by the experiencers themselves? That certainly comes closest to parapsychology's textbook definition of a poltergeist: RSPK (recurrent spontaneous psychokinesis) produced by a human "agent."

Several experiments by parapsychology research groups over the years have appeared to create entities by literally imagining them. Probably the most famous of these is the "Philip Experiment," carried out by a group in the Toronto area "to determine whether subjects can communicate with fictionalized ghosts through expectations of human will."

The project was overseen by two PhD academics, geneticist A.R. George Owen and psychologist Joel Whitton. The group made up the entire life story of a 17th century man named Philip Aylesford. In the end, they claimed they could communicate with Philip by means of séances.

Other groups have conducted similar experiments in the same way, sometimes asserting that they had eventually been able to photograph the entity they seemed to create.

Then there's the "Slender Man," known to be an Internet creation. Yet, regular reports come in about people encountering the Slender Man in real life, especially after séances.

Hmmm. Séances? I have found these to be a louder dinner bell for parasites than Ouija boards. Are we dealing here with thought forms or opportunistic mimics? In my own work, the latter answer seems to be the clearest. And parasites love attention.

THE ALIEN FACTOR

People hear about my theology background and say, "Aha! You must believe that all ghosts, cryptids and aliens are actually demons!"

No, I don't. In fact, I am convinced that most ghosts, some of which I have seen myself, are multiverse intersect experiences, not dead people. I have encountered Bigfoot and experienced it as a sacred event. And the "demons" I have encountered came across as utterly other – and "alien" is the best word to describe them. In fact, I consider most "demons" (parasites) to be alien, not the other way around.

Do I believe that all "spirit guides" are parasites? No. In many or even most cases, I believe they are facets of ourselves from, for lack of a better term, "higher" parallel worlds. And I am a great believer in the enduring love of ancestors, and their occasional ability to help us from worlds where they never "died."

Could some mimics of man actually be from parallel worlds, and somehow have the ability to interact with ours?

CONCLUSION

As for food sources in addition to our negative vibes, all parasites seem to feed on recognition and attention to some degree. Some become "stuck" in certain places because of the conditions there. Interestingly, we've seen this both near homes and in wilderness areas.

As to the parasite version of family farming, the question arises: All families, and certainly every person, have stress and negative experiences. Why isn't every person obsessed, oppressed or possessed, and why doesn't every home have its very own parasite/poltergeist?

Good question. Over the years, however, it became apparent that many factors must fall into place for paranormal phenomena to occur at all, never mind engulf a person or family. And it became clear that parasites don't have *carte blanche* to feed wherever and whenever they please. There seem to be rules in the multiverse, probably depending on the laws of physics. Evidently, Godzilla can't just blunder through a membrane and eat New York. In the same way, parasites apparently can't just come through anywhere or anytime and carry us away. Or can they?

That's another story.

How to avoid parasites? Don't use Ouija boards, séances, or any other occult device that sends out a dinner invitation. Test all comers! If something weird comes to you, be a confirmed skeptic. Don't believe everything you hear. And don't get isolated: Parasites feed on division. Most importantly, use the Peter Pan Theory. Make it part of your daily life. Love your family, friends and the people around you. This creates unity, and unity repels parasites. Remember: Every act of kindness is an act of unity.

Be in unity, and no parasite can touch you.

WOMAN'S TERRIFYING ORDEAL AFTER HEARING "FAIRY VOICES"

She was skeptical about the supernatural world until she heard a high pitched voice that made the hairs on the back of her neck stand up

A Meath woman was terrified when an ordinary walk in a nearby woods took a chilling turn.

She took to Twitter to try and explain her supernatural ordeal after walking through two trees. The woman then became completely lost, without being able to find her way back onto the path.

Others quickly said that fairies were at play and explained that Irish folklore may be far more real than many think.

Thankfully, the former skeptic remembered an old trick that she had heard in stories. She told "Dublin Live" that she would be hesitant to return after her experience, especially after hearing a terrifyingly light female voice coming from both sides.

She said: "I just had to get my steps up for a challenge that we were doing in work. I decided to go walk somewhere nice instead of just doing laps of my estate. It was a nice day so I said I would go for a walk in the woods. What was the worst that could happen?

"It was going fine. Then the path leads through two identical trees. I stepped through and put my hands on both trees. People are saying now that this was a mistake. One was really warm and the other was really wet and cold. I walked on and I think I took a left.

"The main path kind of branched off to the left and it just went nowhere. It went into a really overgrown forest, really high weeds and plants. I knew it wasn't the path. There were lots of people around. It's a really popular spot. So I walked back and I thought that this wasn't the main path and I should have taken the other way.

"I took the other way and then that similarly went nowhere. I went back to the fork to start over. I went back and I think I tried to go back the way I came. That also led me nowhere.

"I walked back up the main path again but it didn't look familiar. It was quite overcast at this point as well. I had pulled up Google Maps and I didn't have a signal on my phone at all, which is not unusual for that area.

"I decided to keep trying paths. There were only three so I thought I'd eventually get somewhere. I kept walking down a path towards a really overgrown area again. At that point then, I heard a really light woman's voice. I don't know how to describe it. It was really high. She was shouting 'over here'. I thought she was probably calling to her kids or something. Then she laughed, and it was just when she laughed that the hairs on the back of my neck stood up.

"I have a very professional job. I'm not crazy. I'm quite logical. But then the call came from the other side of me. I knew something wasn't right.

"Something was just wrong. My first instinct was to run, but I didn't even know where to run. I just remembered turning your clothes inside out is supposed to help. So, I just tried that. I felt like it was just mental. I just had to do it. I turned my t-shirt inside out, put it back on. I was hoping nobody was looking at me because it was a really weird thing to do in the middle of a forest.

"I turned around and walked back and almost immediately came to the two trees again. When I turned around and came back, I came to them quicker than when I had been walking in the opposite direction.

"I didn't even think. I just wanted to get through. Then I could hear the birds again and people and stuff. I didn't know what had just happened.

"When I got back to the car, I looked at my steps. The last time I had checked my step counter I had done 8,000 steps or something like that. I had put on an extra 10,000 steps. I didn't come from a family that would have believed in that sort of stuff. Certain things just stick in your head and that's why I remembered the turning the clothes inside out thing."

The woman admitted she was terrified when she heard the voice and didn't think the laughter was friendly.

She said: "I was scared when she laughed. When she laughed, I don't think I've words in the English language for it. I had never heard someone laugh like that. I knew something was really wrong. I just got this really bad feeling that things were not going to end well for me if I didn't do something.

"I wasn't scared until then. When she laughed, I knew something was very wrong. A lot of people have said that it was a 'stray sod'. I always just thought they were nice stories. I love that collectively as a nation we often acknowledge it as a thing. I don't know where all the extra steps on my Fitbit came from. I was surprised by the amount of people that it had happened to.

"We may not believe but we still don't ever want to run the risk. I think I just got unlucky. I've been in those woods before. People were saying that the two trees on the path were a portal. I've no massive opinion but something really weird happened. We do so many things on a daily basis instinctively. There are open fields, but every so often there will be a ring of trees in the middle of a field. They will plow around them. Even with our modern farming equipment, they still plough around those trees."
Source: Dublin Live - Roisin Cullen

www.dublinlive.ie/news/dublin-news/womans-terrifying-ordeal-after-hearing-25006288

The 1950s contactees said that the alien visitors are secretly living on Earth and are passing as humans. They managed to hold down jobs by visiting their home planets only during work holidays.

INFILTRATION
Tim R. Swartz

"**A** growing number of individuals who have served in military, intelligence or government institutions testify to the presence of extraterrestrial (ET) races that compete among themselves and with clandestine (human) organizations for influence over global humanity."

This is the beginning of Michael E. Salla's "Research Study #4" (May 30, 2003, www.exopolitics.org). Salla states that the paper analyzes the extent of military and intelligence branches of the government that have been infiltrated by different ET factions and the threat this poses to the sovereignty of humanity.

Salla's paper is indicative of the paranoia that has accompanied certain parts of the "UFO Community" since the late 1940s. This paranoia, in some parts, stems from the contactee movement with people such as George Adamski and Howard Menger claiming that UFOs are spacecraft from nearby planets. Not only are these planets home to intelligent life, said the contactees, but this intelligent life appears human enough to mingle with us unnoticed.

For example, according to whistleblower Dr. Jamisson Neruda, who claims to have defected from a clandestine organization embedded within the NSA (National Security Agency), there are a number of ET races intervening on the planet with multiple agendas where simple moral categories are insufficient to fully understand the consequences of their activities and influence.

It sounds like the stuff of nightmares: something other than human, living with us unnoticed, whose ultimate agenda is unknown.

This is not to say that "extraterrestrial infiltration" is the absolute answer to the thesis of this book...that there are "mimics of man" that can interact with us without most people being any wiser. However, right, wrong, or somewhere in-between, it is probably the most popular idea/theory addressing "the others."

This photo is allegedly of a human-looking extraterrestrial involved in the Italian "Friendship Case." The "person" shown here was said to be over 8-feet-tall.

ALIENS ARE HIDING AMONG US

Haim Eshed, who headed Israel's space security programs for 30 years, claimed during an interview with Israel's "Yediot Aharonot" newspaper that Israel and the U.S. have been secretly in contact with extraterrestrials for decades. A respected professor and retired general, Eshed said the aliens signed a contract with us to do experiments here and help us understand "the fabric of the universe."

Eshed made his surprising revelation in December 2020, and considering everything else that was going on that year, it was quickly forgotten after a few days of coverage.

Eshed confirmed that extraterrestrials have been among us for a long time and the cooperation agreements signed between them and world leaders included an "underground base in the depths of Mars" where Earth astronauts and alien representatives could work together.

When asked why he was revealing the information now, Eshed said that it was because the academic landscape has evolved and that he is in academia.

"If I had come up with what I'm saying today five years ago, I would have been hospitalized," he said. "Today, they're already talking differently. I have nothing to lose. I've received my degrees and awards; I am respected in universities abroad, where the trend is also changing."

In his book *"Our Haunted Planet,"* John Keel writes that on August 7,1965, three men in Venezuela witnessed a UFO landing and had a conversation with two tall (seven to eight feet) beings with long yellow hair, large penetrating eyes, and one piece metallic coverall-type garments. The witnesses, who included a well-known Venezuelan doctor, claimed they communicated through telepathy, and among the questions they asked was, "Are there any beings like you living among us?" "Yes," was the reply, two million, four hundred and seventeen thousand, eight hundred and five."

Other contactees have asked the same question, and the answers are wildly variable, from seventy-five to ten thousand (in the city of Los Angeles alone) to up in the millions. (*"Our Haunted Planet"* By John Keel, 1971 – Fawcett)

SCIENTISTS SAY HUMAN-LIKE ALIENS COULD ALREADY BE HERE

Oxford University scientists have been researching to see what aliens could look like and they have discovered that they could look just like us. One of the keys to unlocking the universe and the possibilities of aliens is an understanding of biological evolution and natural selection.

As it turns out, biological evolution should be the same across the entire universe, according to Sam Levin, a researcher in Oxford's Department of Zoology. This means that natural selection on any planet could have led aliens to look exactly like the human race.

The scientists at Oxford are the first to apply the evolutionary theory to predict what aliens could actually look like. One of the hurdles about making predictions of what the aliens may look like is that our only frame of reference is what we know from Earth and our experiences here.

We've all seen the now pop culture-typical humanoid extraterrestrial with the large head and big, black eyes. But considering that these beings are supposed to be from another planet, they still look like an exaggerated version of a human.

"Past approaches in the field of astrobiology have been largely mechanistic," said Sam Levin, "taking what we see on Earth, and what we know about chemistry, geology, and physics to make predictions about aliens. In our paper, we offer an alternative approach, which is to use evolutionary theory to make predictions that are independent of Earth's details. This is a useful approach, because theoretical predictions will apply to aliens that are silicon based, do not have DNA, and breathe nitrogen, for example."

The team hypothesizes that alien life may be influenced by the same environmental factors that take place on Earth, where complex life arises from major transitions. These extreme events force a group of separate organisms to evolve in to one higher level organism, such as cells becoming multi-cellular organisms. This is where the knowledge of biological evolution comes into play. Levin explains.

"By predicting that aliens underwent major transitions, which is how complexity has arisen in species on Earth, we can say that there is a level of predictability to evolution that would cause them to look like us. Like humans, we predict that they are made-up of a hierarchy of entities, which all cooperate to produce an alien."

Levin went on to say that there are "potentially hundreds of thousands" of planets in our galaxy alone.

"We can't say whether or not we're alone on Earth, but we have taken a small step forward in answering, if we're not alone, what our neighbors are like."

Marcus Allen, publisher of the magazine "Nexus," took Levin's idea to the next level when he spoke at the 27th Glastonbury Symposium in August 2017. Allen told the packed audience that "extraterrestrials are now living among us and we may be oblivious to them."

He claimed that there was a difference between aliens and extraterrestrials, and that both of them were already on Earth, but their existence has been covered up by world leaders.

"Aliens do not look like us, but ETs (extraterrestrials) do look like us," Allen said. "There could be some in here now and you wouldn't know."

He then offered the suggestion that all humans could in fact be aliens who came to Earth from another planet in the far distant past.

"In a way we are the extraterrestrials."

CLOSER THAN WE THINK

Dr. Young-hae Chi, an instructor at the University of Oxford, believes that UFOs and the abduction phenomena are real. In multiple lectures he's given at Oxford, he says they're creating alien-human hybrids as a hedge against climate change. However, he theorizes that our concept of "aliens" as creatures from other planets may be somewhat simplistic.

"If they are far, they shouldn't be concerned about us. I don't think they are from far away; they are just next to us, but we can't see them. We can use an analogy of fish which can think and perceive things only in the way they can and humans also perceive only in the way we can, so our perception of the world is limited by our organs."

Dr. Young-hae Chi thinks that "the others" are nearby, but they can't be seen unless they want to be seen. Sally Painter, a paranormal researcher and author, lists several of these "alien species" that are living among humans right now.

The Nordics are described as tall, blond aliens with blue eyes. They are described as being physically beautiful with a slim but athletic body type. These beings were the favorite of the 1950s contactees and claimed to come from planets in the solar system— Venus being the particular favorite. In later years the Nordics were said to come from the star group Pleiades (no planet in particular, just from somewhere among those 800 stars approximately 400 light years from Earth).

Contactees said the Nordics were reaching out to humans in an effort to assist us in transforming to the next level of existence. Aside from their physical appearances, Pleiadians can be distinguished by their personal interests and concerns, such as the planet, the human race's development, and advancing the healing arts. However, their biggest priority is to serve as guides in assisting humans to grow spiritually.

A similar group of extraterrestrials that are said to be with us now are called The Tall Whites. These are a type of alien said to be tall, extremely white, and very enthusiastic about the various Earth cultures.

Substantial information about the Tall Whites comes to us from Charles J. Hall, who, from 1965 to 1967, served as a weather observer at Nellis Air Force Base in Nevada. During this time, Hall claims he often observed extraterrestrials called Tall Whites that moved about freely on the base.

Hall describes the Tall Whites as having thin, frail bodies, chalk white skin, large blue eyes, and nearly transparent platinum blonde hair. Their eyes were twice the size of human eyes. It's believed that older Tall Whites can reach 10 feet in height, while younger ones have a shorter height and can temporarily blend in with humans. It is said to be very easy to pass a Tall White on the street and not notice them as an alien, but as a rather strange looking human.

During one interview Hall was asked if he had any information about the first interaction between the Air Force and the Tall Whites.

"I do not have any personal information regarding the first interactions between the U.S. Government and the Tall White aliens," Hall said. "However, as I describe in '*Millennial Hospitality III - The Road Home*,' the Tall White lady who called herself 'The Teacher' stated that one Tall White named Pamela had been born in Indian Springs Valley during the time when James Madison was the U.S. President. That was back around the year 1812. The construction of the main Tall White hanger was consistent with the late 1940s or early 1950s.

Charles J. Hall, who was a weather observer stationed at Nellis Air Force Base in Nevada, claims to have witnessed interactions between the military and a group of mysterious tall, white, human-like extraterrestrials.

"U.S. President Harry Truman stated that he believed he had met the ghost of Abraham Lincoln in the White House one night back when he was president during the late 1940s. However, it is my observation that his description of the 'ghost' matched completely with any number of Tall White guards that I personally saw out on the Indian Springs Ranges at night. For that reason, I would guess that the first formal interactions between the Tall Whites and the U.S. Government took place during the 1940s or very early 1950s.

"You also should consider the legends of the ancient Greeks, dating back to before 972 BCE, that refer to a group of Tall White 'gods' who were said to have come to Earth from the star Arcturus. For that reason, the ancient Greeks named the star Arcturus 'The Watcher' star. It is very probable that the Tall Whites have been coming here to Earth for at least three thousand years."

INGO SWANN AND THE HUMANOIDS ON THE MOON

Ingo Swann was a psychic, remote viewer and visionary artist who also pioneered the field of remote viewing. Working alongside such notables as Harold Puthoff and Russell Targ, Swann tested his abilities on a remote viewing project, code-named "Project Stargate." This ran from 1978 - 1995 and was entirely funded by the CIA with the aim of developing psychic abilities in others.

Some of Swann's most remarkable discoveries were describing, in 1973, Jupiter's rings and the presence of rotating storms and ice crystals in its atmosphere, years before NASA confirmed their existence. As well, he successfully located targets such as Soviet spy planes for the U.S Department of Defense.

One such remote viewing session of Swann's is probably his most amazing, yet also his most little known.

In his 1998 book, *"Penetration: The Question of Extraterrestrial and Human Telepathy,"* Swann reveals that he was recruited for a covert, "deep black" CIA operation. Amazingly, he was tasked to try and remote view certain areas on the far side of the moon.

After being hypnotized by a special agent known only as Mr. Axelrod, Swann was given various locations on the moon's surface to remote view. Upon reviewing the last location, Swann described seeing what appeared to be track marks leading towards a crater that was filled with a greenish haze of diffused light.

"I found towers, machinery, lights of different colors, strange-looking 'buildings,'" Swann said. "I found bridges whose function I couldn't figure out. One of them just arched out—and never landed anywhere. There were a lot of domes of various sizes, round things, things like small saucers with windows. These were stored next to crater sides, sometimes in caves, sometimes in what looked like airfield hangars."

Swann was shocked to see that alongside the strange lunar structures there were also people busy at some kind of work.

"I saw people, but what they were doing, I could not figure out. The place was dark. The 'air' was filled with a fine dust, and there was some kind of illumination—like a dark lime-green fog or mist. The thing about them was that they either were human or looked exactly like us—but they were all males, as I could well see since they were all butt-ass naked. I had absolutely no idea why. They seemed to be digging into a hillside or a cliff."

Swann was able to mentally shift his viewpoint a little closer to the strange figures, but then realized that his presence had somehow been detected.

"Being there in my psychic state, as I felt I was, some of those guys started talking excitedly and gesticulating. Two of them pointed in my 'direction.' Immediately I felt like 'running away' and hiding, which I guess I, psychically, did, since I 'lost' sight of this particular imaging."

"I think they have spotted me," Swann told Axelrod. "They were pointing at me I think. How could they do that...unless...they have some kind of high psychic perceptions, too?"

At the end of the session, Swann was left with the impression that the "others" he saw on the moon have the ability to trace a psychic probe and kill any Earth-psychic if they were good enough to spy on them.

Ingo Swan said that the figures he saw working on the surface of the moon were human, or looked exactly like us. As well, he noticed that they had the ability to sense when he was remote viewing them.

Even though Swann managed to avoid any negative effects from this lunar session, he did have an unsettling run-in with a strange woman in a Los Angeles supermarket. During August and September 1976, he traveled several times to Los Angeles. On one of these trips, while shopping with a friend at a large Hollywood supermarket, Swann noticed "a ravishing woman."

"She was notable not so much for her excessive female physical endowments, but by the fact that they were barely covered," Swann noted.

"She was dressed in the briefest of halters of pink with big yellow polka dots. Beneath that were short-shorts so short they barely existed. Far beneath that she wore a pair of platform high-heels about eight inches high. She had volumes of gorgeous black hair, and her eyes were covered by purple sunglasses. She was absolutely awesome."

However, despite her physical attributes, Swann suddenly experienced an electrifying wave of goosebumps throughout his body. Without rhyme or reason, he immediately "knew" she was not human, but an extraterrestrial.

"At this point, I realized that I was somewhere I should not be," Swann recalled. "I made a hasty and strategic retreat to the bread section on the other side of the store. By the time I reached the bread section, a considerable wave of TERROR had begun to make itself felt."

Swann left the store and returned to his friend's car. Shortly, the woman came out pushing a loaded grocery cart. He asked his friend about the woman.

"Study that one and tell me what you think," Swann said.

His friend looked briefly at the woman—and then said the most remarkable thing.

"Well, if you mean do I think she's an extraterrestrial, yes," he said in a bored way. "We've got a lot of them here in La-La Land."

Later, Swann was told that there are a lot of "them" and many are bio-androids.

"They're dangerous," Swann said. "They realize that Earth psychics are their only enemies."

BREAKAWAY CIVILIZATIONS

As I've stated before, the "others," even if they are non-human under the skin, may not necessarily all have to be extraterrestrials from other planets. Håkan Blomqvist, in his excellent article "Ancient Breakaway Civilization - A Source Study," quotes his friend Tony Brunt who said, "I have no doubt that there are others living in a more advanced state in hidden places on the planet." (ufoarchives.blogspot.com/2022/08/ancient-breakaway-civilization-source.html)

Blomqvist writes in several books and blog articles that he has worked to answer the question – who are these people? Human-looking visitors who obviously mingle in our society and possess an advanced technology.

"They are physical like us and seem to be Earth-based in their activities," Blomqvist says. "If this is the case, where is their hiding place on this planet? Could some specialized and covert intelligence groups have discovered who these people are and begun trying to deal with this delicate issue in their own way? Disclosure of such a fantastic scenario would probably not be regarded as an option by the people who have a need to know."

One compelling case was offered by Walter Bosley, using the pen name E.A. Guest in his article "The Other Paradigm" ("Fate," April 2005). According to Bosley, his father had worked for a special assignment team in the U.S. Air Force to find and retrieve a crashed craft. He had inspected remains from several crashes, including human-looking aliens, and was briefed at Wright-Patterson about the real nature of the craft and aliens.

"A civilization thrives underground, hidden from the surface world," writes Bosley. "These people are not extraterrestrials. Quite the contrary, they are among the oldest people on this planet... Occasionally, they come and go, emerging in their vehicles, and occasionally they crash. They are human in appearance, so much so that they can move among us with ease with just a little effort."

Eugene Drake, in his 1950 book *"Visitors From Space,"* wrote, "There is an ancient civilization living underground with entrances in Mexico and not such a great distance from Mexico City. They often come to the surface and mingle with the people, but aside from a few mystics, the people of Mexico do not know this, and they would have a difficult time, if they did, in locating the entrances to their underground cities."

There is also a cryptic statement in Howard Menger's book *"From Outer Space to You"* when a space woman tells Menger that there are other, not so friendly, extraterrestrials that use people not only from this planet... but "also other people of your planet – people you don´t know about. People who live unobserved and undiscovered as yet. It is a kind of 'underground' in your popular terminology."

Blomqvist also finds intriguing that esoteric sources, contactees and UFO case investigations often refer to an ancient breakaway civilization hidden on the planet. Our attitude to such controversial data should be neither belief nor disbelief, but keeping an open mind and using the information as an alternative working hypothesis. Only further research can determine what is reality and myth with this enigma.

JOURNALIST PAOLA HARRIS LECTURES ON THE IMPORTANCE OF HUMAN LOOKING ETS

Sean Casteel and John Weigle

On July 27, 2013, UFO researcher and author Paola Harris spoke to a meeting of the Close Encounter Research Organization International, a group founded and led by hypnotherapist and alien abduction researcher Yvonne Smith. The meeting was held in Thousand Oaks, California, a city just north of Los Angeles, and drew a packed house.

Paola Harris is an Italian-American photojournalist and investigative reporter who has worked for many years conducting interviews with military and government officials about their UFO knowledge and experiences, what she calls an extremely "nuts-and-bolts" approach to the subject. She worked as an assistant for the late Dr. J. Allen Hynek from 1980 to 1986 and in 1997 interviewed and became a personal friend and confidante of the late Col. Philip Corso, a military insider who went public with claims of back-engineered alien technology. Her credits also include bringing major figures in UFOlogy to Italy to speak, such as Travis Walton, Nick Pope and the late Dr. John Mack. She has recently launched a new nonprofit association, Starworks Italia, which will continue her efforts to bring topflight UFO speakers to Italy and promote disclosure and exopolitical dialogue worldwide.

Paola Harris

Harris says it is rare for her to investigate cases of claimed contact with extraterrestrials, but the cases she spoke about in her lecture were nevertheless so compelling that she felt they deserved further scrutiny. Two of the primary contact events she covered in her talk took place in Italy, about which more later.

Harris began by saying that UFOs are the most important subject in the world, and also the most hidden.

"It's not science fiction," she declared. "It's science fact. This is not Disneyland. This is the history of humanity, the visitations we've been having."

In the early years, she said, the phenomenon of contact with extraterrestrials involved mainly human-looking aliens. The contactees of the 1950s reported seeing blond Space Brothers with human features, while the now ubiquitous Grays were not widely reported until after the 1961 Betty and Barney Hill abduction case.

"We're dealing with human-type aliens," Harris said, "and this is dangerous, believe it or not. Now ask yourself why."

Harris said that Col. Philip Corso (famous for his revelations about U.S. military involvement with the aliens as presented in his book "*The Day After Roswell*," co-authored with William Birnes) once told her that military officials weren't worried about the crashes or the gray beings, but instead feared the idea of "some of these people walking in-between the halls of the Pentagon."

Harris further stated that, "You're looking at forms that look like us, but maybe we're the standard form of the universe. Maybe there are people out there and maybe it would be nice to meet them. But maybe we're not ready to meet them yet, because evidently these people are so evolved that they can travel among the stars. We certainly aren't. We're earthbound. We're still fighting wars, dealing with economics, dealing with all kinds of disgusting issues, and we can't get off the planet, which is very, very sad."

Continuing her theme of human-looking ETs, Harris related that at a Florida event she sponsored earlier in 2013, a seven-year-old girl named Anna sat in the front row for three days. Anna said that she had had a sighting and met a being that looked like a regular person, a blond-haired man. She was among other children on the craft, and the beings examined her arms and elbows and saw how the children's muscles worked. Harris said she is working on a book called "*Anna and Her Extraterrestrial Friends*," adding that, "If disclosure doesn't happen in our generation, it most certainly will happen in the next one."

Harris dealt in more detail with a case that has come to be called "Friend Ship." She presented a video from YouTube that called "Friend Ship" the incredible story of mass contact between humans and extraterrestrials. Until recently, according to the video, people thought the contactees were a small group. But in 1956, there was a contact case involving hundreds of people. Several of them came forward to discuss their experiences with the late researcher and author Stefano Breccia, whose PowerPoint presentation Harris also included in her CERO lecture.

The eyewitnesses told Breccia that the beings spoke perfect Italian. The beings explained that the Earth "had been created for a positive purpose and that man was turning everything into evil." Humans' morality level was much lower than theirs. The aliens said that their task was to ensure that the situation didn't get out of hand. They had not come to conquer as there was nothing to conquer, but instead emphasized that all things required love and respect and that everything should be done in accordance with those principles. The ETs were familiar with Earth's history and its differing religions.

"They had already been on Earth for many years," Breccia was told, "living at secret bases in various places on the planet. They preferred not to reveal themselves publicly because people weren't ready for the contact."

Breccia himself met with many of the aliens, some of them very tall, including one alien who was 15-feet-tall and was photographed towering over some trees in the background. The aliens were given the name "W56s," because the year was 1956 and they were human-looking in appearance. They sometimes communicated telepathically, and at other times through crystal radio sets.

"We were hoping for an experience with teachers who could help us in love," said one woman who took part.

Meetings between the humans and the ETs continued for several months. A being named Dimpietro was the captain; other names were Sigir, Itaho, Kenio, Sinas, Saju, Meredir, and Romulus.

The names were invented by the humans; the W56s had a different concept of names.

Harris showed a slide from Breccia's PowerPoint presentation that read, "The W56s are a confederation of different people coming from almost all of the known universe. To them, our Earth has a mystical meaning because it has been one among the only fifty Mother Planets that is a planet where life has been born, throughout the whole universe!"

Harris reiterated that we are not evolved enough to meet the cosmic consciousness. "If we're judged by what's on TV, if we're judged by our media, good grief!" she said. "I don't know who in the world would want to meet us. For what reason? We certainly have not very much to share with them."

The Friends started asking for help and wanted industrial quantities of fruit and minerals of various kinds. After taking delivery of a truckload of vegetables, the truck driver was lured away by human beings to have coffee, at which point the aliens teleported the goods off the truck. The driver was surprised to return and find the truck was already empty.

Harris said there were also similar groups in Germany, Chile and Russia in the 1950s. There was jealousy and competition among members of the groups, a fact that did not escape the aliens' notice. Another slide from the PowerPoint presentation said, "The 'help' they (the Friends) were requesting from us consisted mainly in keeping our group compact. To them, cohesion among people was not just an [abstract] concept, but an actual living entity that they were calling Uredda. They needed Uredda's well-being because almost all of their equipment depended on that."

"If we don't react very well with each other," Harris commented, "I don't know how in the world we're to react with cosmic cultures."

It was claimed the alleged aliens known as W56 were humans coming from planets in our own and other galaxies.

The aliens would sometimes admonish the human participants to "stay united." Meanwhile, the W56s said they were themselves fighting a group of "artificial beings" who they called their "enemy brothers." A man named Bruno Sammaciccia named the combatants "CTRs," from the Italian word "Contran."

NOT THE ONLY ALIENS AROUND

In his original PowerPoint presentation, Beccia also claimed that, "In the 70s, 80s and 90s, the W56s were not the only aliens present in our country. Other groups were active here, among them: the Ummites, pretending to belong to the Spanish group (indeed, I do not believe that.) The CTRs, of course. The Elta-BV, a strange group interested in Computer Music. The UTI, a kind of cosmic police, at a higher level, who were taking action against their friends when they were passing limits."

The W56s also revealed the existence of an enormous undersea base in the depths of the Adriatic, almost in contact with the continental shelf. Many smaller bases are located closer to the surface. There is a huge gap in the scientific and technological development between the Friends and human beings.

Stefano Breccia wrote a book about the communal experience called *"Mass Contacts: The 50s Contact In Pascara, Italy, With Human-Looking Aliens."* He wrote the book as a favor to the aforementioned Bruno Sammaciccia, who named the CTRs. A book Harris wrote, called *"Exopolitics: All the Above,"* includes a 2009 interview she conducted with Breccia in which he says, "I do not intend that anybody believes what I've written. I've stated this many times, within the text. It's up to the reader to decide whether I am a fool or not. About photos, I am the first one to state that the pictures are meaningless. I even present a fake, done by myself. I've included a lot of pictures simply because most of them are totally unknown, up to now. Think of the scout craft formation, seen from above! Or the many pictures shot during a landing. I've never seen anything like that in any UFO book; therefore I believe 'Contattismi di Massa' has been the first one to show such things. There are even two pictures of W56 people."

He says he has seen the people he writes about. The people spoke Italian and other languages; the Italian was often corrupted with Abruzzo's vernacular, but they were able to speak Latin and Sanskrit. They made contact by radio sets, telephones or video. "Our friends are living inside small bases, or plainly within our environment. As far as I know, all of them are human-like, with only minor differences, height among them."

When asked why there was conflict with the CTRs, Breccia answered, "You'll find several different motivations about this war, this quarrel, or whatever you'd like to name it, within the book. The main reason is the rage between human and not-human beings. The W-56s are among our ancestors, while the CTRs are an artificial offspring, generated by the W-56s themselves."

He says he interacted with beings who left "a very friendly" impression.

According to Breccia, there are bases near Pescara on the Adriatic Coast, which he finds difficult to describe because of technology we don't understand. He says, however, there are no fixed entries into them; when necessary, a passageway is opened, and then closed, and everything goes back to the "status quo." The large base had a ceiling 300 meters high, and sometimes it rained inside the base. He added, "A lot of our Friends are living among us, interacting at ease with our society, having Earth identities."

In her CERO lecture, Harris also spoke extensively about the case of Maurizio Cavallo, who wrote a book called *"Beyond the Heavens"* and says he photographed the aliens he met. "I was blown out of the water with his contact case," Harris said.

According to Cavallo, "They (the aliens) don't live here, but they're people." They're from the planet Clarion and were growing vegetables in a villa between Turin and Milan, Italy. When Cavallo took Polaroid photos of the aliens, they told him to keep them hidden for ten years. There exists a tape recording of the aliens speaking, made when the tape recorder turned on by itself. The spacecraft in a film of one of Cavallo's contacts "manifest as light ships and then become metal craft." PhotoShop had yet to be invented when the film was made.

In a 2006 interview that Harris conducted with Cavallo, he said, "We only see what we have learned to believe is reality. When humankind will be able to look through this other window, will look at reality with new eyes, perceiving the real universe we live in, we will go insane or we will evolve. There are no alternatives."

His story began in 1981, when Cavallo had been on a picnic with family and friends and he saw a UFO go behind some nearby mountains. He returned home, but felt compelled to go back to the location of the sighting the following night by an "internal and imperious voice." After hearing the voice, he tried to wake his wife, but she did not respond.

"It was like my house was entrapped in something," he told Harris. "I don't know how to define it. It was almost like being frozen. I don't know if that is the correct word. I went to the bathroom to have a glass of water, and the glass slipped from my hand and fell on the ground, but it fell in slow motion, very, very slowly." The glass broke, but he heard no noise.

Cavallo calls his experience an abduction, but has come to feel differently about it.

"In my book, I say that those who were my controllers— I call them abductors –those who imprisoned me, were the same ones who gave me my new freedom. They showed me that the Cosmos is not what we believe; that life is not what we live; that everything we call reality is a pure illusion. They opened for me a window on the Cosmos. They brought me to the edge of madness and they destroyed the Maurizio of the past. The old Maurizio existed no more; they had skinned him, lapidated him, but they permitted to the new Maurizio to look beyond the borders of what we call reality. They gave me an immense gift; they gave me freedom."

The aliens showed Maurizio recorded images of his mother, who had died when he was 13, walking in a graveyard when she was a young girl. He later encountered his mother at home, thinking at first that he was dreaming, but then realizing that he was in fact awake.

"I saw my mother not with the appearance that I remembered," he said. "She was physically different. I knew she was my mother, but she did not look like her."

Cavallo told Harris that he has met people from Clarion at a café in a large Italian city, which he was told not to name. His primary contact, an alien named Suell, gave him a little black card that emitted pulses that gave him instructions on what to do or not to do. They are here to help us in our evolution, to offer helpful influence. Some of the aliens were born here and have both extraterrestrial and human DNA. Others arrived here as adults and have only alien DNA. Their females are uniformly gorgeous.

He showed Harris photos of the aliens, including one in which he claims "you can see those in the Bible who were called 'Cherubs.' They are astral beings."

Cavallo issues the same warning as most contactees: that we are at a crucial moment in history where we must raise human consciousness to a higher level in order for our species to survive.

"We have no more time," he told Harris in the interview, "and so our duty is enormous."

Harris concluded her lecture by again emphasizing the importance of recognizing that we've been contacted by human-type creatures in several countries, yet these contacts are ignored. In spite of the prevalence of images of gray aliens, we have been contacted by many different cultures. It is necessary for us to evolve to the point where we can meet people who look like us and communicate with them.

"I hope you enjoyed it," she said of her presentation, "and I hope it opened up your minds a little bit. And you never know who's sitting next to you."

THE "PEOPLE" NEXT DOOR

Lon Strickler

Over the years I have amassed an abundant collection of anecdotes and inquiries that explain a variety of subjects and interesting observations. The most captivating narratives, in my opinion, involve the writers' personal perceptions of other people, in particular...the neighbors. I present to you a few of these brief accounts:

THE SMITHS

I grew up in a bedroom community outside of New York City. It was the 1970's and all the fathers in the neighborhood commuted to work while our mothers were stay-at-home "moms." All the moms were busybodies and basically had their noses in each other's business. The talk of the neighborhood was the family that lived beside us - the Smiths.

The Smiths were very strange. There was Mr. and Mrs. Smith who looked like they were in their 40's and their kids, a son and a daughter. The kids were in their early teens and we never knew their names! They didn't go to school so we assumed they were home-schooled. The only time we saw them was when the whole family would walk single file to the garage in the back of their house and drive away in their Rambler station wagon. My Mom talked to Mrs. Smith once right after they moved in, but that was it. They never answered the door and there was no telephone listing.

Mr. Smith never drove to work and Mrs. Smith was never seen shopping or doing any chores. The yard work was taken care of by two men who would drive up in a gray service truck once a week during the spring and summer. They would cut the lawn and trim the hedges. There were no flowers or trees - no lawn furniture - nothing.

One of our neighbors called the Mayor's office about the kids and school - but we never saw anyone ever come to the house. In fact, they never received mail (the postman told us) and there were never any deliveries.

The Smiths lived there for about 4 years. We didn't even know they had left until another (normal) family moved in. They told us that the house had been on the market for several months and that it was purchased through a government auction - but that seemed strange as well.

WHAT ARE THE ODDS?

Hi Lon - what are your thoughts on possible alien habitation among the human population? Please keep an open mind when reading my email.

I live in a moderate-sized borough in Pennsylvania. I live in the same house where I grew up. In fact most of the neighborhood has remained the same for the past 20 years or so. This includes the family that lives across the street.

This family, who I refer to as the Odds, is not normal by any stretch of the imagination. There is the husband and wife who are in their seventies and their daughter (Carol) who is now my age, 52. They have lived there as long as I can remember. Carol and I went to school together though we barely knew each other. She has always been very attractive though I never recall her ever having a boyfriend (or girlfriend).

Her parents maintain a very nice house and seem to get along quite well together. In fact Carol and her parents are always a trio. They are never seen separately. They do not go to church and are not involved in any civic activities. But this isn't the strange part.

Every spring since I can recall, they dig up a huge hole in the backyard. It's in the same location every year. The size I estimate is about 15 x 10 foot and about 4 foot deep. As soon as the hole is dug they cover it with a huge tarp that is staked into the ground around the perimeter. It remains like that for two days, and then it is quickly filled in and topped with new turf. Every year! It's almost like a harbinger of spring. The Odds are digging the hole!

The Odds don't talk to anyone. Never. Carol never talks to anyone. I have only heard her voice on a few occasions and that was when we were in class together and she'd be answering the teacher. I attempted to talk to her a few months ago during the holidays and she simply looked at me, smiled and said nothing. I have never heard her parents say anything. That brings up another point; Carol doesn't look anything like her parents. She must be adopted or, as I suspect, something else is going on here.

I remember when I saw the movie "The Truman Show." That is the Odds. Everything stays the same. One summer I took a photograph of a family member on our front lawn. In the background was the Odd's front yard and house. A few years later I was looking at the photograph and was amazed at how similar the house, shrubbery and flowers were at the present time! It looks like the flowers came up the same way a few years later!

They seem to follow a routine for each day of the week, but the one thing they do every morning is really strange. The three of them 'tour' the outside of the house. There are specific places on the perimeter of the house where they stop, hold hands in a circle and look into the sky. It's very strange because each time they perform this ritual I get a static feeling in the hands and feet. It affects my mother the same way - even when we are not watching them and are somewhere else!

There are other oddities as well. None of them has a job, no one ever visits and they get a lot of deliveries (it seems like every day something comes).

I'm convinced that these "people" are not entirely human. I know it sounds nutty but I'm not the only person in the town that thinks that something nefarious is going on with the Odds.

Source: Phantoms and Monsters

www.phantomsandmonsters.com/2012/04/people-next-door.html

TWO "VERY SPECIAL" WOMEN ENCOUNTERED IN DETROIT

Two out-of-place blonde women are seen at a local yard sale in a gated community. The witness states that they were possible Nordic EBEs because of their odd behavior.

The following account was recently reported to MUFON:

Detroit, Michigan - "On Saturday, October 24, 2020, my wife and I, as well as our next door neighbors, were conducting a yard sale in front of our respective garages.

At about 1:00 PM that day, I noticed two young women coming down the street from the left toward our yard sale. These two young women were both in their mid-twenties and did not live in our gated-entrance and partially-fenced community (Town Square Cooperative). I immediately sensed something strange about these two young women. They were both very attractive - one was taller (approx. 5'9") with medium length blond hair, and the other was shorter (approx. 5'7") with light long hair. Both women were dressed very stylishly in what appeared to be brand new clothes and shoes.

These two young women spent about 10 - 15 minutes looking around before leaving. While they were at our sale, my wife offered

186

them donuts, which they both refused. However, the shorter young women did take a small Snickers candy bar that my wife offered but did not eat it while at our sale.

I watched as the two young women departed our sale. They started to walk back the way they came, but instead of going back to the left - the way they arrived - the taller one raised her right arm and pointed to the right - as if to say let's go that way.

This is where it gets strange. I know for a fact that you cannot get out of our community if you go off to the right because it is fenced in over there by a 7' tall metal fence with no gate or any other opening to go through. As I watched them proceed to the right, they got off of the road and onto the sidewalk that leads up to, and dead-ends into, the fence. There is a public pathway on the other side of the fence that goes to the main road (St. Aubin St.).

Once they got onto the sidewalk and were walking toward the fence, I decided to go to them to tell them that you cannot get out that way because of the fence. I was only about 10 seconds behind them and could not see where the sidewalk dead-ends into the fence until I got closer. When I got closer and could see where the sidewalk meets the fence the young women were not there! I expected to see them either standing there trying to figure out how to get out or walking back toward the way they came from.

When I arrived at the fence, I looked around for them and, to my amazement, saw them on the other side of the fence walking down the path toward St. Aubin Street. I immediately looked back at the fence area for any kind of opening (and there was none) and then looked back down the path and they were not there.

These two young women would have to be "very special" to have gotten on the other side of the fence in less than 10 seconds. The metal fence is seven feet high with spikes on the top and vertical metal bars about four inches apart.

So how did these two young women get to the other side of the fence? Were they super-human and jumped over the fence or climbed over it all within 10 seconds? After doing a lot of thinking about this, my conclusion is that these two young women were actually Extraterrestrial Biological Entities (EBEs) that either: 1) dematerialized and then rematerialized on the other side of the fence, or 2) shape-shifted and passed through the 4" space between the vertical bars. I have read that there are certain Nordic-type EBEs that can dematerialize/rematerialize and walk through walls. I believe I encountered two of these   s -nothing else can explain this strange event in my mind. - MUFON

Source: Phantoms and Monsters:

www.phantomsandmonsters.com/2020/12/possible-ebes-2-very-special-women.html

"MANNEQUIN MAN"

Location: Ottawa, Ontario, Canada

Date: Summer 2016

Time: Early morning

The main witness and her boyfriend had gone to a mall before work – in the very early morning hours when they had just opened – and as they walked into a store, they both noticed, at the very same time, a very odd-looking man sitting on one of the benches, reading a newspaper. He had one leg crossed over the other at a right angle with his arms outstretched, holding this newspaper with a small smug smile on his face, but there was something very, very wrong about him. He had a baseball cap on over hair that looked like a wig and mirrored sunglasses, but even so, they could both tell that his facial features were not normal, in that beyond the thin, smug smile, that never moved, never changed, there were no other discernible features

– no freckles, no wrinkles, no pores, nothing. His entire posture was all wrong and unnatural and he did not move even in the slightest as they walked by.

He was also oddly dressed – it was an incredibly hot summer day, and he was dressed in long heavy pants and a flannel long sleeve shirt, buttoned right to the top. Her boyfriend and the witness actually turned to one another at the same time as they passed this man and entered the store and simultaneously commented on the oddness of the fellow. They agreed that the person looked like a "mannequin" (well was it?). They then both turned around to look at him again together and he was completely gone. They exited the store immediately and looked all around, but the "mannequin" man was nowhere in sight. For the rest of the day, they laughed about how Mannequin Man's experimental day out "blending in" with us humans had not gotten off to a good start and it would be back to the drawing board for the aliens or what have you. Throughout the entire duration of the encounter, it was as if everything in her body, mind and soul was screaming at her that something was very much not right and that this was something unique. Pure primal instinct.

Source: Anne Charbonneau in "Beyond Creepy" YouTube Channel

STRANGE RIDE BY THE RIVER

I have a strange memory that has stayed with me for many years. I believe it took place in 1971, near the Missouri River. I didn't remember it right after it happened. It came to me a few months later.

In this memory, I am sitting in front of the TV and it's a hot summer night. We didn't have air conditioning and all the windows were open. I was watching TV alone very late and the house was very quiet. This in itself was strange because my parents did not allow us to watch TV late, even in the summer. It was also next to impossible to be any place in the house without a crowd, because I come from a large family, and the house was always noisy.

I remember having a strong feeling to look outside. I went to the front door and looked out the screen. I saw a large dark vehicle parked outside. It wasn't right in front of our house, but was closer to an empty house.

I couldn't see the make of it. It was black, and the windows were too dark to see inside. It looked like a gangster car out of maybe the 1930s. I thought it weird that it was parked on our street, but some of the guys in the neighborhood were into muscle cars, so maybe it wasn't that weird. It was very quiet outside, and there were no lights at the neighbor's houses. The night air reminded me how it feels right before a thunderstorm.

Suddenly, I'm in the car. But oddly, the light is on inside, and there are a number of people with me. We are sitting on rows of seats, and there is a yellow orange light filling the vehicle. I look around to the faces in the car, but no one is looking back at me. They seem familiar, but not like relatives. The vehicle appeared to have a large number of us inside, maybe 15-20, but the inside is not that big. Suddenly I am aware that the vehicle has been moving, although I couldn't feel anything at all. Soon I realized we were stopping, and at another house. I remember standing inside as a tall thin figure held the hand of a person in pajamas leading them out of the room. Two people were sitting on a couch watching TV, as I stood there, but they seemed in a daze, totally indifferent to us being there. Then I was in the vehicle again and we were sitting inside very still.

Somehow, I was able to look out the wall of the vehicle, and saw we were moving over a grassy area that was very muddy. It was very dark outside but it smelled like muddy water, and it occurred to me that we were near the river. There were no buildings around us, just overgrown areas of trees and grass. I saw some cat tails in some gorges under us. There must have been streams off of the river. At this time of the year you would often be hearing the crickets very loud at night and see the fireflies all over. But it was dead silent, and I didn't notice any of the fireflies around. The vehicle was moving, but not rolling like a car; it seemed to be hovering above the ground.

I turned from looking outside to looking back inside, and realized there was a front seat to the vehicle, and there were two people sitting in front. All of a sudden, one turned and looked back at me, and it was a beautiful golden haired child. He couldn't have been more than a year or two old, wearing a diaper. He resembled statues of the baby Jesus I have seen in Church. There was a warm glow about him, and I remember the curls touching his pink rosy cheeks. He was talking to us, and some of the people next to me seemed to relax and a few sighed.

But as I am sitting there, I am thinking something is wrong. Something didn't feel right. The words he was speaking were in my head, but they were bothering me. The sounds bounced around my skull and echoed, giving me a headache.

For a baby, there was something cold and distant about him. I shook my head and looked at the figure speaking. There was fuzziness in front of him. It was like a television screen in front of him that was losing its signal. I reached out to touch him, and he backed away. As the image flickered in front of me, I saw another figure. It was small and brown, and the head was a weird shape. It had large eyes, wider than long, and ridges around its eyes like over-sized lids.

I had a frightened thought that something really terrible was standing in front of me. The face of the Baby Jesus stabilized and I felt my body go cold. Baby Jesus looked deeply into my eyes and leaned toward me and I broke loose and punched it in the face. I didn't think about punching it, I seemed to do it instinctively. I think I saw a flash, and then I must have blacked out.

I guess I forgot about it until a few months later. My family drove down to a riverfront park to celebrate some relative's birthday. I was walking on a path close to the river and could smell the strong smell of the muddy water. I glanced around and saw a bunch of cat tails. Suddenly, I remembered it: The gangster car, the yellow orange light, the people watching TV, the Baby Jesus, the strange headed being, and the punch.

I never told anyone about this event. There were so many things about it that are too ridiculous. In 1971, I couldn't make any sense of it or place it in any category if I tried. I have never considered it a dream, because it was too real. I have other strange memories about the house I grew up in, but many are not as vivid as this one. I recently moved back into the house and started thinking about this event again. I don't really know what to do with the memory. I made some sketches about what I remember.

The Baby Jesus figure was like a little glowing angel, with but there was something very distant about it. The weird being had tan, light brown dry skin. It didn't look like any of the grey aliens I've seen in pictures. When I hit it, it was like hitting a turkey with dry skin. The black car seemed to dip in the back and seemed to hug the street when it was parked outside the house.

Thank you for what you do. GU

Source: Phantoms and Monsters

www.phantomsandmonsters.com/2017/07/daily-2-cents-strange-ride-by-river.html

THE STRANGEST STRANGERS

Chris Holly

Over the years of writing about the unknown there has been one story I kept putting off writing as it is by far one of the strangest things I have ever encountered. It is the story of the oddest being I have ever met. I would have continued to pass over this story due to its high strangeness if it were not for a conversation I had with a paranormal researcher I know who told me of a string of strange events he had with a similar odd being. I decided the time was right to write about both of our odd encounters with two very strange beings.

As the title states I think of the man I met as a very strange stranger. My fellow paranormal investigator friend described the person he told me about in the same way.

Let me start by telling you what my friend told me about his odd encounters with the man he felt was the strangest person he ever encountered.

It was a few years ago and my friend was running a chat room for those interested in the UFOs and space. He would often notice the name ID of Professor Star joining his chat group. However the person did not join in with the others in the chat room.

One night when the chat room was empty this man entered the room. My friend engaged the man to see if he could draw him in to a conversation. The two of them started talking. The man who called himself Professor Star was a soft spoken man who was extremely intelligent and well educated in the areas of science and space. My friend talked to him for a long time, convincing him to return and join in with the others when the chat room was full of people.

The man did return, but only when the chat room had only one of two other people in it. The man would talk to the people, explaining many things to them about the universe. His knowledge was vast and those who spoke with him were always impressed.

Soon the man would visit my friend's chat room specifically when only my friend and two other people he came to know were there. He would not show up when the chat room was full. Over a few weeks' time, the three people he choose to talk to decided to form a smaller chat room where they could use their web cams as to see and hear each other in a better environment allowing for a more personal conversation.

These private sessions were the strangest conversations my friend and the other two chatters ever encountered with anyone on the internet. Not only were the conversations odd, the group of people soon learned via web cam video that the appearance of this man was also very strange.

PROFFESSOR STAR REVEALS HIMSELF

He was a big man with broad shoulders. He did not seem to have much, if any, neck, making his head look like it was sitting directly on his shoulders. He was bald with very small ears and extremely white. His eyes were very large and light colored. He was an extremely odd-looking man.

He told the people he had chosen to talk to that he needed them to listen to him, as he was going to tell them something hard to believe. He told them that he was one of the last star babies born who were developed to see if it were possible to create hybrid humans who would be better able to travel in space. He told them that he was an experiment as were the other children born to see if they would be better suited to deal with the physical trauma of space travel.

He talked to this group of people about worm holes being a mode of transport through space. He also told them that dimensional travel did happen, however humans were not well suited for it.

This strange man was very bright but mainly wanted to talk to them about being one of the last of his kind. This strange man was as white as an albino but was not one. He was very smart but also very strange. His voice could have passed for either male or female. His tone was always moderate and with little or no emotion.

He did not want to become involved in any conversation beyond what he wanted to discuss and would leave as soon as the group tried to question him about his odd appearance or odd message.

Shortly after telling them what he wanted to say he disappeared into the internet wilderness never to be heard or seen again. Of course this could have been a hoax on this group but the makeup and time to make this man appear as he did for only three people seems a bit extreme.

The fact he was extremely educated concerning our universe makes his being a fraud a bit of a strange thing to do for only three people to witness. Why would a highly educated man want to waste his time with only a handful of people? Once he told the three UFO/space room people what he wanted to say this strange man was never seen or heard from again.

This is an odd story and one that could be passed over with a shrug with those involved left wondering what he was all about. I would think it a questionable encounter. However I, too, met someone very similar to the man described to me by my paranormal investigator friend.

CHAT ROOMS

In the early days of the internet, chat rooms were far more civil, bringing in people who actually wanted to use the chat room systems to discuss topics that interested them. I frequented a few different science topic chat rooms during that time.

At the time voice chat and web cams were first being used in the chat rooms. The rooms would draw people who were interested in the subjects and topics of the room titles. If a room was listed as a science room that discussed space or physics that is what you would find the people talking about in the room.

I enjoyed the science rooms as at that time they were filled with intelligent people who understood what they were discussing and offered a great deal of knowledge to those who wanted to understand the newest topics in the field that the chat room represented.

You could sit and listen to scientists from all over the world talk about the newest theories or explain the complex workings of space, time and dimensions, to list a few of the subjects that were covered.

While visiting the science rooms you would get to know the people who frequented them. I enjoyed the rooms and told a few of my friends who work in science about them. We would all visit the rooms to listen to the debates or views of the interesting people who took part in them.

During this time two of my friends and I noticed that a man using the ID Siriusbound would come in almost nightly and sit and listen without taking part in the conversation. Now and then he would text a remark in to the chat room that would always stump the other scientists in the room. This man would not use the voice option and for a very long time was very low key.

Finally one night when only a few chatters were in the science room the topic of space travel came up. The man speaking on the voice option in the room was talking about his opinion of space travel, discussing rather old views without much modern thinking or science involved.

Siriusbound did not agree at all with the man speaking and tried in text to disagree with him. Since most people used the voice option his points written in the room were going unnoticed.

For the first time Siriusbound used his voice option and talked to the small room of chatters. The man had an androgynous voice, making it difficult to determine if he was a man or woman. He was extremely smart and could discuss every point the other scientists brought up, often correcting their facts or thinking. He was impressive and by far one of the smartest, if not the smartest, participate in the science room.

Both of my friends, who were highly educated working scientists, were very curious about this man and would try to engage him in conversation often.

It was soon realized that Siriusbound would only talk in the room when there were limited people there. As soon as the room filled with people he would simply sit in the background and listen.

My friends wanted to talk to this man so I came up with the idea of forming a private chat room with invited speakers only. About five to seven people, including Siriusbound, were invited to our private room and our trip to high strangeness began.

SECRETS IN THE CHAT ROOM

Siriusbound became the most sought after speaker in the private room. The other scientists would wait in line to ask him questions and test his knowledge. Soon it became apparent they were not dealing with any ordinary person. No matter what question he was asked on any subject, this man had an immediate factual, sometimes incredible, answer. That however was not the strangest part of this strange man.

While in the small private room Siriusbound would use his webcam to communicate with the small group of people he now felt comfortable with. He would turn on his webcam and talk to the small group of people gathered so we could visually see him as well as talk to him.

We were all rather shocked when we got our first look at this man. Siriusbound was extremely odd in appearance. The only other people I have ever seen who were similar to this man were the unexplained tall albino family with large blue eyes I wrote about who once lived on the Atlantic Ocean coastal area of Long Island, New York, in the 1960's.

Siriusbound was very thin and lanky. He appeared to be about six-feet-tall but could have been taller. He was completely hairless. He did not have a hair on his body. Not an eyelash or eyebrow, much less hair on his head. He was completely and utterly hairless.

Sirusibound had overly large eyes that were brown. The most striking thing about this odd being was that he did not have any pigmentation at all, leaving his body as white as fresh snow. At first we thought he was an albino but he quickly told us he was not.

We tried to keep him on the subject of his strange appearance. However, he would avoid it or give us a nonsense answer like being in a tragic accident that removed all his hair and skin pigment.

He was thin to the point of it being disturbing. He would appear nearly flat when standing sideways. His ears were close to his head and if you watched him long enough his neck would at times seem to sink into his shoulders making him look like a human snake. The man was the strangest, most alien looking person that I had ever seen. This was the opinion of everyone who was able to view him in the private room. His appearance was upsetting.

I asked two medical doctors I know to visit the room and look at this man on his web cam. Both doctors were annoyed that I wanted them to do this; however, both were fascinated by this man once they sat and carefully looked at him.

Neither doctor knew of any disease or condition that would cause the strange appearance this man displayed.

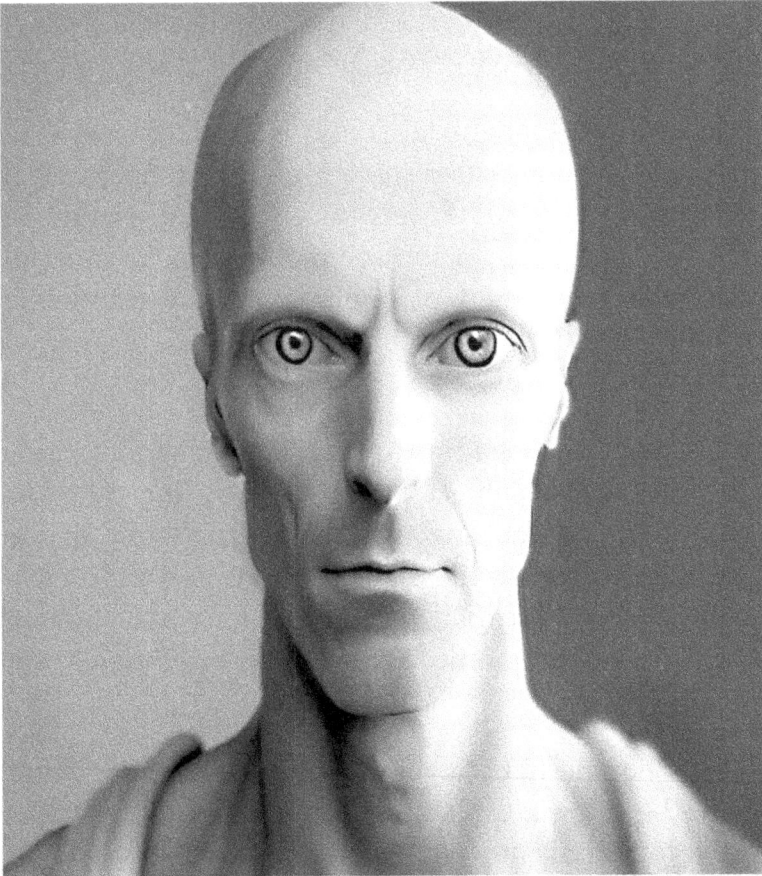

According to Chris Holly, Siriusbound was the strangest, most alien looking person she had ever seen.

I understand that there may be explanations for this man's appearance. However, not the scientists who were part of this private room, the doctors who viewed him nor I could find one.

Siriusbound told us he was not able to go outside during the day as he could not tolerate the sun at all. He spent most of his life indoors.

The strangest thing about this man occurred when the small private chat group discussed books or science journals. It did not matter what book was mentioned Siriusbound would quickly turn to the bookcase behind him or reach beyond the web cam view and return holding the book we were discussing up to the camera.

At first we all thought he simply had an extensive library of popular books but soon learned something far stranger was going on. No matter what title we would mention, this man would display the book. Soon the scientists in the room would make great efforts in mentioning titles of journals or books that were extremely rare or unknown and still this man would step away returning with that journal or book in his hand.

This strange man had an incredible science background and could talk about every subject brought up by the other scientists. During one of the private chat room gatherings one of the people brought up the subject of chimeras. At the time I did not know the meaning of this term but that did not last long; the moment it was mentioned, Siriusbound jumped on the voice option and explained it fully.

He did not hesitate or even blink an eye. He simply went directly in to the subject, explaining it in full as a mix of two different DNA's mixed to become one person or creature. It is why a handful of people in the world have one blue and one brown eye. They were to be two different people or twins when developing and one fetus absorbed the other instead, forming one baby with two sets of DNA.

Of course this is a simplistic description of the subject of chimeras but it gives you the idea. The fact is that at the time years ago this was not a known subject, yet this man was fully versed about what it was and how it worked.

It was like this all the time with Siriusbound. He was incredibly smart with what seemed to be the largest library of books owned by anyone we had ever known. The book situation gave way to long discussions when Siriusbound was not around concerning how he was pulling off showing every book we mentioned on his web cam.

The scientists involved thought he may either be in an office in an actual library. However, that was decided against since he would show us immediately whatever title we talked about, discounting the library theory. This man would walk off from the web cam view and return immediately with the book we mentioned in his hand.

A great deal of thought and discussion was given to the idea that he somehow was able to group hypnotize those in the chat room in to thinking they were seeing the books when in fact he did not actually have the books.

The small group of people who took part in this private chat room knew they were dealing with a very strange being. His actions, knowledge and appearance were unlike anything we had ever seen before.

TIME TO LEAVE

The encounters with this man ended abruptly one day when my friend and I were alone in the chat room with this man.

He told us it would be the last time we would be seeing him as it was his time to leave. When we questioned him as to where it was he was going, he stunned us with his bizarre answer.

He told us he was returning to his home far away as his mission was over here and it was time for him to return to his own kind, his family and his home. He told us it was his mission to live here and watch our culture, but his mission, which had lasted many years, was now over and he could finally go home.

While he talked to us at this last meeting we both were shocked as we watched this man on his web cam. His neck would seem to lose length and form and his head would slide down onto his shoulders, giving him a very snakelike appearance. Frankly, this frightened me and I sent a private message to my friend who was also watching this man on the web cam at the same time.

My friend is a scientist, a physicist, and told me not to panic or turn off my web cam connection. He told me to keep watching, in fact to not take my eyes off of him and to try to remember everything we were seeing.

I did what he said and listened with care as this strange stranger talked about how he was leaving and watched as his body melted into different forms and how he would become aware of it and pull himself back together again to only start to melt down again. It was the strangest most bizarre thing I have ever seen.

This odd man said goodbye to us, turned off his web cam and left the chat room. That was the last any of us who belonged to that private chat room ever saw of him.

LEFT WITH A LOT OF QUESTIONS

Of course we talked about the encounters we had with this stranger for a few weeks after his last appearance in the room.

Those who saw him and spoke with him all agreed he was the oddest being they had ever had contact with. His knowledge on all things was astounding. The oddity of his displaying every book or journal we mentioned was hard to believe.

The appearance of this man will stay with me forever. He was so white, so hairless, with large dark eyes and a long thin body. I do not know how he was able to walk around in public without a great deal of attention. I assume he wore clothes that covered him along with hats and sunglasses. He would appear to be an albino if he covered his large dark eyes. The fact he was hairless, including the absence of eye brows and eyelashes, would only be noticed if he removed his hat and sunglasses.

I do think his time walking about out in the world was limited. However, the people who lived around him had to be curious about this odd man's appearance. I discussed this with my friend the physicist. He thought it was possible we were somehow mind-controlled or shown a hologram and never were seeing this man as he actually appeared in the first place. He also thought it was possible he was not a human and could have been some other type of lifeform who simply wanted contact with a group of humans

I know all of this sounds really strange and hard to believe. All I can tell you is that this did happen and he did appear to us as I described and did do the things I have told you.

I have no idea what or who this stranger was. I have no idea how or why he looked as he did or knew what he knew. For years after our encounter with this strange stranger we talked about him and the possibilities of what and who he could have been and how he did the things he did.

He disappeared after that last visit. One of the members of the private chat room claimed he had the address of this strange man which was located in the southern part of the United States. The chatter claimed he sent him an article and that the strange man displayed via web cam that the mail did arrive by showing him the article he had sent him. This is where the strangeness of this man goes beyond strange to high strangeness.

Once this man told us he was leaving, the man who sent him the article sent him a note in the mail. The note was returned stamped "no such address." The man then tried to locate the address he had sent the article to on Google Earth. What he found was a large open field with nothing around it. He tried reverse look ups with no luck at all. Finally, he called the Post Office that belonged to the zip code to be told no such address existed. The man was truly confused as to how the strange man could have received and shown him the article he mailed to an address that did not exist!

I admit this is a very strange story. I may not have believed it if it had not happened to me. I think many strange strangers are walking around with us daily all over this world. Maybe it is time we all pay close attention to who and what surrounds us so one day we will all understand who or what these strange strangers are.

Be careful out there. You never know when you will be the next to find you are looking straight into the eyes of the unknown! Know if there are two strange strangers out there – there must be many more of them seeking the attention of many more of us.

THE HUMAN FACE OF THE UNKNOWN

Sean Casteel

The cover art of Whitley Strieber's 1987 number one bestselling book, "*Communion*," did a great deal to popularize the now ubiquitous image of the gray alien, bald and with large black eyes. While Strieber has had numerous encounters with that sort of diminutive, embryonic creature, he has also had a goodly number of experiences with human-looking aliens.

JUST YOUR AVERAGE BOOKSTORE SHOPPERS?

But first an account that came to Strieber secondhand. In 1988's "*Transformation*," the first sequel to "*Communion*," Strieber recounts the experience of Bruce Lee, a senior editor at the publishing company Morrow, which occurred in January 1987.

"Absolutely incredible things began to happen after I published '*Communion*,'" Strieber writes. "The first of these took place in a bookstore on Manhattan's Upper East Side. Morrow senior editor Bruce Lee and his wife walked into this store on a cold, windy Saturday afternoon. Mr. Lee showed his wife the display for my book, which was facing toward the front of the shop in the fifth or sixth rack behind the store's entrance."

Mr. Lee noticed two people enter the store and move without hesitation to the display for "*Communion*." The book had only recently come out and yet this couple went right to it, which suggested it was already receiving some word of mouth notoriety. Mr. Lee moved closer to the couple.

"They were both short, perhaps five feet tall," Strieber writes, "and were wearing scarves pulled up to cover their chins, large dark glasses, and winter hats pulled low over their foreheads. They were paging through the book and making such comments as 'Oh, he's got that wrong!' and 'It wasn't like that.' There was gentleness and humor in their demeanor – at least for the moment. Mr. Lee also noticed that they were turning – and apparently speed-reading – the pages at a remarkable rate."

Mr. Lee approached them and introduced himself as being associated with the publisher and asked them what they found wrong with the book. The couple looked up at him and said nothing. At that point, Mr. Lee saw that behind their dark glasses both the man and the woman had large black almond-shaped eyes. Mr. Lee compared their manner to a dog about to bite.

"That was the feeling I got from their eyes," he told Strieber. "So I moved away."

Strieber writes that that would not be how Mr. Lee would respond in a more normal situation. Mr. Lee had been a reporter and correspondent for "Newsweek" and "Reader's Digest," and had covered the White House, Capitol Hill, the Pentagon and the State Department. He was used to confronting tough people.

"But in this instance," Strieber writes, "he felt decidedly uneasy, deeply shocked. He went over to his wife, pointed out the couple while mentioning the similarity of their eyes to those on the 'Communion' jacket, and urged her to leave the store. Nobody, least of all myself and the Lees, knows what to make of this experience. Was it an example of the visitors' odd sense of humor? By simultaneously confirming their existence by appearing to a man of high credibility and reputation but also saying that 'Communion' was full of perceptual errors (a revelation that certainly didn't surprise me), they proved me right and wrong at the same time."

In the above story, the visitors don't seem to have changed their form to something completely human, appearing instead in their usual short stature and with the often reported almond-shaped black eyes. But they were able, using only minimal aids like scarves to conceal their elongated jaws, to pass among people on a winter's day in Manhattan as sufficiently human-looking to not be noticed as "alien."

Behind her dark glasses the woman had large, black, almond-shaped eyes. Bruce Lee compared her manner to a dog about to bite.

THE MASTER KNOCKS

Many years later, Strieber would have an encounter with an entity who looked completely human and yet possessed a wisdom far beyond the limits of mortal knowledge. Strieber has written a complete account of the meeting in a book called *"The Key: A True Encounter."*

"I did not know it at the time," the book begins, "but on the night of June 6, 1998, one phase of my life was going to end and another begin. At around two thirty in the morning, I had a most extraordinary conversation, indeed a life-changing conversation, with a man I have come to call the Master of the Key."

Strieber was in a hotel room in Toronto, having just completed a month-long tour to support his book *"Confirmation,"* and was exhausted. He had eaten a room service dinner and gone to bed. When he heard a knock on the door, he assumed it was the waiter coming to take the tray back.

"Not realizing it was long after midnight, I opened the door and let him in," Strieber writes. "He ignored the tray sitting on the desk and began talking. For a moment, I was confused, then I understood that this was not, in fact, the waiter."

Strieber next thought the person might be someone who wanted to engage with him about the new book and had somehow found his hotel room.

"A reliable rule of thumb," Strieber writes, "is that no stranger who calls or arrives after midnight is going to be somebody you want to talk to, so I immediately began to try to get him to leave. He said something about mankind being in chains. Thus began the most extraordinary conversation I have ever had in my life."

"At this point," Strieber continues, "I think that I am right to assert that I cannot make conventional sense of this man, whom I have come to call the Master of the Key. This is because his words were a key for me that unlocked many doors, and his mastery lay in the fact that they were often either brilliant distillations of complex ideas, or were entirely novel, and they were delivered with calm assurance."

Strieber describes the man as displaying a "twinkling good nature." His hair was white and close-cropped, and his eyes were a light blue. He wore a dark gray turtleneck and charcoal trousers. He seemed rather slight to Strieber, perhaps five foot eleven, weighing maybe a hundred and seventy to a hundred and eighty pounds. He looked to Strieber like an ordinary physical individual.

"I know what he was," Strieber further declares. "He was one of us. No matter the mystery of his identity, his humanity was immediately familiar. Had I asked him, though, I suspect he would have revealed himself, also, in radiant form. I do not think that he walks the streets of Toronto, that he eats his dinner and reads his book. I think that he is either a man who has, in life, attained the ability to live and see beyond the limits of the physical, or somebody from beyond the physical who has perfected the skill of walking among us when he wishes."

A DIALOGUE FOR THE AGES

The ensuing conversation between Strieber and the Master of the Key took the form of a classical student/teacher dialogue in which the unknown guest provided lessons in human potential, esoteric psychology and man's fate. The visitor shone a light on why man has been ensnared in a cycle of repeat violence and self-destruction and offers a slim, but very real, possibility of release.

One of the questions Strieber asked the Master of the Key was "Could aliens walk among us without our noticing?"

The Master of the Key replied: "By bending light, they can be invisible, and walk here to some extent, and also by using means to prevent you from looking at them by influencing your mind from a distance. But there are also those patterned on the same template as you, and they walk freely here. It is their job to enforce secrecy. This is the source of all the confusion about this. They appear, for example, to be part of your government, but they only use it as a camouflage and as a source of power. Human institutions do not control the secrecy. It is controlled from a higher level."

A STRANGE YOUNG BOY LIGHTS UP

Strieber has also encountered human-looking aliens who are not so wise and benevolent, at least not on the surface. A website called Uqbar Calling, dedicated to reporting on "the high strangeness of reality," tells the story of a young human-looking man who haunted Strieber and his family for some time.

According to the website, "In 1993, Whitley Strieber realized that a mysterious young man was lurking around his cabin in New York. When the Striebers heard sounds of movement in the woods around their cabin and caught whiffs of cigarette smoke throughout the summer of 1996, they decided he had become a permanent fixture. On several occasions, Whitley discovered piles of cigarette butts beneath trees close to the cabin.

"Strieber suspected the man was a human-visitor hybrid," the site continues, "because, although he had all the physical characteristics of a human being, he exhibited the 'same testy, frantic quality that characterized the grays that I had previously encountered.'"

This tendency was so pronounced in the young man that Strieber wondered whether the boy suffered a mental illness, like schizophrenia, or was perhaps a failed genetic experiment the visitors left behind to watch over Strieber as their "asset." Later, in an online journal entry, Strieber described the "guardian" as looking like a child who had grown to adulthood without ever entering puberty, and his erratic behavior, combined with his stunted stature, led Strieber to think of him as a "sinister chain-smoking dwarf."

There were indications that the guardian sometimes entered the Striebers' cabin and spent the night in a guest room. The rest of the time, he seemed to occupy a series of crude little sheds he built in the woods around the cabin. Strieber sensed that not only was the young man shy, but that he found people too emotional and too unpredictable for his tastes and was unhappy overall.

THE SMOKER FOLLOWS THE STRIEBERS TO TEXAS

In the late 1990s, the Striebers suffered severe financial setbacks that forced them to sell their cabin and move to a small, rather drab apartment in Whitley's native San Antonio. It was a depressing, discouraging time for them. Their new neighborhood was a typical urban setting, worlds removed from the quiet and isolation of their cabin.

"One night," the Uqbar Calling site says, "Strieber detected the familiar odor of cigarette smoke. A short time later, a neighbor told him that a boy about 12 years of age had been lurking around the building, even climbing up an exterior wall that had no toeholds whatsoever. Strieber caught a glimpse of the guardian dashing away from his apartment one night. Thereafter, he would lurk in the shadows every night, smoking and watching just as he had done in New York."

At this point, Strieber picks up the story in his 2020 book "*A New World.*"

When Strieber and his wife Anne were living in their small condo in San Antonio, and the bizarre man who had been living in the woods behind their cabin in New York showed up with two companions, strange events immediately followed. Those events most notably included demonstrations of the interlopers' ability to control minds.

As the nights in San Antonio passed and the strange youth continued to linger just outside the Striebers' bedroom, just a few feet away from them, Strieber and his wife became aware of two strange men living in the apartment immediately below theirs. The feral "child" was living with them beneath the Striebers. One day, Strieber saw one of the men in a local drugstore loading shopping bags with smoking materials of every kind, which were in those days still sold on open shelves.

"Anyone in the store could have seen him doing it," Strieber writes. "He walked out in full view of the clerks with two bags full of cigarettes, pipe tobacco, cigars, you name it. Every clerk in the store stood silent, staring straight ahead. Except for me, the customers were all in the same condition. As he passed me, he gave me a look that was at once knowing and venomous, and from that moment to this, I have known that there are people who can do as they please in this world, because if you can control the minds of the people around you, you can control your world."

Strieber soon discovered that the youth and the two men were squatting in the condo complex. When he reported this to the owner of the condo they were crashing in, the owner had them evicted.

"The last I saw of them," Strieber writes, "the two men were canvassing the complex, trying to sell the rest of us the owner's furniture. Of course, as everyone knew they were squatters, nobody bought it. One morning a couple of days later, the 'boy' strode out of the space between our condo and theirs while I was working in our garden. He went marching off down the street.

"And this is why I know there are people," Strieber continues, "who can control the minds of others. One would think that this would confer on them almost unlimited power, but one glance at the seething, desperate world of the human elite and it is obvious that, whoever they are, they do not rise to the top of our societies. Judging from the way these men were, so very weird, and, in the case of the small one, apparently schizophrenic, one can see why."

Some human-looking entities can offer world-changing wisdom, while others seem to be able to control the minds and bodies of "mere mortals" and disable their force of will completely. Whitley Strieber here bears witness to creatures who look ordinary enough, but possess powers and strengths we more normally associate with the grey or Nordic aliens frequently reported by abductees.

Perhaps it is the human-looking entities who can walk among us unnoticed that we should fear the most.

Dr. Roberto Pinotii, author of the book *"UFO Contacts in Italy,"* claims that in October, 1958, two men were allowed to enter a landed UFO and take pictures of the interior and the very human-looking pilot.

WHY THEY ARE HERE

Timothy Green Beckley

Some people seem to be natural magnets for the intelligence behind the UFO phenomenon. Robert Short is a prime example, as his warm smile and shimmering blue eyes reflect his genuine sincerity. Although his claims of contact with extraterrestrials may seem farfetched to some, documented evidence points to the fact that his astonishing claims are authentic. And yet we cannot explain how it is that he might have been chosen out of millions to speak for them on a regular basis.

A CHANNEL FOR SPACE INTELLIGENCE

Robert E. "Bob" Short has probably had more close encounters with UFOs and their occupants than any other man alive today. The California-based contactee has been receiving messages from UFO entities for almost 30 years. A friend once said, "Bob draws UFOs like a bowl of jam draws flies."

This is no exaggeration. During lectures held across the United States, Short's presence has somehow triggered valid sightings.

Short, who is the founder of the Solar Space Foundation of Joshua Tree, California, is an untiring researcher of archaeology, Indian cultures, customs and prophecy.

Bob's first experience with being a channel took place in 1952. A year earlier he had been experimenting with automatic writing, achieving some success. Then he heard about a man who had spoken to aliens in the desert. Bob felt compelled to find him. The man was the controversial George Van Tassel, who lived in the Twenty-Nine Palms area and had claimed to have gone onboard a UFO that landed a hundred feet away from where he was sleeping on a sweltering night.

Eventually, the two did meet. Bob told Van Tassel about his automatic writing and about how his writings told him to find the man who spoke with space people. Van Tassel was interested. He invited Bob to stay for a session in which Van Tassel was to communicate with aliens.

"There were a lot of people present," Short remembers. "I sat in a big chair and the lights were turned off. I was ready to do my automatic writing, but my hand started to shake. Then my arm shook. My whole body started shaking and I couldn't stop it. And all of a sudden, I passed out cold. When I came to, the lights were on. I thought I'd fallen asleep and I apologized.

"The people were staring at me with a strange look in their eyes," Bob recalls. "Then George Van Tassel told me I wasn't asleep, that the aliens were using my voice box to communicate with the people in the room. My wife says that just before the voice came through there were peculiar clicking noises in my throat."

SECRETLY LIVING WITH US

During an interview with Bob after one of his lectures, I asked him if aliens, or space people, were here, secretly living among us.

"Yes," he said. "I believe they are with us now...they walk our streets, they work with us...if we were open to them, they would stop and talk to us."

"Can we recognize them?"

"Yes. The eyes are very peculiar. They're more hollow, or sunken, than ours, and they seem to have a strange side vision. But there are others who look something like the Indians of Peru. High cheek bones, high foreheads, almost Oriental, with swarthy skin. They seem to be ageless."

"Do they have bases?" we asked.

"Here? Yes, although they can't stay here very long because of the chemical differences in their bodies. Their bone structure is different. They don't have our boney look. And their bases are in the southeastern part of the country. There are some off our coastal shelves and perhaps some in the Bermuda Triangle.

"Look, I am in touch with them. I don't want to lose contact. And that could happen if I reveal too much, that is, be too specific about where they are."

We asked, "What would happen if we confronted one of them?"

"He wouldn't say anything," Bob says. "He'd probably just smile. If you were alone with him in an isolated area, and you were receptive, that is, meant him no harm, he might lay a whole thing on you. He might tell you about your life, what you've been doing, what you hope to do." Space aliens, it seems, are very psychic.

STRANGE COUPLE

Short relates a unique incident which occurred in February, 1962. He was in the Glinton Restaurant in Yucca Valley with a group of people prior to a communication he was to have that evening in a desert area near Death Valley. After some time, a couple came in, a man and a woman. They had to stoop over to get through the seven-foot-high door.

Even though "extraterrestrials in disguise" is the favorite explanation
for the "others," it may not necessarily be the only explanation.

Diners were frightened by them because of their height, but
Short said that their presence had been predicted during an earlier
communication. He had been told that the entities would meet him in
person. Bob felt instinctively that this was the moment.

There were plenty of seats available at the counter, yet the couple elected to occupy a table close to Bob's. He described the woman as being exceptionally beautiful, with a sort of scooped out face. She wore no makeup. Her eyes were very pretty, wide and alert. Her nose was straight.

Short said the man was handsome in a rugged sort of way, much like the Clark Gable type. He wore a moustache. His slacks were dark and he wore an Eisenhower jacket with a winged white shirt collar which went all the way to his shoulders.

The man sat with his back to Bob's group, but the woman faced them and smiled often at Bob and his friends. They ordered toast and coffee but did not touch the food. At the cash register later, the woman turned and again smiled at Bob and the others.

As soon as they went outside, Bob Short bolted from his chair and hurried out after them. He was too late. They were gone. There was nothing outside. He saw no car on the road. There was no other building they could have ducked into. It was as though they had vanished from the face of the Earth.

WE WANT YOUR BABY

One of Bob Short's strangest experiences deals with a pregnant woman. She had heard of Bob's reputation in the field and had come to him for two reasons. One was that she had a disorder in her tubes which the doctor had described as a tumor. The other was a contact with a couple who wanted her baby.

The woman told Short that while she was in her doctor's office in Oakland, California, a couple came in. They spoke briefly to the doctor. When he approached her, she said, he was visibly frightened. The doctor said, "There are people here who want to talk to you." He then ushered the woman and the couple into an unused office.

According to Bob's visitor, the couple was wearing brown street clothes. The woman was pretty. She had an aquiline nose, no makeup. The man had short, reddish hair, and very penetrating eyes.

He did all the talking. He told the pregnant woman her life history from the moment she was born to the present. He then mentioned the child she was carrying, about how he wanted to adopt it and take it back where he came from, which was Tibet.

Bob Short frankly did not know what he could do about helping the woman to keep her baby, but he did hope that the space people would cooperate with him on the matter of the disorder in the woman's tubes.

"I did communicate in the woman's presence," says Bob. "They did something through me which healed her. I was nothing more than an instrument. But she had X-rays taken later and her doctor described her as a walking miracle. There was nothing there, not even scar tissue. He was absolutely floored. She had her baby, a beautiful child, and now I understand he's very much interested in UFOs."

The inference in this business about the baby was that the woman might have copulated with an Ultra-Terrestrial. However, Bob Short apparently did not know the father and therefore chose to remain silent on that aspect. In any case, the baby was not adopted by the mysterious couple who showed up at the doctor's office.

*Originally published in *"UFOs - Wicked This Way Comes"* - 2003, Inner Light/Global Communications

WHO WERE THOSE STRANGE, TALL ALBINO PEOPLE? OR SHOULD I SAY *WHAT* WERE THEY?

Chris Holly

I was sent an email by a woman who lives on the end of Long Island, New York, at Montauk Point. She told me that she often walked her two large dogs on the beach along the Atlantic Ocean coast on the end of Long Island; the woman told me that she often reads my articles and remembered one I wrote years ago about a strange, tall, very white, odd-looking family that lived on Long Island in the 1960s.

This lady told me that while walking her dogs during the months of December and January she witnessed a strange family with a huge strange dog also walking on the beach. She told me they were extremely tall and seemed to be two couples of albinos with about four or five children with them running along the beach as the adults walked the dog. She told me she remembered my article and wanted to know if I had any other reports of this strange family being seen on Long Island.

I contacted the woman, who told me she stopped seeing the strange group of tall albino people at the end of February. She told me she found them to be so very odd that she asked the people in the town shops and her friends and neighbors if they had seen the group. The only other person who claimed to have seen them was an older man who would feed the birds along the shore, but he only noticed them once and did not recall ever seeing them again.

I questioned her and found the woman to be concerned about the people because she believed they were something other than human and felt very uncomfortable when walking near them. She told me her large dogs, who were very protective and a bit on the aggressive side, would whimper and stick their tails between their legs, dragging her away from the group and refusing to stay close to them. She was finally dragged in a half run down the beach away from the strange group of people by her frightened, protective pets.

In the many decades since my family and I encountered this same type of tall, albino-looking people, it was the first time anyone in my area had ever talked about seeing them – not only on Long Island, but anywhere.

What follows is the original article I wrote about these strange, tall, white, blue-eyed people. I wonder if they are being seen anywhere else in the world and, if so, who they are, where did they come from and where do they disappear to?

THE STRANGE CASE OF THE ALBINO FAMILY

Years ago I was sitting on my deck with my mother having lunch when my mother looked over to me and said "Remember the Albino family that used to live in our area that always shopped at Gertz Department store?"

I hadn't thought about Gertz Department store, which had long ago gone out of business, for years, and much less the Albino family.

My mother went on about how striking they were and how well dressed and groomed they were. My mother commented many times back when she saw them how beautiful the family was and always noticed what they were wearing. I never thought much about it then as I was in my teens but, as my mother went on and on about the Albino family, I realized how very strange they really were.

Each member of the "Albino Family" had completely white skin and hair. Their eyes, rather than being pink, were a clear, light blue.

The family consisted of two adults and three children. All of them were albinos. I have only seen a few other people who have this albino condition and really did not note the differences in this family and the other albinos I have seen. In talking to my mother about this family, I began to realize they were truly unusual people and not like other albinos.

The five members of this family all were 6ft in height, including the mother and daughter. The male members stood between 6ft–3 inches to 6ft-5 inches. They were extremely tall people. When they walked through the department store, they stood a head above most of the other shoppers.

Each of them had thick, full, pure white hair. They were beautiful people with high cheekbones and straight model-like features. Their skin was white – pure white. They all had the same color eyes, which were clear, big, and very light blue. They kept to themselves. They would stay together when they shopped and seemed to be quiet, polite people.

It wasn't until years later, when I had that conversation with my mother about that family, that I realized they were a very different group of people. I thought about the possibility of two beautiful albino people who looked so much alike in height, looks and facial features meeting and marrying. Although this is possible, I knew the odds had to be nearly impossible. I then recalled reading an article while in college in the late 1970's that talked about all the eye problems that went hand-in-hand with those who were albinos. I also read that eye color for the typical albino runs towards the pinkish, reddish tint. I know that there are degrees of the condition which would have a lesser or greater effect on things like eye and skin color (or lack of it) in those who are albinos. I did not read about any who had clear, big, blue eyes.

I tried to find out if there were blue-eyed albinos that could run in an entire family but came up empty handed in my search. I am not qualified to answer the question to the chance of this happening but feel at best it would be a very rare occurrence.

I thought about this family and had to admit that finding two tall, beautiful, blue-eyed albinos who married and had three tall, beautiful, blue-eyed children was either an incredible happening or they were not a family of albinos!

Years after discussing this family with my mother, I came across a few articles on the Internet that talked about the tall whites. I was scrolling down one of the pages of the site I was looking at when I came to an artist's drawing of the alien species called the tall whites. I was completely taken aback as I sat and looked at the same tall people with the same beautiful faces – white hair, blue eyes and high cheekbones – as the albino family that use to shop for their clothes and housewares in Gertz department store in Bay Shore, Long Island, New York, in the 1960s.

I will never know if that strange, gentle family of tall, beautiful people was simply a very rare family of human albinos or if they were a group of entirely different beings.

I often wondered over the past years about that family or group of people. I have tried to search for them a few times but cannot find anything anywhere that would explain this odd group of people. Maybe they just moved away to another state – or planet!

I did learn to not be so ambivalent about things and pay attention to people and my surroundings far more than I once did. I wish I had been more curious at the time. I wish I considered how odd those people were and thought about things instead of just blindly skipping along without considering what was going on around me. I learned many lessons during my life. Being alert to my surroundings can be the most important thing I can do for my safety and that of my family. I will tell you one thing: if I ever see a group of tall, white aliens again with those huge light blue eyes – I am going to pay attention.

Part of both paranormal and UFO lore is the shapeshifter; a being who
can disguise itself as a human in order to blend in unnoticed.

THE CURIOUS CASE OF DAVID DANIELS, THE REPTILIAN MAN

Philip Kinsella

Are there aliens walking among us? Well, that's a good question, and one which I will try to address. Dealing with the theoretical aspects of alien contact, (something I have been exploring for well over thirty years) has led me to conclude that there appears to be an interaction of so-called alien contact on a conscious level of projection on *their* part, most notably the Grays which are so famous within the annuals of Ufology. This is to say that the phenomenon presents itself in an almost ethereal state, leaving very few clues as to the reality of just such a singularity. My exploration into the Grays confirms for me that we may be dealing with an interdimensional species which permeates our reality from time to time. However, the question of whether aliens walk among us is another point in question, and something which I believe is a reality, and for very personal reasons which I will explain.

As an author and researcher into UFOs and consciousness, I happened to meet with Brenda Butler, who was the first British author to release a book surrounding the famous Rendlesham Forest UFO Incident, which had occurred within the Christmas period of 1980. The book was called *"Sky Crash, A Cosmic Conspiracy,"* published by Neville Spearman Publishing Ltd back in 1984 and co-authored with Dot Street and Ufologist/author Jenny Randles.

Anyone remotely interested in UFOs will know of the famous event which occurred at the American twin bases here in the UK surrounding the forest of Suffolk. However, for the content of this chapter, we will not be focusing upon this occurrence, but just to make the reader aware that Brenda, along with many other prominent figures within the world of UFO research, had been touched by this very strange phenomenon, and one which attests to the fact that aliens do appear to be walking among us, and for the most part largely undetected. This alien, however, appeared in the guise of a Reptilian, and not your classic Gray! Although there appears to be a plethora of different extraterrestrial species gracing our planet, the difficulty is trying to establish where they come from, and just why they appear to elude detection. The events described are true and actually occurred, no matter which way anyone tries to change the narrative. As you will see, this Reptilian had no interest in the preceding events at Rendlesham but was more concerned with his species' own plight. In a strange twist of fate, myself, along with my twin brother, Ronald, and good friend, Susan, may have also met this elusive individual, and many long years after Brenda's interaction with this creature. This will be described at the end of the chapter. Here, then, is a brief overview of what occurred back in 1984 with Brenda Butler and the Reptilian.

A PANICKED PHONE CALL

On the evening of the 23rd of November, 1984, Brenda received a distraught telephone call from Dot, who seemed to be in a state of complete shock. Dot proceeded to tell her that a strange man had come to her door, asking for Brenda. What scared Dot the most was the fact that one minute the man had been standing in front of her, and the next he'd simply vanished, and had then appeared in her living room! Dot's voice had the urgency of a very frightened individual. Brenda begged her friend to get to her house as fast as possible. At first, Brenda refused point-blank, but after listening to Dot's pleas, she relented and drove the thirty miles to her house. Dot told her that the man had particularly requested speaking with Brenda personally.

When she finally arrived, Brenda was presented to a tall, slim man with blonde, cropped hair, neatly parted in the middle. His eyes were the bluest she'd ever seen. His hands and fingers were, as she observed, exceedingly long. He looked to be in his late thirties and was extremely handsome. What shocked her more was his calm and confident nature. He wore a long, leather coat which almost touched the floor, giving him the appearance of some old, war-time soldier. As Brenda entered the house, Dot tried to convey something to her in secret without speaking, because the man was directly behind them, but Brenda could not understand what she was trying to say or warn her about.

Brenda observed the man for a while as they sat in the living room after they had been introduced. She was puzzled as to why he'd wanted to see her. "*Sky Crash*" had only recently been released, so she was in two minds as to whether he was here to discuss the book, along with its revelations. He could have done that with Dot, she thought. It was obvious there was another reason, and one Dot couldn't understand. She was both nervous and frightened of him. She felt threatened by his presence alone and wanted him out of her house.

The man eventually spoke. He said his name was David Daniels, and incredibly proclaimed that he was from the Pleiades, and had arrived in a spacecraft. It appeared to Brenda that he had no discernable accent. She thought at first that he was American. After all, she knew enough of them at the base, but she wondered why this man had sought out Dot at her home in the first place, and not gone straight to hers instead. His statement, '*that he was from the Pleiades star system*' seemed rather far-fetched. After all, the constellation of the Pleiades is in far excess of roughly 440 light-years away from Earth. But with what they'd all discovered in regard to the appearance of a UFO at Bentwaters, it seemed just about anything was possible!

David told Brenda that he had been waiting a long time for this moment. In a strange way, Brenda felt drawn to him. She would give anybody a fair hearing, but it appeared Dot was on the other side of the fence. She wanted anything other than his company. She kept picking arguments with them both. Why she reacted in this fashion was beyond her. She'd never seen her friend using such hostility towards anyone like this before.

David requested that he and Brenda go for a walk because of the bad atmosphere brewing in the house. Dot begged Brenda not to go. After all, the man was a relative stranger, and she feared for her friend's safety. His apparent ability to move from one place to another in a blink of an eye had obviously shaken Dot to the point where reasonable logic went straight out the window. Also, with the recent publication of 'Sky Crash,' it was no wonder tensions were high, and it was difficult to know who exactly to trust.

After much debating between both women, Brenda decided to take David up on his offer to go for a walk. As Brenda recalls, they walked some miles and felt an immediate bond with one another. David continued by reiterating that he was, indeed, who he claimed to be - a traveler from the star-system, Pleiades, and that he'd arrived in a spacecraft. He also explained that he was part of a group of nine others, five of which would soon meet up with Brenda herself. He was on a mission, and one which would be made apparent in time. He spoke about the Second World-War, and of the 'Foo-Fighters,' (UFO's), which were so famously recorded as following Allied aircraft when in trouble to help guide them to safety. These, he claimed, were drones, operated by Mother Ships hovering high in the skies, and not advance machines created by the Allies, or the enemy for that matter, as once thought by all those high-ranking officials during the Second World War.

Brenda recalled that David seemed a very spiritual person. By the time she checked her watch, it had just gone past 10.15 pm, and she suggested they had better make tracks back to Dot's. On returning to her friend's house, however, Dot had been beside herself with worry, and was furious that Brenda had been gone for such a long time. Brenda decided at this point to say her goodbyes and leave.

THE MYSTERIOUS STRANGER

Over the next week, Brenda made repeated journeys back to Dot's to further her understanding and friendship with David. On each occasion, however, she found that the tension between Dot and David was becoming increasingly hostile. Dot wanted him out of her house. She didn't like David at all, least of all what he claimed to be. Brenda knew this was totally unlike her friend to go off the wall about someone. The curious fact was this: why did she let David stay in her house in the first place? And why hadn't he sought out Brenda's address? This was still a puzzle to Brenda, but the open-minded and understanding person that she was, she was prepared to let this go for the moment. She felt she had to learn more from this strange man and see what he was about and what he was after.

On one occasion, David asked if both he and Brenda could go out for a drive. Dot and David had had a terrible row that day. He couldn't understand human emotions. He was puzzled by Dot's hostility towards him. Quite what the arguments were about, Brenda wasn't sure, but she felt that she needed to get out of the house and see if she could help David in some way.

Once again, and while driving, he continued to talk about the stars, space, and of his home, people, and way of life. He also reminded Brenda that things would be made clear to her all-in good time. Her home would also be used as a 'Staging-Post,' and Brenda could not work out what he meant by this. For some strange reason, he never spoke about the Rendlesham UFO incident in 1980 which Brenda, Dot and Jenny had written about in '*Sky Crash*'. This was a very curious point indeed, and something else which Brenda could not fathom. After all, her years of research and investigation into the case would be anyone's dream to talk about, yet he made no mention of it whatsoever. He seemed more concerned for Brenda's safety than anything. Was she in danger?

On one such occasion, Brenda was going up to Woodbridge to meet with two Americans who had phoned her and asked to meet her with regards to Rendlesham and the UFO sighting. David, on learning this, did not want her to go alone, and asked that he accompany her. This she agreed to, but on leaving Dot's house to make the journey to the base, they found that a vehicle was following them. Nerves set in when Brenda discovered that the car, (a red Mazda with two occupants in it), had, apparently, been tailing them for some time. She drove into a pub's yard not far from Woodbridge to curtail them. They waited in the car for about fifteen minutes in the hope that it had gone, but Brenda was shocked to find that it had taken its position far up the road, and had been sitting patiently, waiting for her next move. As she drove past the Mazda, it once again continued its pursuit. Brenda decided to stop off by a chip van and waited there. She knew at this point that her meeting with the two Americans had to be cancelled, and both she and David decided to return to Dot's. The car which had been following them had disappeared. Was it possible that these occupants knew of the meeting between Brenda and the two Americans at the base?

Their return was anything but pleasant. Dot had got herself so wound up due to them getting back late again that she started shouting at them both, telling Brenda that she was frightened of David and his weird ways and that she wanted him out of the house at once. This prompted David to go to his room while Brenda tried to defuse the argument. Brenda didn't agree with Dot's outburst and duly told her that she liked David and that perhaps Dot was over-reacting. Dot explained that David only ate greens, loads of them, along with sweets to keep his energy-levels up, and was repeatedly appearing and disappearing in front of Dot all the time. Even her daughter, Sue, backed these claims to a shocked Brenda. Dot kept telling her that David was dangerous, and that she feared for her life.

Brenda took herself up to David's room and knocked on the door. He'd said that if it was Dot, he wouldn't see her. As Brenda entered the bedroom, she found David lying on his bed, looking very sad and upset. Once again, he couldn't understand why Dot was so against him. He wanted to leave. Staying in this house would, so he explained, kill him. He then asked Brenda to lock the door. It was time for him to reveal his true appearance, and that he felt she was ready to accept him for what he was in order that she trust what he said about him as being the truth.

What happened next was, to say the least, bizarre. David asked Brenda to not be frightened by what she was about to witness. She was not to talk, and on no occasion to touch him. Quite what he meant by this, Brenda wasn't sure. She remembers the event well and was not scared in the least.

David began to shake. Brenda noticed that the veins in his hands, neck and temple rose to about half an inch. This was followed by his appearance changing into what she could only describe as a Reptilian. His skin was like that of a snake. This shape-shifting episode lasted for about two minutes, and while in this state he began to talk in a strange language which Brenda could not identify. As David came round, his alien appearance disappeared. He was shaking, felt cold, and remained silent for a moment while a shocked Brenda gathered her thoughts. There was no telling what was going through her head while all this took place, but there was no doubt in her mind that David was exactly what he claimed to be - an alien! This was performed with no equipment, or hidden cameras, and there certainly weren't any machines in the room capable, during this time, that could create the bizarre special effects needed for someone to transform themselves in such a manner. It happened quickly, as Brenda recalls from memory, and left her completely speechless.

It took a while for David to compose himself. Sitting up, he proceeded to tell Brenda that he was here on a mission, and that

233

Brenda was an important key to the initial landing which was to take place sometime in the future. She had nothing to fear. They would find her when the time came. Brenda was then shown a strange Star-Chart which he'd mapped out with various signs of the constellations. Quite what this all meant, she wasn't sure. She knew enough, however, to realize that she was in the company of someone far more advanced than anyone she had ever met before, and she had to protect him at all costs.

Dot knocked on the door and demanded that they both come downstairs. Brenda decided to go, but David pleaded that she take him with her. Brenda didn't live in a large house, so there was no room to put him up, save from a caravan in her yard. Dot was becoming hostile again, and so, despite David's pleas to go with her, she drove the thirty miles back on her own, her mind in a tangle. Shocked, amazed and certainly convinced that she was dealing with someone who was not human, Brenda hoped that she'd see him again.

DAVID MOVES IN

The very next morning, Brenda was shocked to find David knocking on her door. How he'd managed to find where she lived was a mystery. Evidently, he'd hitch-hiked and walked most of the way. Within an hour of inviting him inside, Dot phoned Brenda to tell her that he'd gone, and was even more surprised to learn he was now at her friend's house. Her reply was curt; she never wanted to see him again and was rambling on about his weird ability to teleport from one place to another in the blink of an eye, his strange eating habits, and his non-stop talk of his important mission on Earth and of the planets, stars, and constellations. Because Brenda had formed a close bond with David, she put this to one side. The overall fear that David was a plant (whether for the Military/Government or any other organization) didn't seem to make any sense. After all, the lid on the Rendlesham Forest incident had been blown wide open with the release of 'Sky Crash'. And, anyway, David had no interest in the incident whatsoever, which was even more puzzling. There was, however, much more which would become apparent in proving beyond any shadow of a doubt that this stranger was wanted by Higher Authorities and had even penetrated the British government with a plea to understanding of his apparent Intergalactic plight!

Over the course of many days, Brenda had become closer to David, but it would soon appear that many others would also begin to fear this man, for one reason or another. There were many curious factors which Brenda needed to address, and which had unnerved her then partner, Chris Pennington, who was living with her during this time. It was decided that David would stay in the caravan in the yard. He could not bear to be cooped up inside a small house and needed freedom, and he made this fact very clear to Brenda, although he was humbled by her offer for him to stay on her property in the first place.

Chris Pennington is a very down-to-earth individual, having no flights of fancy whatsoever. In fact, he was to play an instrumental role in grounding Brenda. A musician at heart, he'd been witness to many strange things, but none more complex and amazing as what was about to occur. Chris constantly feared for Brenda's safety, and, like Dot, found that David Daniels was a menace to him also. This was due to the many threats Brenda had received from unknown sources during and after the publication of 'Sky Crash'. Remember, during this time, the Cold War was still on, and tensions within the world governments and militaries were high.

To prove that David was indeed not from this planet, and to convince Chris of this fact, he would take a random book from a shelf, flick through it speedily and hand it over to Chris.

"Pick a page, any page," David said.

Chris chose a page at random, and was shocked when David began to recite, word-for-word exactly what was written in the book. He demonstrated this ability on many occasions. He could also mind-read, knowing exactly what Chris was thinking at any given time. Chris didn't like this at all, and constantly warned Brenda about his fears. The atmosphere in the house was becoming tense, and it appeared that David saw Chris as a threat towards his relationship with Brenda.

Chris feared this man so much that he slept with a gun under his pillow. Astonishingly, David approached Chris and told him he'd seen in a vision the gun and what his intentions were if he became hostile towards him. It appeared, through Chris's recollection, that this person was indeed a danger. The mind-games he played and apparent demonstrations of super-human ability were enough to convince Chris that he wanted him as far away from them as possible. He demonstrated the ability to mind-read constantly, and Chris feared that it was David's intentions to get him out of the way - for good. Through our interviews with Chris, it became apparent that this no-nonsense and remarkably intelligent man admitted himself that he did, indeed, feel that David Daniels was more than human. His emotional reactions when talking about David were enough to convince the most hardened skeptic that he was indeed what he claimed to be.

This ability in creating problems between Brenda and Chris was displayed on another occasion by David, when Brenda had made them all a lovely meal. Waiting to see if their guest would eat anything other than greens, David took the pepper from the table, heaped it onto the potato and other greens which graced his plate, and simply stirred the whole lot together in a mess. David was, currently, watching Chris for a reaction. All the effort and trouble Brenda had gone into cooking a nice meal meant nothing to him at all, and this had infuriated Chris. After all, human emotions confused David, and he didn't seem in the slightest bit worried how other people felt about him. Chris, however, knew what his intentions were. David wanted him out of the picture - completely. As with anyone taking the precaution of protecting themselves with a gun, David must, surely, have unnerved Chris to the point where Chris felt physically threatened.

David claimed to be a shapeshifting reptilian. He was always seen wearing a very long leather coat which came down to his ankles.

There were some other bizarre factors both Brenda and Chris observed with their strange guest. He never had any change of clothing and never washed but was always clean-shaven and immaculate. This would seem an impossibility. He never needed the toilet either. There were no amenities within the caravan to provide for such hygiene, or anywhere else for that matter. On almost all occasions, David donned a very long, leather coat which came down to his ankles, and wore sunglasses in the daytime to shield his eyes from our light. He would constantly be observed by the locals wandering up and down the street in the early hours of the morning, scaring many who lived nearby. This was brought to Brenda's attention, and she asked him to stop these midnight excursions.

Dot had indeed been right. The only thing he ate were greens and sweets, perhaps to maintain his physiology. If David was indeed a Reptilian, (as he claimed), then he would need to maintain high levels of energy at all times. He carried no money and no change of clothing. The only items he had were a strange, blue crystal and a toy bear. Anyone with a rational mind would throw such notions right out the window. A man who purports to be an alien carrying a strange crystal and toy would not go down very well among serious investigators, but the fact of the matter is, this is all he had on him. It has been suggested that the bear could have been a decoy, and that it was perhaps used to hide something within it. Still, it is baffling why an alien would have such a ridiculous object in his possession.

On one occasion, Brenda and Chris were horrified to find that the outside paint from the Caravan in which he stayed was peeling away. With no means of generating much heat within the mobile unit, it was thought that David had generated this energy within his apparent reptilian body to maintain his physiology. Both Brenda and Chris had never seen anything quite like it.

Things seemed to add up and lend credence to the story that David was what he claimed, a Reptilian! Chris had examined the caravan, and, on closer inspection, found that the paint was crisp, almost burnt, as though someone had placed an enormous blowtorch around the whole of its perimeter. This was an impossibility, at least to his logical mind. Chris had built the caravan himself and knew enough to assume that an incredible amount of heat must have been generated from the inside to cause the exterior to decay. After all, the only source of heat David had was a small camping stove, nothing large enough to create such a puzzling enigma. There were no razors, soap, water, or toilet in there in which to clean oneself. The amenities were sparse and very basic. How, one wonders, did he appear so clean and fresh every day without entering the house which was always locked when both Brenda and Chris went out. Upon returning home and after checking to make sure there was no way for David to gain secret entry, Brenda and Chris found that absolutely nothing had been touched. And why, we must question, would someone go to all the bother of secreting themselves inside Brenda's house in the first place, when all he had to do was ask if he could use the bathroom?

STRANGE BEHAVIOR WITH BOOKS

Another odd factor with David was books. He would steal and then bury them. A bizarre act, to say the least! However, Chris was furious when he discovered that David had taken two of his Ordnance Survey books. David had deliberately marked out lines around the Rendlesham area within the pages, (carefully constructed with patience and accuracy), showing where certain portals (dimensional openings) were located. This is how UFOs were able to gain entry within the Earth system, or so he explained to Brenda. This would make sense many years later when it would be discovered that these lines led to Ireland where a hidden, underwater base of some kind was supposed to exist, discovered through the deciphering of certain binary codes Jim Penniston recorded during his initial encounter with the UFO in the forest in 1980.

One book which had captivated David was, 'Briefing for The Landing on Planet Earth,' by Stuart Holroyd. He'd told Brenda that this was the closest thing to the truth regarding UFO contact. In his words: "A true book - the only one!" This he also buried, much to Brenda's shock. The book describes extraterrestrials who wish to contact humans. Certain psychic mediums were involved, along with a peer and other prominent individuals. It is an apparent true account which explores the psychic realm in greater detail.

David requested that he be taken to a Sunday church service. He was interested in human theology. Brenda took him to a small church in Aldringham. During the service, David was fascinated by the hymn book and Bible. So much so, he helped himself to the two books upon leaving the church, secreting them within his coat. Brenda was mortified and demanded that he take them back. This was duly done, and in doing so he, along with Brenda, had a meeting with the vicar at his home where David explained who he was and why he was here. The vicar got on very well with him, so Brenda recalls, because he had an open mind. David was especially fascinated in the concept of God and of creation through "human" interpretation of the facts recorded within the Bible. He had made an in-depth study of the book, and the vicar was astonished by David's ability in quoting references from any part of the Bible. The vicar believed in UFOs and explained that the children of God would welcome brothers and sisters from other systems which supported life.

What was also interesting, and will become apparent, is the fact that David showed Brenda pictures of himself dressed as a priest, along with an identity card. She didn't think much of this at the time but was to realize much later the relevance of this very strange guise.

The crystal he carried was used on Brenda to re-establish past-life links. This he did by placing it upon her head while taking her into a light trance within the outer building he occupied on Brenda's property. It seemed that David had a vested interest in the concept of reincarnation, and that he was keen to discover whether Brenda could recall these events to establish a stronger bond with him. Instead, Brenda saw her Spirit Guide, Raah. In this vision, Brenda saw Raah's world. Beautiful people dying from starvation and disease. The images (according to Brenda) were very clear and upsetting. These aliens had come to our world, and had brought diseases with them which, so she was shown, had infected our planet. They had come to Earth in order that a cure be found, but the mission failed.

Another oddity was the midnight telephone calls David was making. He claimed these were to his government, and that he could also communicate with his people by other means, namely telepathy. These calls were witnessed by both Brenda and Chris, but strangely never showed up on the bill. The calls were real, and on many occasions Brenda recalled hearing someone replying on the other end of the line. However, on checking the list of numbers which had been called, not one of his contacts came up!

With his inability to sleep, along with midnight excursions outside the house, the neighborhood residents approached Brenda and asked that this strange man leave immediately. He was scaring the locals too much. In total, he spent three months there. But within that period, he had furnished Brenda with information on all that he understood about space and the heavens, along with the knowledge that Mankind was not alone in this infinite universe, and that there was purpose to our existence.

It was, so he had told her, time for him to leave. There were people in authority who now knew about his craft and whereabouts, and that 'they' were looking for him. David said that others would come, and these people would not be as close to her as David had been, but he reassured her that they would meet again later. Although many of the residents breathed a sigh of relief when this strange man had left, Brenda was heartbroken.

MORE STRANGE VISITORS

Not long after David had departed, a woman named Suzanne turned up at Brenda's door. She said she too was from the Pleiades, and that Brenda was a contact point for them, and that she had been chosen as a child to perform this duty. Suzanne proceeded to tell her that there were nine of them in total. They had come, so she explained, to understand about human life here on Earth, along with emotions which they found hard to deal with. One wonders at this point just exactly *why* Brenda had been selected to perform such a task. She was none other than a down-to-earth woman with no real political status within society. However, the general theme with regards to alien encounters does prove that extraterrestrials do tend to link with people who are not connected in seats of high power, which goes to prove that they are not here for global domination as the film industry would have us believe.

Suzanne only stayed one night with Brenda, which gave her the chance to take her up to see Dot. Once again, Dot took an instant dislike to her, the same attitude she had adopted with David Daniels, and wanted her out. Brenda decided to take Suzanne to the forest where they talked for a time. She had to go but explained that others would come. Suzanne was going to see Billy Meier, (a farmer from Switzerland who was also a UFO contactee and prophet, and who was also in possession of some very controversial photographs of apparent alien spacecrafts which he had caught using a simple camera). Suzanne explained that the humanoid Nordic aliens who contacted Billy were indeed from a star system beyond the Pleiades, and that those in authority wanted to make him appear as a fraudster.

When Suzanne left, two other people came. These were Michael and Alana 'O'Legion, who claimed they were also from the Pleiades and were here to go on Anglia TV to talk about their planet's struggle with water and how our governments were looking for them. They stayed for a few hours. The couple also described how our governments won't let them land on Earth - that it was forbidden - and that a carefully controlled program by the military was in place to prevent this from happening, or so they claimed.

David Daniels got back in touch with Brenda. He phoned to ask whether she'd go to London to the House of Lords to see Admiral Lord Hill-Norton to persuade him to help his people on the Pleiades. Lord Hill-Norton was Chief of the Defense Staff of the UK and became Lord of NATO's Military Committee, a very high official within the world of government. David had organized a meeting with the Lord and was keen to discuss his plight. What's amazing is that a peer from London was willing to listen to someone who purported to be an extraterrestrial! However, the meeting was set, and Brenda went up to Liverpool Street Station to meet with David.

At the House of Lords, Brenda was searched by security guards. She had with her a briefcase which contained a copy of her book, '*Sky Crash,*' along with some other documents about the Rendlesham case. What's strange is that David was not searched at all. They were taken down some corridors and then into a room within the complex where Admiral Lord Hill-Norton was seated behind a huge, oak table. Both David and Brenda sat on the opposite side. Lord Hill-Norton talked about his house in the country and other light topics before David went into his discussion about interplanetary problems. Strangely, Brenda recalls that the peer seemed more interested in David than her. He listened as David explained about the Pleiades, of the Middle Earth People, and of his culture, along with the problems they were experiencing and the need for our world to intervene. David went on about other dimensions, of the British government knowing about UFOs and alien intervention, along with a real need for the Earth people to take his pleas seriously.

Lord Hill-Norton reflected over what David was saying and asked many questions regarding the Pleiades, taking immense interest and pity upon his plight. However, the peer explained that he could not help in any way, because he had his job and pension to consider. Getting involved in this kind of thing would, so he explained, ruin him, even though he had a great interest in the subject of UFOs and their reality.

Brenda took from her briefcase the copy of '*Sky Crash*' and pushed it across the table towards the peer. He glanced at it and pushed it back. He curtly told Brenda that if it had anything to do with the Americans, he wanted to wash his hands of the matter, and that 'they' - meaning the Americans - were bound to make more of it than what it was.

After the meeting, Brenda and David went to a small cafe to discuss what had just taken place. There was the distinct possibility that Lord Hill-Norton knew more about the Pleiades than he was letting on. It was clear from the meeting that his hands were well and truly tied. After their discussion, Brenda asked David to come back and stay with her. David replied by saying that it would be too dangerous for them both but relented after Brenda kept on. She wanted him to meet some other people whom she thought he'd find interesting and were also involved in a UFO incident which had become very famous. Little did Brenda know that things were about to get more heated and difficult with David Daniels around.

UNDER SURVEILLANCE

Unaware to her, Brenda's movements during the period of 1984/85 were being monitored even more closely by government officials, along with the police. During her investigations in the forest in the beginning of 1981, she had acquired a vast amount of information, along with some physical evidence which she had concealed very cleverly within her house. Since the release of 'Sky Crash' by Neville Spearman, all three women found themselves in a bizarre world of lies, deception and paranoia. One can only wonder, then, how they were able to keep their sanity and wits about them. Brenda was now in touch with aliens who purported to have come from the Pleiades system, and that one of them, their Group-Commander, David Daniels, was here on a mission which apparently seemed thwarted due to governmental intervention.

Higher officials wanted David, and it would appear they would do anything in their power to get him, whatever the cost. These faceless, unknown individuals who worked tirelessly behind the scenes were orchestrating their own version of events to silence not only the biggest UFO story in England, but any interaction with seemingly alien beings. This is nothing new within UFO cases. Time and time again, witnesses are always intimidated and harassed in order that their version of events become twisted and distorted. The media machine hardly helps either. By the time they get their version of events highlighted on the news, or documentaries for that matter, the whole subject is made to appear almost laughable.

Brenda was happy to have David back, even though it was just for a week or so, as he had other pressing duties to deal with in London and couldn't stay for very long. She decided to take him up to some friends who were having a party. This couple was John and Susan Day.

It is well documented that they, along with their three children, were subjected to a famous UFO encounter on the 27th of October 1974 in Aveley, Essex. It is best known as 'The Aveley UFO Case.' As the family was driving home, their car ran into a green mist upon a lonely road, and they subsequently lost two hours of time. John started to have recurring dreams, and this led to an investigation by a Dr. Leonard Wilder, who performed hypnotic regression. Upon examining the suppressed memories stored within John's mind over a period, it was found that the family had been taken onboard a UFO and been given a medical examination by strange beings who appeared to look like doctors. The case has been written about extensively and is considered genuine.

When Brenda introduced David to John, there was an immediate air of tension between them. What's strange is that both men seemed to recognize one another, even though they had never met before. Brenda found this shocking. A terrible row then ensued between them. John claimed that David was an enemy, and that they were rivals in a past alien life and had been at war with one another. Brenda had to get David out of there in case the argument turned nasty. The way they were shouting at one another indicated they were not welcome.

Brenda got David into her car and started the long drive home. David seemed quite affected by the encounter. In fact, Brenda was forced to stop while he composed himself. She had never seen him like this before, displaying signs of trauma, confusion along with surprise. This was indeed something strange, considering he didn't understand human emotions.

Was it possible that John Day had, through his abduction in 1974, remembered some form of past life; that the episode of his initial UFO encounter had, somehow, opened an area of his mind which had previously been closed to any such notions? It seems plausible. We know enough about the survival of the soul and its ability to transmute from its physical life upon the Earth-plane into what we term the 'Spirit World,' whereby some form of new incarnation takes place after a soul chooses to return to any number of worlds or dimensions for another experience.

This is common with abductees. They appear to be more consciously aware and seem to have a greater understanding of their purpose within the grand scheme of life. We also understand that there are many other dimensions just being discovered by our scientists, and that a soul can choose whether it is to experience not only a human life but an extraterrestrial one too. The fact of the matter is that both John and David recognized one another, and of their dealings from past incarnations upon other worlds. Both had been at war within the Pleiades star system. This is something which, we believe, will be more understood by scientists through the discipline of the mind and when we begin to understand the complex multi-layered dimensions of consciousness.

After a week, David returned to London, where more work of his had to be done. He never spoke about his movements to Brenda, or what exactly he was up to, but he maintained contact on a regular basis.

Ralph Noyes was also to play an intricate part in Brenda's life. A former MOD (Ministry of Defense) official, he'd attended one of Brenda's lectures in 1984, which centered on '*Sky Crash.*' He'd specifically asked to meet Brenda after the lecture, whereby she furnished Ralph with knowledge about David Daniels. Ralph found the information intriguing and wanted to meet this David to see what he could make of him.

It appears that David had gone to stay with Ralph over a three-day period. In that time, and on one memorable occasion, David had taken the ex-MOD official to a bridge in London, not far from Elstree Studios, to demonstrate his unusual powers. Dressed in his usual long, black coat and wearing sunglasses, (even though it was dark), David raised his arms upwards to the sky while Ralph watched, and was amazed to see three luminous white lights in the shape of a perfect triangle hovering above them before disappearing.

Ralph later explained all of this to Brenda through several correspondences, telling her that he was, indeed, impressed with this man's ability in performing these seemingly incredible feats. Strangely, Ralph did not feel threatened by David in the least. However, there was cause for concern among certain peers in the House of Lords about David's pleas. A letter from Norman Trent, (another researcher), on the 14th of January 1985 to Brenda outlines this fact clearly:

"….Ralph Noyes has promised to deal with the House of Lords people and warn them not to have any more dealings with David Daniels." Norman goes on to say that: "I do not think that I have told you that 'D.D.' (as he was constantly referred to by all those who met him), asked for some guided meditation, as he felt tense. I discovered a very unpleasant layer in his inner consciousness which may explain quite a lot. We all hope that we can forget him, but we would like our books back!" The book incident was yet another example of David's fetish in stealing them, whomever they belonged to.

However, Ralph Noyes shows no such remorse towards David, as others had, in a letter he wrote to Brenda on the 10th of February 1985. Whether Ralph had followed up on these claims to warn those peers in the House of Lords about David Daniels is not clear. He makes no mention of this in his letter:

"....It certainly must be said for David Daniels that people don't forget him! The odd thing is that although I felt distinctly uneasy during my two meetings with him, I certainly didn't <u>dislike</u> him, and I found him, in his way, a strangely impressive character. The unease springs, I think, from the fact that he very obviously carries some powerful and important idea within his head, but won't say what he wants, (not to me, anyway). Despite the things that his American contacts say about him, I would certainly see him again if he ever turned up. I assume from your letter that he hasn't been in touch with you again, though you and Lady Clancarty were the only two people of whom he spoke with any warmth when talking about his experiences in the UK."

Lady Clancarty was the wife of Brinsley Le Poer Trench, the 8th Earl of Clancarty. From 1956-59, the Earl edited the famous "Flying Saucer Review" magazine and founded the "International Unidentified Object Observer Corps." He also served as a Vice-President on the board of BUFORA, (The British UFO Research Association) and later organized celebrated debates in the House of Lords regarding the validity of UFOs. The Earl also wrote books on the UFO subject.

Another meeting occurred. Ralph's letter to Brenda dated the 12th of March 1985 explains as much:

"As it happens, David Daniels came to see me last Saturday, having rung me on the Friday evening. It's the first I've heard from him since January. (How did you know we were in touch again?) He seemed very relaxed and cheerful, but I had no more idea than on the two previous occasions why he had really come. He is a strange man! Anyway, he gave me a London telephone number on which he said I could reach him if necessary. So, I phoned him this morning and gave him the message you had had. He thanks us both."

Ralph went on to write a science fiction novel based around the events of Rendlesham Forest entitled, 'A Secret Prophet,' which had been published by Quartet Books in June of 1985. It was speculated that Ralph's book, which ran alongside the publication of 'Sky Crash,' was an effort to somehow discredit the real UFO case and sway public opinion regarding the events which had really occurred at Rendlesham. This is mere conjecture but was felt by many to be the case at the time.

It seems odd that David was seeking all those who had been involved in the Rendlesham mystery, even though he appeared not in the least interested in the case at all. He made a brief visit to Jenny Randles, only to be sent away by her because she felt unnerved by his presence.

A WANTED 'MAN'

Around 20th August, Brenda received a distraught telephone call from David, asking her if the C.I.A, M.I.5 or Scotland Yard had phoned or been round to see her. Brenda replied that they had not, and David assured her that they would be in touch. He explained that 'They' had found the whereabouts of his craft and were monitoring his movements. David also went on to say that she was not to believe what they would relay to her. He had to keep moving for fear of being caught. Then, quite abruptly, he hung up.

At this point Brenda feared for David's life. She felt he was indeed in trouble. No sooner had David finished his call when her phone rang again. This time a man introduced himself as Detective

Inspector Letterman, (real name changed), from Scotland Yard, and was looking for a certain David Daniels. He also said that he was working alongside M.I.5. Brenda made out that she didn't know what he was talking about, but the Inspector assured her that he, along with his team, was aware of their movements and had been watching them for some time. Brenda asked him to prove that he was who he claimed to be, and he duly gave her a number to ring. After putting the phone down, Brenda rang the operator, who confirmed that the number was indeed from Scotland Yard. She rang Inspector Letterman's office and, after being transferred via his secretary, listened very carefully to what he had to say.

Inspector Letterman continued by saying that David was a dangerous man, and that he had killed someone, a man in London who he'd been staying with. Apparently, the police had found UFO literature, along with an address book which contained Brenda's contact details inside the man's flat. Inspector Letterman gave no mention who the deceased was, or if he'd been connected to Brenda in any way. He also went on to explain that both Brenda and David had been under surveillance for quite some time. She asked how it was, (and indeed, if their movements had been monitored by Scotland Yard), they didn't now know as to his whereabouts? This seemed strange considering the situation. Inspector Letterman did not answer her question, but merely insisted that she get in touch with him as soon as David contacted her.

About one hour after the call from Scotland Yard, Brenda received yet another one from a man claiming to be from C.S.I. (Crime Scene Investigations). He, like the Inspector, asked Brenda whether she knew the whereabouts of David Daniels, and that he had indeed murdered someone. She duly told the man that David was not dangerous and knew the real reason why they wanted him. In no uncertain terms, the gentleman warned Brenda to be on her guard, and that they would be sending someone around to interview her. The caller hung up. No such person turned up to take Brenda's statement!

The very next day, David telephoned and explained that he would not phone again, or come down, as people were closing in on his movements. He also told Brenda that her phone was bugged for 'them' to discover his whereabouts. He was being set-up with trumped-up charges which were not true. The call was hurried so no trace could be found on David. He merely said that he would be in touch again when things had cooled down.

There was never any mention of a murder in London, and nothing came up with regards to the police's supposed investigations into the case, which seemed to Brenda to be just a little bit suspect. After all, in any form of murder investigations, all witnesses are interviewed extensively by the police. And, indeed, if both she and David's movements had been monitored, (as Inspector Letterman had claimed), why didn't Scotland Yard, or M.I.5 go in and arrest him straight away?

BIZARRE VISITS

A while later, Brenda had a call from a man named Jim who was a TV producer from Somerset. David had been staying with him. Jim asked whether Brenda would go down and meet up with them so that she could tell her side of the story. Jim was equally impressed with David's super-human ability in reading minds, finishing sentences, along with the art of disappearing. Brenda declined the offer because she feared detection, and of David being caught because of this.

David then visited a retired USAF Lt. Colonel Wendelle Stevens in the United States. Wendelle was also a prominent UFO researcher, spanning an incredible 54 years, and was the author of, "*UFO Crash at Aztec - A Well Kept Secret,*" along with many other books on the subject. A highly-decorated man, Wendelle became Director of Investigations for the Aerial Phenomena Research Organization, (APRO), in Tucson, Arizona. He'd also amassed the largest collection of UFO photos which, subsequently, have been used in many journals across the world.

Wendelle was serving a prison sentence for some trumped-up charge, and always maintained his innocence. One wonders, then, if he was getting too near to the truth with regards to his research concerning UFOs, and was therefore set-up. He was also a man who had many contacts, some of them very high-up, especially in governmental circles. He'd collected an impressive list of credentials and had also won numerous awards for his UFO research.

During the time that Wendelle was serving his prison sentence, Brenda had befriended another author and UFO researcher, John Hanson, along with his now ex-wife, Dawn. John is an ex-CID Officer and has also published some beautiful books on UFOs, most notably his series entitled: "*Haunted Skies*," which chronicles UFO sightings around the world since the 1940's and up to the present, and a series which has taken him well over sixteen years of painstaking research to complete.

Brenda had been in touch with Wendelle for many years. She had also briefed John about her "implant" and experiences within the forest, along with David Daniels. It was also Brenda who was instrumental in getting John to communicate with the retired Lt. Colonel through emails. John helped Brenda in bringing her information as and when she needed it through his own interest in UFOs.

An unexpected email was sent to John and Dawn on the 20th of July, 2005. In it, Wendelle Stevens describes in more detail about his first meeting with this David Daniels, or rather, "Father Daniels," as he called himself. Note the identity card he'd shown Brenda much earlier as him dressed as a priest in her caravan. It seemed that David used this guise to gain easy access anywhere he wanted.

The email from Wendelle Stevens' reads:

"....Oh Boy! This may take some time to tell. I first met 'Father' David Daniels when he came to see me in prison. I was expecting retired FBI Agent, Jim McCoy, to visit me, as he had sent word that he would be out on this Friday. I had known McCoy for years. We both sat in the old APRO Board of Governors Meetings here in Tucson while APRO was active and before the deaths of Jim and Coral Lorenzen. (Jim and Coral had originated the Aerial Phenomena Research for UFOs which started in 1952, and which was also a scientific study into the subject). Bob Dean was another Senior Board Member at the time. At about ten minutes to twelve, I heard my name called over the speaker system to come to the visitors' center. I thought Jim McCoy had arrived a little early and went on over to the center. He was not there yet, but they let me in anyway as 'My Visitor' had arrived. As I entered the room, I noticed a Catholic priest sitting at the first table talking to some other visitors. Not seeing McCoy, I went on past to the back of the room where I could observe all who entered, to wait for McCoy, and sat down at a vacant table. He seemed slow in arriving. As I waited, I saw the priest get up and begin blessing people at every table as he came towards the back. When he got to me, he pulled out a chair and sat down.

"I said: 'I am sorry, Father, but I have a visitor coming.' He said: 'I AM your visitor.' I replied by saying: 'No, I am waiting for Jim McCoy, I am sorry,' and I pulled my chair back. He repeated: 'I am your visitor. I am Father David Daniels, and I have come to see you.' 'To see me? Where are you from?' I was a little confused, because I was a Catholic myself, and I didn't recognize his Order. Each order of Catholic priests has some distinguishing part of their vestments, and I thought I knew them all.

"He repeated it had taken some time to get here, but he had come a long way to see me. I said: 'Where did you come from?' and he replied: 'Yugoslavia, by way of New York.' I said I didn't know anybody in Yugoslavia, and no priest or Catholic orders from there. He continued: 'Actually, I came from London, through Yugoslavia,' and he pulled the chair out again and sat down. He took out a small, pocket notebook, along with an elaborate pen. This made me even more suspicious, because what Catholic Priest (who is not allowed to own property), has anything but an expensive pen?

"The notebook was a tiny one you can buy in any discount store for under 25 cents. His Crucifix wrapped around the Bible he was holding was different from any I had seen before. It was of dark wood, a little bigger than most and bound in silver around the edges. He had this wrapped around his Bible, which I suddenly recognised as the Green Grosgrain version put into hotel rooms by the Gideons. This roused my suspicions even more and I asked to see some identification, which he promptly produced in the form of an American passport. It had his picture and a signature in it, and a permanent home address of 414 N. 44th Street, New York, NY, an easy one to remember by the number 4's in it.

"Now the name of David Daniels: two first names, which struck me as odd. It also had an endorsement written in cursive English. It read: 'Please extend the usual courtesies of the Church to the bearer,' and was signed in cursive by an indistinct name, Vicar of...., (Wendelle cannot remember the name), but he said it was the head of this man's Anglican Order in London. That explained the vestments, which may have been correct, but unfamiliar to me. About that time, I saw Jim McCoy enter the room at the far end, and I said to Father Daniels that I would have to spend some time with my anticipated visitor, and that he should leave. He got up and said he would be back, and he went around the room blessing people again before leaving. I expressed my suspicions to Jim. He said he would see what he could find out, and I gave him the name, address and number punched in the top pages of his passport which I had memorized.

I suggested Jim wait out in the parking lot and try to see how the priest got to the prison.

"He thanked me and left. Jim waited, as suggested, and told me later that he'd come out of the building and got into an older car that he was driving, and which he drove out of the parking lot and back to Tucson and downtown. Jim cautiously followed him to a pizza parlor in the south city-center, where the priest parked the car and got out. He entered the building and returned the car keys back to the owner of that shop. The priest then came out and caught a city bus downtown where he duly got off in front of the Congress Hotel, across the street from the railroad station. I knew the Congress as a cheap hotel, costing at the time no more than $10 per night. And, of course, they have the Gideon Bible in every room. That answered a couple of questions, but many remained.

"This is getting long, and I may lose my connection [obviously the timing of his writing and since Wendelle did not want to sever a link with the computer server], so I will send this on now. If you want more, then I will be glad to continue. Give my best to Brenda. She put up with a lot from this same impostor, and there is much more. I have included my daughter Cece in this addressing, so that she will know what I have already said. She has a lot more she could add if she cares to do so. With all my best respects. – Wendelle Stevens"

It appears that David had gone to see Wendelle with no discernable reason, or so we are led to believe. Wendelle was both surprised and unnerved by this man's sudden appearance. In another email which he sent to John, Wendelle goes on to describe more of his thoughts on the matter after yet another visit from "Father Daniels." This was sent on the 24th of July 2005, four days after his previous communication with John. Wendelle had asked John to send Brenda's full report on her dealings with David for his own personal perusal after discovering from John that she too had dealings with him:

"Dear John, yes, I would love to see a copy of Brenda's report on David Daniels. I shall continue with my narrative account of his visits to me. He came back to the prison to see me the next day, Saturday, (still a visiting day), and I went over to the Visitor's Center, thinking my daughter, Cece, had come out to bring me some mail. When I got there it was not Cece, but David Daniels! He was a smiling, youngish-looking man, sandy haired, about six-foot-two in height, tall, slender, and healthy looking, like he worked out regularly. He wore his hair clipped short, military style.

"He greeted me with: 'You know, we should be friends, we were born under the same sign. As a matter of fact, we have the same birthday!' I said: 'What is yours?' and he replied, '18th January - as I said, like yours.'

"This seemed incredible, and I asked to see his driving license. He responded by handing me his passport again, and I opened it and looked at the front page with his picture and signature. Sure enough, it showed an 18th January birthdate, but just twenty years after mine, showing him born in 1943, making him about 40 years old.

"I said: 'Just what are you doing here, Father?' He replied: 'I came to get you out. You have some important work to do, and you cannot do it in here.' I said: 'Look, I do not want any help. If they opened the doors wide, I would not leave. I have my home and business to think of, not being a fugitive, unable to even use my right name.' He said: 'You are not thinking right. I can take care of that.' Then he said something strange. He continued: 'I was going to join you in Harare, (Rhodesia), to meet Cynthia Hind, to go down to Pinetown, South Africa, to interview Edward

White on his contact with the Koldasian.' I had told nobody but Cynthia about that - not even my daughter! And then he added, (equally surprising): 'I wanted to get an introduction to your courier, Flight Captain, Rodolfo Caselatto, and have him take me to Mirassol to meet Antonio Fereria on his ET contacts, with whom he fathered an alien, hybrid daughter.'

"This really floored me, as I had told nobody about that case, which I was still writing up. He stayed for about an hour before leaving. My daughter, Cece, came out the next day, (Sunday), with my mail, and she said that a priest had come to her home to ask about me. She said my neighbors had seen him at my home in Tucson, looking it over. She asked me why I had given him her confidential addresses. I told her that I had not done so. She said he had bought a couple of my pictorial coffee-table books on the Pleiadian Contact Case in Switzerland. He watched Cece go into a bedroom in her house where she kept them. That same night, he came back about midnight and tried to open that bedroom window from the outside, but the neighbor's barking dogs discouraged his efforts and he left.

"He never told me he was a Pleiadian, but he had a very special interest in that case. He came back to Cece's again and bought more Pleiadian pictorials. The following day, (a non-visiting day), I was in my cell typing, when I heard a key knocking on the small glass port of my door, and I looked up to find a small face with round spectacles peering in. I went to the door and opened it to see a short, overweight man in white shirt and black trousers out there with the priest. He said he was the Chief of Chaplains for the prison complex, and that Father Daniels had come a long way to see me, and he introduced us. I could see that the priest was pretending to meet me for the first time and had extended his hand. I shook hands with him and said: 'Good to see you, Father.'

"The Chief of Chaplains took us over to the Visitor's Center and unlocked the door and took us in. He put us in a sound-protected Attorney-Client room and locked us in, saying someone would come to let us out in an hour. When he left, I asked the priest again: 'Just what are you doing here? I have asked for no priest!' And again, he said: 'To get you out. You have some important things to do.'

"I repeated my statement that I would not leave if they opened the doors wide! I considered myself innocent of my charges and would show them so by being the best model prisoner until I was officially released. And I really was, which I think is why the warden granted an exception and allowed me to have a typewriter in my cell. By now, I was quite certain that this man was no priest. I asked him how he found my daughter, and he replied by saying: 'Oh, that was easy. I had hoped she would give me a letter to Captain Casellato. I wanted to get to Brazil unnoticed.' He seemed to know everything I had been doing!

"A couple of weeks after he left Tucson, Cece got a letter from Christina, (Captain Casellato's daughter who was living in New York), saying she had met the nicest young man. A clean-cut gentleman who drove a red Ferarri sports car and took her to an elegant, expensive restaurant. She had introduced her to her father when he was in town, and they got along well.

"While we were in the Attorney's room in the Visitor's Center, I asked him how he got in on a non-visitor's day, and he said: 'You know your Yard Captain's name is Daniels?' I said 'yes,' and he raised his eyebrows. I got word that Jim McCoy would be out to see me that coming weekend, and he did come. He advised me that the priest's passport number was, in fact, one assigned to the American Embassy in London, but that it was not 'property issued!' Now I knew that my priest was an imposter! He came to see me one more time, and I told him that I knew his passport was invalid, and that if he ever came back, I would turn him in and have him detained. That was the last I ever saw of him. The next I heard, he was back in London and was staying with Brenda. – With all my respects - Wendelle Stevens."

One of the key facts is that he also unnerved all those, bar from Brenda, with whom he met. This would also suggest that people could "pick up" that he was different. Wendelle Stevens had nothing more to do with "Father" David Daniels and remained confused by his visits.

SIGHTINGS OF DAVID

David was seen again, this time in Hawaii and Australia. The sightings of David Daniels in Hawaii are interesting. His movements are nothing less than astonishing! The email came through from a Glennys Mackay on the 17th of August, 2000, and was sent to a Robert Stewart. Brenda was sent the relevant information. It reads as follows:

"....This David, I must comment, sounds the same as the David that turned up in Hawaii and wanted to join our tour group. He was accompanied by a female, about five feet in height, who never talked. He always answered on her behalf. He used to read our minds and was very strange. After five days he disappeared. Called himself David Sutherland! And he would not let anyone photograph him. One of the girls did manage to get a shot of him. The film, however, came out white and cloudy. His whole body was covered with this light!"

Another email from Glennys to Robert was made on the 28th of October, 2000. In this report, Glennys goes on to describe her journey in Australia, but reflects again on her meeting with David during a trip around Honolulu in more detail, as follows:

"....Now with regards to this David! I would not be surprised if it was the same one, tall, hard to gauge the age - mid-twenties to early thirties. Disappeared as he came, the mystery man, and a woman who disturbed all 15 in my tour group."

Her report continues: "....We also feel that we have received implants. I experienced mine going in between my shoulder-blades. This was verified later when I got back to the hotel and friends checked it out. They could see the pinprick and feel something under my skin. It was about the thickness of two matchsticks, and about half the length. The strange man and his partner were sitting in the back of the tour bus, which we'd hired for our trip around Honolulu and the outer islands. After David and the woman left, we tried phoning the hotel where they claimed to be staying and was told there was no one by that name registered. He said his name was David Sutherland, and the woman's name was Jane, I think. It was very disturbing, as he could read our minds and correct our thoughts. Very strange."

She finishes by saying that she was looking forward to hearing about Brenda's experiences.

This was followed up by Robert writing to Brenda for further information which he would send to Glennys. What's interesting is that David does not seem to have aged. Could the female also have been Suzanne who had gone to see Brenda previously? One can only speculate. The last anyone heard about David was that he was somewhere in Australia. His mission was a mystery, along with himself. His ability to transform into a Reptilian suggests that he was anything other than human. Today within UFO literature, there are claims made about these so-called higher beings. Once you get past the bogus material, you will find there is some truth to these supposed allegations. During the period of 1984/85, there were hardly any accounts of Reptilians. Indeed, within our history, it is believed the Serpent was honored, and that these so-called gods had made frequent visits to our planet.

Many years later, during the 1990's, I had belonged to a UFO group. It was here where we had met with American Ufologist and author Peter Robbins, who informed me, Ronnie, and Susan that we had to go to Rendlesham to check the place out for ourselves, as there was still weird activity happening there. This had been long before I'd met with Brenda or had any real interest in the 'British Roswell' case as it is commonly known here in England. Although much of this has already been documented in *"Sky Crash Throughout Time,"* there had been one memorable experience which indicated that we may also have encountered this so-called Reptilian!

The UFO group had decided to do a "Sky-Watch" at Rendlesham. Susan, Ronnie, and I were excited to see the famous military bases and surrounding area where the American troops had experienced UFO activity over the three-night episode during the Christmas period in 1980.What most of the public are not aware of is that UFOs had been witnessed long before, and, after the famous Rendlesham incident, within the region of Suffolk. These have been documented by Brenda herself. However, just before darkness, our group stopped at a pub not far from the location of the forest to get some refreshments and a meal before our long night vigil began in the forest.

It had been while we had seated ourselves around a table that a tall man approached us. He had not been part of our group and had been seemingly loitering around the entrance, looking for someone. As soon as he clocked us three, he came over and introduced himself as Joseph. The man was relatively handsome, being around forty-years of age, and had dark-blond hair which appeared slightly cropped. He wore a long coat and simple clothing. Joseph attached himself to us immediately and was curious to know more about us on a personal level, something which made me feel uncomfortable, especially when meeting someone for the very first time! As he was talking, both Ronnie and Susan saw his hand change, as though becoming plastic before returning to normal again. This alarmed them greatly, and although I didn't see this personally, I believed them completely.

Joseph also appeared to know a lot about us and had no interest in the Rendlesham UFO event whatsoever. When we had finished our meal, he got into his car and followed our minibus to the forest, where he immediately attached himself to us three again. To be honest, I was getting a bit fed up with him, and had been relieved when he started to approach other members of our group while settling to sky-watch. We didn't know what happened to him afterwards, as he obviously departed in the early hours of the morning. On our journey back to Bedford, every single person within our group spoke only about Joseph and how strange he'd been. Had we encountered this elusive David Daniels using the alias "Joseph"? That's something which we will never know, but I am certain he'd been one of the same.

You decide!

A PEEK UNDER THE MASK

Gene Steinberg

Are we alone in the universe?

It has become more and more clear that there are uncountable numbers of planets that have the conditions to spawn life. The common UFO theory goes that some of them have advanced space-faring civilizations and that they have come to Earth for reasons best known to themselves.

NEITHER GRAYS NOR INSECTOIDS

If this is true, what form do they take? Do any of them look like us?

That takes us to perhaps the greatest conspiracy theory of all among people intrigued by the UFO mystery: The possibility that, walking amongst us, are beings from other planets. But they are not small grays or grotesque insect-like beings, common in UFO contact and abduction claims. Instead, they can and have readily passed for human.

What might this mean? Could you tell them apart? Would there be a subtle physical aspect that would provide the clue, such as weird eyes or an extraordinarily large head in proportion to the body? A weird gait when they walk? What?

It's fair to say, though, that genuine humans (I assume they are genuine) have differing physical characters. Sometimes a genetic anomaly, an injury or physical ailment can significantly affect one's physical makeup.

Maybe it's something in their behavior.

So I think of my next door neighbor, a woman in her indefinite 30s who says she works at a nursing home. While I haven't had any lengthy conversations with her, I do see her walking her dog every so often.

So why do I consider such a possibility? Well, her apparent lifestyle seems odd. Passing by her apartment, I've never seen a visible light passing through the blinds. It's as if she always lives in the dark. Periodically I see restaurant delivery people placing her meal on the welcome mat, but that's nothing particularly strange nowadays. Besides, it's likely that she's the sort of person that, while outgoing in a work environment, just prefers to stay alone while at home so she can unwind.

Now some people might regard me as strange, and I surely resemble that remark, but I do not believe that I was born on another planet. I can trace my birth to a hospital in Brooklyn, New York, many, many years ago. My birth certificate, correctly I presume, identifies by name my parents, both of whom were born in New York City.

At least, that's what I assume. Yes, I realize birth certificates can be falsified.

Now way back in the early days of my nationally syndicated paranormal radio show, The Paracast, my co-hosts and I would sometimes wonder if any government agents were forum members. I mean, it was a perfect way for them to keep tabs on us, right? That assumes, I might suggest in an egotistical way, that we do anything at all that intelligence agents or alien infiltrators would regard as important.

Now, in the early days of the UFO field, the FBI watched over some notables, particularly those who claimed contacts with ETs. They weren't concerned so much with possible interactions with alleged visitors from outer space. Instead, they were concerned with issues of national security, such as exposing communists or communist sympathizers. George Adamski is a prime example, because he did reportedly have such proclivities.

THE STUFF OF SCIENCE FICTION

But one thing not considered is that, if ET is truly in our midst, would they attempt to pass as human and quietly live among us?

It is the stuff of fiction, of course, and it depends on being able to assume a human appearance with a disguise, some form of genetic/physical manipulation, or shapeshifting. Or perhaps they are human to begin with but were born on another planet.

Maybe the humanoid is a common form across the galaxy. Maybe we are descended from the same origins, by some advanced race that seeded us all around the universe.

Consider the classic 1951 sci-fi film, "The Day the Earth Stood Still," where an alien entity, Klaatu, appears to be perfectly human. The film never gets into whether his appearance was natural or engineered in some fashion.

In any case, after being shot by a nervous soldier shortly after his arrival on Earth, he is taken to a hospital, where they are amazed that he is far older than he looks, but do not cite any nonhuman physical characteristics. He asks whether he could walk among the people to learn more of our world and is told that he can't.

So he escapes, borrows a suit with the name Carpenter on a tag, and uses it to identify himself. Now some suggest that this is a Biblical reference to Jesus Christ, a carpenter.

Perhaps the reason the "others" look so much like us is because they are distantly related to humans.

Regardless, other than displaying an obvious naïveté about Earth culture and norms, Klaatu passed perfectly as a human being. It was only when he revealed himself to people that they began to recognize the implications of his presence.

Now this is fiction, but it also fueled at least some of the contactee claims of the 1950s, in which alien visitors from nearby planets were also perfectly human. George Adamski allegedly met Orthon, who wore a silvery uniform reminiscent of Klaatu's costume.

So such beings could just as well live quietly among us without being recognized for who they really were.

ARE THE EXTRATERRESTRIALS HOSTILE?

But not all depictions of ETs in human form represent beings that are, basically, peaceful. It's a nasty fact largely ignored by the contactees influenced by him, but Klaatu did threaten Earth with destruction if

266

we didn't abandon our evil ways. But he had our best interests in mind, right?

When it comes to ET hiding its evil ways, there was "V," which appeared first as a TV mini-series in 1984.

In the show, aliens arrived in human form, claiming that they were here to obtain a chemical substance that they required on their home world and they wanted to help us produce it. In exchange, they would teach us about their superior space-faring technology.

But they were actually wearing a disguise that shielded their true reptilian form and their real motives, which were to steal our water and turn humans into frozen food to feed the populace of their home world.

Again, to all intents and purposes, they appeared human so long as they weren't subjected to physical examinations.

A revised version of "V" appeared in 2009 and ran for two seasons on ABC. The premise was similar. The aliens were reptilians who wanted to take over our planet. However, the plotting was more nuanced, introducing sleeper agents among the aliens who wanted to save humanity from the machinations of their fellow beings.

That's all fiction of course, and pretty entertaining. In the real world, is there any evidence at all that ET is here in human form, integrating with our society?

THE THEORIES OF DR. DAVID JACOBS

According to Dr. David Jacobs, a retired historian who specializes in UFO abduction research, there are alien-human hybrids afoot who are busy infiltrating our society. Their goal? To quietly take over our planet, all without firing a shot.

If any of this were true, it would represent the ultimate alien conspiracy. As I said, it's all allegedly being done covertly, unlike the overt displays of violence on many of those aliens-on-the-loose films and TV shows, such as "Independence Day" from 1996. No buildings will be destroyed by death rays, no people will die, or at least that's what's implied.

According to Jacobs, some of the subjects of his abduction research claimed to have been recruited by our invaders to teach the hybrids how to blend with our society so that they are indistinguishable from humans. Worse, this infiltration isn't being accomplished in a single country. It's happening all over the world, involving millions of abductees.

So is your neighbor actually one of them? Not to be paranoid and all, but how could you possibly tell? Would it require a DNA test, or is that manipulated in a way that scientists couldn't tell the difference?

Now Jacobs has appeared on The Paracast on several occasions, and the conversations were both revealing and, at times, disturbing. So I asked him during one episode whether the hypnotic regression process he employed in his research was fine-tuned to avoid leading questions. This is regarded as a proper and essential process by therapists. In response, though, Jacobs said, to paraphrase, "There are no leading questions!"

As you can see, I'm highly skeptical of his views and his approach to employing hypnosis to examine flying saucer abductees. He may, of course, be right after all. Besides, if ET intends to take over Earth peacefully, quietly, it may not be such a bad thing considering how we humans have messed up our planet. In the end, we might benefit substantially if the atmosphere of constant chaos cooled down, but it would come at the expense of our freedom of choice.

THE PRESIDENTIAL ALIEN

Imagine one day awakening to a news announcement from a U.S. President who admits he is not from this planet and that his people are now in control. In the TV show, "Supergirl," that's precisely what occurred in one episode. The President, portrayed by Lynda Carter, best known for her portrayal of Wonder Woman in the 1970s, was revealed to be an alien infiltrator who only wanted peace.

Of course, that might present a problem, since the U.S. Constitution limits the people who can occupy the Oval Office to natural-born citizens. Then again, it doesn't specify that a President can't be part-human/part-alien, so long as he or she is 35 years of age or older and was born in this country.

Other than fakery, like creating false birth certificates, that would merely involve impregnating an Earth woman, via the usual method or via implantation, and having her give birth under the usual circumstances in the United States. A genuine certificate of birth is issued, so the spawn of this hybrid relationship is regarded as a genuine citizen.

Such is the stuff of paranoia.

MONSTROUS TRANSFORMATIONS

But perhaps the most frightening, or at the very least disturbing possibility is that some ETs may be capable of mimicking the shape of a human in ways that aren't detectible.

They are shapeshifters.

Now you can trace legends of shapeshifting throughout literature. Through one of many methods, from native capability, to influence via demons, sorcery or spells, one is able to change one's form at will, or under special circumstances.

Such as someone becoming a werewolf when the moon is full, best depicted in the classic 1941 horror film, "The Wolf Man."

But even vampires supposedly possess the ability to change form. In the famous 1931 film, "Dracula," featuring Bela Lugosi in the title role, he was capable of turning himself into a bat or a wolf. He used his shapeshifting ability essentially for surveillance, to keep tabs on his followers and to seek out more victims.

Shapeshifting was a key plot element in the gory vampire TV series, "True Blood," and in "Star Trek VI: The Undiscovered Country," model-turned-actress Iman played a chameloid, a shapeshifter who was able to take on different forms at will.

Another variation of the aliens-among-us theme was depicted in a 1988 film from director John Carpenter, "They Live." The film's protagonist is an unnamed drifter who acquires special sunglasses that reveal the dreaded secret: The ruling classes of Earth are actually alien invaders concealing their true appearance. They manipulate the populace to breed and conform to proper, to them, behavior by employing subliminal messages in the mass media.

SUBTLE DECEPTIONS

It is certainly true that social networks are consumed by billions, and the posts they see can influence their behavior in different ways. The power of these posts can exacerbate an individual's propensities, violent or peaceful. Members will seek out, or be sent, the messages that conform to their beliefs or enflame them in the appropriate ways.

Polarizing people may also help in generating conflict, making us less able to see what's really going on as well as making us susceptible to some grand alien design.

But perhaps it's all about a bunch of wealthy and greedy tech executives doing whatever they can to earn advertising dollars and enhance their power regardless of the results.

And who took over Twitter in a very controversial move in 2022, and is now trying to advance a political agenda?

Yet another danger is inciting people to turn violent, warlike, hoping that humans will eventually destroy themselves and leave this planet ready for another species to terraform and take over. Again, they do not have to stage an overt attack; they just have to observe the proceedings and patiently allow sufficient time for their evil grand design to be fulfilled.

Then again, if their intent is to make us a more peaceful race, wouldn't that be a good thing even if it's due to the machinations of covert alien visitors?

In the meantime, is it reasonable at all to consider whether your next door neighbor, a friend, perhaps a coworker, or even your boss, is an alien or half-alien? How would you know? Would you notice eccentricities in their behavior, demeanor, or their looks? Nevertheless, people can act in mighty strange ways and still be 100% human.

What about your personal family tree? Can you trace it back several generations? Are you absolutely certain the clan wasn't spawned on another planet and that you may, yourself, be a direct descendant of ET? How would you know?

Or would the suspects seem so normal, look so normal, act so perfectly, that their behavior would defy logic? Do you know anyone like that?

The "others" have apparently been with us since the beginning of history, playing the roles of gods, angels, demons and other types of paranormal entities. Their true origins and purpose remains unknown.

THEY STILL WALK AMONG US
Hercules Invictus

Viewing the Olympian Powers of old as Heavenly Beings, Celestial Visitors, Ancient Aliens or even Ancient Astronauts requires no great stretch of the imagination or suspension of disbelief.

The associations between the starry sky and Greco-Roman Mythology are quite old. The planets of our solar system are named after the Gods in their Roman guises. The days of the week (in the Romance languages) still honor the Olympians and their planetary correspondences. And 48 of the constellations in our night sky, codified by Ptolemy, are based on the old Hellenic tales. The art of Western Astrology is steeped in Olympian symbolism and the Zodiac itself, our sun's annual cycle through 12 constellations, celebrate the Labors of Hercules as well as a handful of other ancient stories set in or around the domains ruled by Zeus on Mount Olympus.

During the legendary past, some heroes (such as Hercules and Perseus), notable personages (like Andromeda and Ganymede), animals (Zeus' Eagle and Orion's Hounds come to mind), fabulous beasts (Pegasus and Krios the Golden Ram), monsters (such as the Nemean Lion and the Hydra) and even objects (the Argo and Orpheus' Lyre for instance) were immortalized in the night sky. Storytellers, artists, navigators and astrologers drew from and contributed to this living lore. This idea of Apotheosis (the process of acquiring a planetary body and becoming a god) established in the myths eventually evolved into the Path of Ascension, which involved navigating (or conquering) the Planetary Spheres (or Levels of Being or Cosmic Rays) and their Archons (Rulers) to transcend this reality and move beyond it.

Though still studied by the literati during the Dark Ages which followed the Classical Era, and still utilized in secret by a handful of practitioners, much of the Astro-Mythological lore went underground and was guarded, obscured and experimented with by both occult orders and lone metaphysical practitioners until it was safe to make it public once again. The ancient wisdom survived this ordeal, and has flourished in our world ever since.

THE FORGOTTEN PAST

Moving forward a bit, Erich Von Daniken, who popularized the notion that the world's mythologies were the distorted memories of early extraterrestrial visitations, focused on the Olympian pantheon in *"Odyssey of the Gods."* And W. Raymond Drake, who wrote many books on the subject, penned one on the *"Gods and Spacemen in Greece and Rome."* Despite the entire data still being debated that is presented in these and other works, they all make a good case for the existence of advanced presences spreading civilization and guiding human evolution. They also demonstrate that superior technology was indeed operant in antiquity. Beyond reminding us of Talos, the robot guardian of Crete, and the golden female automata assisting Hephaestos at his Forge on Lemnos, these inquiries also point to surviving accounts of actual animatronics, vending machines and other technical wonders in Alexandria, plus the war machines of Archimedes (which included a solar Death Ray)! And then there is the reality of the Antikythera Device, an actual analog computer that was manufactured during the Hellenistic Era (between Alexander the Great and Cleopatra).

Science fiction, which is a wellspring of modern-day myth-making, has also explored (and continues to explore) the Olympians in Space theme through numerous books, comics, TV shows, movies, cartoons, games and other entertainment vehicles. Star Trek (the original series), Battlestar Galactica (both original and re-envisioned) and Stargate SG-1 are some examples of sci-fi TV shows that played with the idea of the Dodekatheon's origins in space, their having visited our earth, their past (and sometimes present) relationships with earthlings and their enduring mythic legacy. It is evident that the Olympians are still very much alive, well and thriving in our collective imaginations!

Beyond popular culture, our scientific attempts to expand our influence beyond our terrestrial sphere and venture forth into the heavens themselves have been assigned what are clearly mythological names by NASA, our premiere Space Agency: Project Mercury, Project Hermes, the Apollo Program and Space Shuttle Atlantis for example. At the time of this writing, NASA continues this proud tradition with the Orion Rocket and Moon Base Artemis.

BEINGS OF LIGHT

The Olympians and their lore, as we have seen, have always been (and still are) heavily associated with the Heavens, and as Gods the Olympians have often been believed to be Heavenly Beings.

So, what are the Olympians and what do we actually know about them?

The Olympians are Beings of Light. We cannot perceive their true forms with our terrestrial senses. These secrets are preserved in the tale of Semele, Dionysus' mother. Semele was impregnated by Zeus and the Lord of Dark Clouds offered to grant her a boon, her heart's desire. Hera, the Queen of Heaven and wife of Zeus, tricked her into requesting that the King of the Gods reveal to her his true form. Zeus tried to dissuade her from making this her actual request, but failed. Semele was destroyed and Dionysus was subsequently brought to term in Zeus' calf (as Athena was in his head). Dionysus, after a life of revelry and adventure on Earth, made it to Olympus and rose in prominence until he became one of The Twelve (Dodecatheon).

The Olympians are shapeshifters. They can assume a wide variety of guises, animal, human and elemental. Zeus assumed the form of a bull to abduct Europa from the Phoenician city of Tyre, a swan to seduce Leda and a cuckoo bird to win Hera's heart. Zeus could rage as a thunderstorm or gently caress Earth Goddesses (and at least one mortal) as a soft spring shower of rain, encouraging and quickening fertilization and growth.

The Olympians have strong (and very real) terrestrial as well as Celestial connections and associations. This is clearly true but only makes sense when you explore and seek to comprehend more ancient (and now considered erroneous) understandings of this planet and its night sky. Some of the keys exist in the Astro-Mythological literature and practices. The rest are cleverly hidden in plain sight.

The Olympians walk among us. They establish and monitor certain traditions, practices and cultural institutions. Zeus and Hermes often wandered as humans to monitor our adherence to the Laws of Hospitality they established. According to the tales, those who followed the Laws were rewarded and those who did not were severely punished. Demeter, who wandered among us during her grief over losing her daughter Persephone to Hades, established the Mysteries of Eleusis, which helped humanity overcome their fears, including the threat of death itself. Poseidon and Apollo helped build the walls of Troy (and were cheated out of their wages by Troy's miserly King Laomedon). Apollo was punished by Zeus to labor as a shepherd for King Admetos of Pherae. Some of the gods were said to be strict about the proper performance of their rituals and the observance of their celebratory feasts, which were meant to benefit the greater human community.

It is said that the Greek gods are shapeshifters. They can assume a wide variety of guises, animal, human and elemental.

The Olympians can assume the semblance of the people you know. Athena took the guise of Mentor to instruct and guide young Telemachus, son of Odysseus on Ithaca. Zeus transformed himself into the semblance of Amphitryon to lay with Alcmena and plant the seed of Hercules in her womb.

As you probably noticed by now, if you didn't already know, the Olympians have always sought to establish relationships with us. They can mate with us and produce viable offspring. Through selective breeding they created heroic bloodlines and produced individuals for specific purposes. For example, both Hercules' mother and terrestrial father were of the blood of Perseus, another son of Zeus. Hercules was expressly created to help Olympus defeat the Giants during the much anticipated Gigantomachy. Athena inspired and guided the heroes, individuals who shaped the destiny of humanity. The deeds of the heroes were observed by the Olympians and the gods often sought to influence the tide of events. Also keep in mind that the royalty of the time could and did claim divine descent and boasted of being instruments of divine action.

The Olympians incarnate among us as Wanderers (born into human vessels) or enter our vehicles as Walk-Ins should we choose to vacate. And they can also serve as invisible Advisors or Spirit Guides.

And lastly, the Olympians never left. They still watch over us, guide us and exert their behind-the-scenes influence on the destiny of humanity. They gave us both Democratic and Republican forms of government. Their images adorn some of our most valued civil structures, monuments and seats of power. A classical component in our educational process was until fairly recently considered essential as it provided a firm foundation for better understanding our culture's rich symbolism, including countless literary references as well as the meaning behind much of our medical, psychiatric and scientific terminology. Why not learn from the past and avoid the errors of our forefathers? Socrates, wisest of the Greeks, warned us that Democracy can often lead to Tyranny, something we are now learning anew through the unfolding of current events. Transpersonal psychologists, neo-Jungians and devotees of Joseph Campbell have shown us how we unconsciously live out the ancient tales. These stories can show us what to do (and what not to do) in times of conflict or crisis.

OLYMPIAN STARSEED

I have had more than several personal encounters with the Olympians throughout my earthly sojourn, several of which I've shared in print, and have met numerous other people over the years who have interacted with them as well.

I've reached out to and interacted with whatever Olympians I can find, in person, at workshops and meetings, by phone and on my Olympian podcasts to better understand these enigmatic entities. Here is one of my outreach approaches, often posted online or on the bulletin boards in one of the public places where I am speaking:

An Adventure in Living Mythology – Are you an Olympian Starseed? And if you were, how would you know?

Olympian Starseeds are embodied reflections of Olympus' Light that have chosen to drink the Waters of Forgetfulness and enter the Dream of Mortality to assist in the Great Awakening on Gaia.

The Olympian Starseeds Initiative (OSI) is tasked with locating and liberating incarnate Olympians ensnared by the Dream of Mortality and reminding them of their personal Olympian Mission.

The OSI, mindful that archetypal Olympian patterns have been programmed into the human psyche, believes in assisting all people on Gaia with actualizing their maximal potential. The OSI supports all of humanity's efforts to transcend this world and venture forth into the great beyond, be they metaphysical, mechanical or even imaginal.

If my words resonate with you, or if you would like to learn more, please contact me on Facebook: Hercules Invictus or via email hercules.invictus@gmail.com

Onwards!

© Hercules Invictus

STRANGE FIGURES SEEN DURING PLAGUE TIME

At one time it was thought that comets were heralds of either fortune or disaster. The first outbreak of the Plague in Europe followed an unusual series of events. Between 1298 and 1314, seven large "comets" were seen over Europe; one was of "awe inspiring blackness." One year before the first outbreak of the epidemic in Europe, a "column of fire" was reported over the Pope's palace at Avignon, France. Earlier that year, a "ball of fire" was observed over Paris; it reportedly remained visible to observers for some time. To the people of Europe, these sightings were considered omens of the Plague which soon followed.

According to Johannes Nohl in his 1926 book *"The Black Death, A Chronicle of the Plague,"* at least 26 "comets" were reported between 1500 and 1543. Fifteen or sixteen were seen between 1556 and 1597. In the year 1618, eight or nine were observed. Nohl emphasizes the connection which people perceived between the "comets" and subsequent epidemics:

"In the year 1606 a comet was seen, after which a general plague traversed the world. In 1582 a comet brought so violent a plague upon Majo, Prague, Thuringia, the Netherlands, and other places that in Thuringia it carried off 37,000 and in the Netherlands 46,415."

From Vienna, Austria, we get the following description of an event which happened in 1568. Here we see a connection between an outbreak of Plague and an object described in a manner remarkably similar to a modern cigar or beam-shaped UFO:

"When in sun and moonlight a beautiful rainbow and a fiery beam were seen hovering above the church of St. Stephanie, which was followed by a violent epidemic in Austria, Swabia, Augsberg,

Wuertemberg, Nuremburg, and other places, carrying off human beings and cattle."

Sightings of unusual aerial phenomena usually occurred from several minutes to a year before an outbreak of Plague. Where there was a gap between such a sighting and the arrival of the Plague, a second phenomenon was sometimes reported: the appearance of frightening humanlike figures dressed in black. Those figures were often seen on the outskirts of a town or village and their presence would signal the outbreak of an epidemic almost immediately. A summary written in 1682 tells of one such visit a century earlier:

"In Brandenburg [in Germany] there appeared in 1559 horrible men, of whom at first fifteen and later on twelve were seen. The foremost had beside their posteriors little heads, the others fearful faces and long scythes, with which they cut at the oats, so that the swish could be heard at a great distance, but the oats remained standing. When a quantity of people came running out to see them, they went on with their mowing."

The visit of the strange men to the oat fields was followed immediately by a severe outbreak of the Plague in Brandenburg.

This incident raises intriguing questions: who were the mysterious figures? What were the long scythe-like instruments they held that emitted a loud swishing sound? It appears that the "scythes" may have been long instruments designed to spray poison or germ-laden gas. This would mean that the townspeople misinterpreted the movement of the "scythes" as an attempt to cut oats when, in fact, the movements were the act of spraying aerosols on the town.

Similar men dressed in black were reported in Hungary:

"...in the year of Christ 1571 was seen at Cremnitz in the mountain towns of Hungary on Ascension Day in the evening to the great perturbation [disturbance] of all, when on the Schuelersberg there appeared so many black riders that the opinion was prevalent that the Turks were making a secret raid, but who rapidly disappeared again, and thereupon a raging plague broke out in the neighborhood."

Strange men dressed in black, "demons," and other terrifying figures were observed in other European communities. The frightening creatures were often observed carrying long "brooms," "scythes," or "swords" that were used to "sweep" or "knock at" the doors of people's homes. The inhabitants of those homes fell ill with plague afterwards. It is from these reports that people created the popular image of "Death" as a skeleton or demon carrying a scythe. The scythe came to symbolize the act of Death mowing down people like stalks of grain.

Source: *"The Gods of Eden,"* William Bramley - 1989, 1990 by the Dahlin Family Press

PARAUFOLOGY: A WEIRD ROAD LESS TRAVELLED

Brent Raynes

August 10th, 1975. It was a busy summer. I was burning up the roads from Maine to Florida in my green 4-door AMC Hornet. Once again, I rolled into the small town of Brooksville, Florida, where my friends Ramona and Duane Hibner had taken up residence because it was a hotbed of anomalous activity – UFOs, Bigfoots, ghosts, poltergeists – a perfect example of what John Keel had come to call a "window" – an area that seemed rife with high-strange encounters.

FLORIDA FRIENDS BEAR WITNESS

Ramona and Duane had been particularly drawn to this region because of the ongoing reports of Bigfoot, although they were well aware of the other anomalous activity that had been associated with the area going back to March 2, 1965, when a gentleman named John Reeves really put this place on the map. He claimed to have encountered a humanoid figure who approached Reeves, and who, while facing him briefly, held a small square object up to his chin, followed by a bright flash of light [Reeves would wonder if his picture had been taken], after which the being would soon climb aboard a dull, silvery-gray saucer-shaped craft approximately 30 feet in diameter sitting on the ground nearby and hastily retreat skyward for parts unknown.

So while this couple had set themselves up in this area to investigate reported Bigfoot encounters, they were well aware [and may I emphasize very, very well aware] of the other anomalies. During my visit, I was brought up to speed on a number of peculiar episodes that they had experienced. Duane had recently seen the apparition of a tall thin man, who appeared to be in his 40s, with dark brown hair, seen on two occasions.

THE MANY APPEARANCES OF THE WOMAN IN WHITE

Several times, often in the daylight, Duane had recently seen a woman in a white gown, like a wedding dress with a white veil. Often, he would first catch her out of his peripheral vision, at which time he could see that she was looking directly at him. But when he would turn to look back at her she would turn and move away, soon vanishing into thin air.

This reminded Ramona of an experience she had had years earlier. It happened while she was pregnant. She was lying on her back in bed one day while also praying. Her mother was in a nearby room. Suddenly, Ramona felt like someone had brushed her hair back from her forehead. Her eyes had been closed. "Mother, is that you?" she asked. Her mother, still in another room, hollered back: "No, what's the matter?" At that point, Ramona opened her eyes and said she saw a woman with long black hair dressed in a long white gown [no veil], standing by her bed, with a "warm and gentle expression" on her face.

Back in October 2019, while attending Nashville's first Strange Realities conference, I was listening to a speaker named Timothy Renner, a folklorist, author and artist from York County, Pennsylvania, whose talk on Bigfoot and various other high-strangeness soon had me wracking my brain to remember any similar details that I may have come upon in the past. It felt strangely familiar but after half a century in the field I needed to prime my memory a bit.

One of the things that stood out prominently was these "woman in white" cases.

A few months later, I interviewed Tim in a follow-up about his Bigfoot investigations. He was recalling the time he spoke to a man who claimed he had seen two Bigfoots on the other side of a pond on his property. After getting a good description, Tim then asked him what else odd might have been going on.

"Oh well, my house is haunted," the man replied. He asked if Tim wanted to see some pictures! "Absolutely," Tim replied. "The interesting thing about them is he kept saying, 'I think I'm being haunted by bikers. Look at these guys. They're big hairy guys.' And when he showed me the pictures of them, they didn't look like bikers. They looked like Sasquatches! They were very big. Big eyes. He said, 'Look, he's wearing sunglasses.' They looked like big hazy ghostly pictures of Sasquatches. He said, 'I have another one. A spirit manifested in my mirror. I took a picture.' He showed me a picture of what looked like a woman in a wedding dress. A woman in white and, without knowing anything about it, he sort of presented this woman in white spirit."

"I was on another investigation in Maryland and again waited till they told me all the Bigfoot stories. And at the end of the day I said, 'Okay, what else weird?' and they started telling me stories of UFOs and said their house was haunted and this woman said, again without knowing anything about this: 'One night my husband said he saw a woman in a white dress walk up our driveway and disappear.'"

One Bigfoot site Tim investigated was less than half a mile from a pond where, according to legend, there appeared a ghostly woman in white who had drowned her baby. In his research of folkloric accounts, Tim has found a good deal of woman in white descriptions in various parts of the world, like the European legend of the Frau Perchta witch, also called the Christmas "belly slitter." As the legend goes, after cutting her human victims open she'd sew up inside of them rusty nails and dirt. Tim added how she had "a horde of wild men that followed her" and was also associated with will-o-the-wisp orbs said to embody the souls of children. Tim furthermore stated, "Many, many folkloric wild men across the world have wives or female counterparts that were either white in color or were ghostly white apparitions."

Linda Sigman, claims that when she was 16 she observed a very large winged black figure [estimated at 10 foot in length] flying through the air close to a UFO she and a boyfriend were watching at close-range on the evening of April 18, 1967, on a hilltop in Mason, West Virginia [only 13 miles driving distance to Point Pleasant]. In my interview with her she also recalled how when she was three-years-old she was alone playing outside when she noticed a black haired woman in a white dress standing beside her. The mysterious woman instructed her to follow her to the backyard. There she told the little girl to look down at the ground. She did and was puzzled when she saw tunnels underneath the ground, like she had X-ray vision or something.

The beautiful woman then told her that one day when she was older she'd understand. Years later, when she was about 14, there was a bad rainstorm. Part of the river back in front of the house had collapsed and there was severe flooding, taking out part of a railroad track and trees. Soon afterwards, authorities arrived and informed the family that the damage happened because there had been so much rain water that had filled up in old coal mine tunnels under their backyard!

SPIRITS LIVING UNDERGROUND

In their book "*Where the Footprints End, Vol. 1*," Tim Renner and co-author Joshua Cutchin point out how Bigfoot has often been associated with subterranean sites, with caves and mines. But it doesn't end there. "Moreover, mines are regarded as the domain of faeries throughout the world, from Cornish Knockers and German

Kobolds to the Mondong, diminutive aboriginal spirits believed to haunt Australian ochre mines," Cutchin wrote. [1]

In Anthony Peake's *"The Hidden Universe: An Investigation into Non-Human Intelligences"* [2019] [2] he touches upon the archetypal Marian apparitions that have long figured so prominently in Catholic tradition and beyond. Here, if you take a moment and blur the lines a little, you'll begin to take notice of similar parallels and crossover events and manifestations.

"Many encounters with religious figures such as the Blessed Virgin Mary also take place in caves or grottoes," Peake wrote. "We also know from historical reports that elementals such as the Irish Tuatha De Danann were banished to live in the 'hollow hills,' another underground, chthonic place of darkness. This underground of elemental entities is yet another cultural universal, found across most cultures across the globe. Like shamanism itself, the belief seems to be hardwired into human belief systems."

MYSTERIOUS RANCH-DWELLING CREATURES

Meanwhile, back in early 1974, Ramona and Duane began to initiate some serious investigative work on a ranch in Brooksville. They took me there on one visit in October and shared with me what they had learned. For example, on February 15, 1974, around 10 p.m., Ramona was walking through a wooded area near a small pond when she saw a 7-8 foot tall dark brown haired muscular figure with long arms and legs walking nearby. She said she got a side view where she could see how the "back of the skull was flat" and its head was pointed. A 19-inch-long 5-toed footprint would later be found.

A month afterwards, on March 11th, at about 9:45 PM, Ramona and Duane both observed several of these creatures with short light and dark hair on their bodies kneeling on their hands and knees at a garbage pile. Making "smacking, sucking sounds" and "chatter and clicks," these creatures were described as having pointed heads and pointed ears, leathery looking faces with fangs, sunken eye sockets, with what appeared to be frail-looking long arms.

At this same ranch, around 11 PM one night around August, Duane was out in the driveway when he said that a silent, roughly 100-foot diameter craft and with what looked like large, 20-foot wide square illuminated windows, flew slowly overhead an estimated 60 feet above the ground. In addition, Ramona drove me over nearby Route 491, a two-lane paved road, out in an isolated area, where one night a "big ball of light" seemed to touch down on the road about 200 feet ahead of her vehicle and then immediately shot straight back up into the sky.

Ramona and Duane even stumbled upon cryptid cases that Keel himself might have taken notice of with a gasp of surprise. In the nearby community of Nobleton, about a 12-mile drive from Brooksville, in May 1977, this couple had reports of flying "silver disks," as well as a 7-foot-tall red eyed lizard like creature with a long tail crossing a road, bird-like creatures with up to 15-20 foot wingspans and "skin like leather" flying as if in slow motion and...oh yes...Bigfoot was reported too!

Even on my 1975 visit with them, Duane would share how during the third week of May, around 3 AM, responding to a commotion outside, he left the house with his flashlight shining down on the ground so that he wouldn't trip over anything when suddenly, and quite unexpectedly, he noticed a light-colored thing descending from the air. It came within about 20 feet of the ground and had an estimated 20-foot wingspan! Becoming aware of his presence apparently, the creature soared off in another direction. About a week prior something had been killing two or three of their ducks every night. After that night they had no more ducks being killed.

According to mythological traditions across the globe, caves were often referred to as entrances to an underworld of deep tunnels, lost races and great cities.

EARLIER STORIES FROM RAMONA

I first met Ramona a couple of years earlier in 1973. I was in the Navy then and my ship, a destroyer escort [USS Paul, DE-1080] was homeported in Mayport, Florida. I remembered how the year before I had briefly corresponded with Ramona [her last name then Clark]. She described having had a close encounter with a classic domed disc-shaped UFO near the Mayport Naval Base, along with her 13-year-old son and her husband, on July 29, 1967, after which within 3 or 4 days their home erupted with poltergeist activity and beginning on August 11th entity activity, with balls of light and humanoid apparitional figures in their bedrooms, and how the bedroom episodes always seemed to happen around 3 AM.

As Ramona had initially written me from a PO Box in Jacksonville Beach, I tried to locate her there, several miles away, but was soon to discover she lived in residential base housing just a short walking distance from my ship. Her husband was also in the Navy.

1973 turned out to be a big year for UFOs. The newspapers, radio and TV were full of stories. I got to investigate some of the stories firsthand with Ramona and I even flew out to New Orleans to meet a researcher she put me in touch with who kindly drove me over to Pascagoula, Mississippi, to meet Calvin Parker and Charles Hickson only 10 days after their international headline-making account of being taken aboard a small hovering oval-shaped craft by very strange looking pale, wrinkled, roughly humanoid looking beings with lobster-like claws.

I learned a great deal from Ramona. To this day, I still mull over in my mind the various things she shared with me. "During my numerous investigations of varied phenomena, it was apparent that there were members in each family situation that had psychic abilities other than the person who was involved in an encounter," she once shared. "My eldest brother, his middle daughter and I appear to be the only ones in my family who are psychic (my brother is very psychic). We all three look exactly alike! It is very hard to find a difference in my niece and I. We look and act just as twins would. We all three have had the same health problems, etc.

"In some of the cases we studied, usually a sister, mother or grandmother had psychic abilities. Usually only one male member of the family had it. Sometimes it was a child.

"Odd as it may seem, it was usually someone with hair coloring that was dark and who had an olive complexion. As is true within my own family, the female members were more dominant personalities!

The male members aren't passive or meek but allow the women to take the lead. Both of my grandmothers were very dominant figures within the family as a whole. This strong-willed, determined-to-survive-against-all-odds trait has been passed on to the younger women in our family, as I am sure it has been for hundreds of years among mountain-bred women. Though most I have met are very passive, shy and backwards."

STORIES FROM ATHENS, OHIO

I shared with Barbara A. Fisher of Athens, Ohio, the host of "6 Degrees of John Keel," both a researcher and experiencer herself, Ramona's statement on family psychic dynamics and genetics. "I do believe that some of this is genetic," Barbara stated. "There is some predilection or affinity for contact with the Other that runs in family lines." In her own family she noted how "the psychic stuff runs on both sides of my family. In my experience there isn't a 'look' that goes with the psychic genes. That's what I'll call them. There's no consistent physical 'type.'" She described to me the different physical traits in her family, the various skin complexions and hair and eye coloring.

In the meantime, Athens sounds like one of those "window" areas John Keel wrote so much about, and why not? Athens, Ohio, is only about 38 driving miles from Point Pleasant, West Virginia, which played center stage to Keel's *Mothman Prophecies*," and, remember, the reporter Mary Hyre worked for The Athens Messenger. Barbara and others in Athens have many bewildering tales of high-strangeness.

"One night a friend and I were sitting on this hill overlooking my house. She was smoking a cigarette and I was watching three female looking entities dancing around the three apple trees that stood about twenty feet from the little house. I didn't say anything to her about them. I seldom do when I'm with people because I don't want to influence what they see if they see anything. They looked like they were spinning around and dancing in flowing dresses. The light they were made of was sparkly, kind of gold white. They seemed to have long hair or veils that flew as they leaped and danced.

"Finally, she speaks up. 'So, uh, do you see anything down there?' I said, 'Like what?' She said, 'Oh, three ladies dancing around those trees – kinda spinning?' And I said, 'Yeah.' And she said, 'Why didn't you say anything?' And I said, 'Because I didn't know if you could see them.' And she said, 'Oh. Damn. Well, I can. So this shit happens out here a lot?' I said, 'Yeah.' She was like, "Damn. You need to move."'

On another occasion, Barbara describes how she and a friend named Dave, who she said was very psychic, were one night watching a group of small balls of light approaching them up a hill. These lights had been flashing on and off. One of them came within an estimated two and a half feet from them and, when it flashed back on at that distance, something incredible happened. "It turned on and it looked like a naked little lady with moth wings and it looked right at us," Barbara told me. "All but posed. Just looked at us to make sure we got this great look and then turned off and became a ball of orange light again and zipped off towards the woods."

A MORE INCLUSIVE APPROACH

So many times, and for so many years, researchers and students of so many different fields and disciplines have broken these various inexplicable accounts down into different branches of study and "understanding." But could it be that these things we've long treated individually, in separate categories, could instead be somehow interconnected, over a vast spectrum of interrelated phenomena?

Typically, over the years, the psychical researcher, the parapsychologist, ignores things like UFOs and cryptids. The cryptozoologist typically ignores the UFOs and psychic phenomena. The "nuts-and-bolts" ufologist ignores the psychic, apparitional and cryptid data. Such researchers are guilty of misjudging these phenomena based simply upon their surface appearances and how they fail to conform to their preconceived beliefs and expectations. But, as the old saying goes, looks can be deceiving. These phenomena cry out for a far more penetrating and extensive examination.

Gradually I feel as if a shift is occurring and there is a growing realization of how seriously we need an expanded multidisciplinary perspective and approach to be applied to our continuing study of these perplexing anomalies.

Increased openness, cooperation, and objectivity are the order of the day.

References:

1. *"Where the Footprints End: High Strangeness and the Bigfoot Phenomenon,"* Volume One [2020], by Joshua Cutchin and Timothy Renner.

2. *"The Hidden Universe: An Investigation Into Non-Human Intelligences,"* by Anthony Peake. [2019].

A highly controversial DNA study indicated that Sasquatch could possibly be a human relative that arose some 15,000 years ago.

ALL THE WILD MEN

Tim R. Swartz

Sightings of giant, hairy creatures are both an ancient and global phenomenon. Many of these myths have prevailed for hundreds of years, being passed on from generation to generation as people swear to have seen evidence of the humanoids themselves. Going by many different names (Sasquatch, Yeti, Alma, etc.) their descriptions are eerily similar; hairy, big and human-looking. In fact, some hunters have reported to have had the chance to shoot one, but couldn't because they feared they would be shooting a human.

Because of its chief characteristics, covered completely in hair and usually over 7-feet-tall, there is little chance that one of these creatures could be a modern human...however, their descriptions bring to mind representations of archaic humans based on fossil records.

Over the years, an effort has been made by researchers to find and catalog any biological specimens that could have come from a Sasquatch (barring getting a hold of a complete living or dead creature). Hair, tissue and fecal samples have been taken from areas where these creatures have been spotted, but often the samples were from familiar wildlife.

In 2012, the news was filled with the fantastic announcement from a Texas science team that claimed to have successfully sequenced genomes from Sasquatch biological samples.

The team, led by Dr. Melba Ketchum, claimed to have sequenced three nuclear genomes from Sasquatch and found that the species split off from humans 15,000 years ago.

"Our study has sequenced 20 whole mitochondrial genomes and utilized next generation sequencing to obtain three whole nuclear genomes from purported Sasquatch samples," says Ketchum.

"The genome sequencing shows that Sasquatch mtDNA is identical to modern Homo sapiens, but Sasquatch nuDNA is a novel, unknown hominin related to Homo sapiens and other primate species.

"Our data indicate that the North American Sasquatch is a hybrid species, the result of males of an unknown hominin species crossing with female Homo sapiens."

The "hominins" which mated to produce Bigfoot are not Neanderthals or any other known pre-human hominin.

"The male progenitor that contributed the unknown sequence to this hybrid is unique as its DNA is more distantly removed from humans than other recently discovered hominins like the Denisovan individual," explains Ketchum.

"Sasquatch nuclear DNA is incredibly novel and not at all what we had expected. While it has human nuclear DNA within its genome, there are also distinctly non-human, non-archaic hominin, and non-ape sequences. We describe it as a mosaic of human and novel non-human sequence. Further study is needed and is ongoing to better characterize and understand Sasquatch nuclear DNA."

Dr. Ketchum is a veterinarian whose professional experience includes 27 years of research in genetics, including forensics. Early in her career she also practiced veterinary medicine, and she has previously been published as a participant in mapping the equine genome. She began testing the DNA of purported Sasquatch hair samples in 2007.

Ketchum said that, genetically, the Sasquatch is a human hybrid with unambiguously modern human maternal ancestry. Government at all levels must recognize them as an indigenous people and immediately protect their human and Constitutional rights against those who would see in their physical and cultural differences a "license" to hunt, trap, or kill them.

Others are naturally more openly skeptical. Yale neurologist Dr. Steven Novella says the samples may be contaminated samples of normal, human DNA.

"The bottom line is this," he writes on his blog. "Human DNA plus some anomalies or unknowns does not equal an impossible human-ape hybrid. It equals human DNA plus some anomalies."

(Source: Yahoo News UK - Rob Waugh, November 2012)

HUMAN OR NOT

The legend of the wild man persists as a part of European and Asian folklore and culture. Surprisingly, these legends also continue in North and South America. In the 9th century, Irish folklore describes how a pagan king is driven mad when he attacks a Catholic bishop, eventually transforming into a beast who roams the woods. The Konungs Skuggsjá, an educational Norwegian text from the 13th century, describes a creature very similar to other descriptions of wild men. The text says the strange creature was like a human but with a great deal of coarse hair. It says the creature was captured in the woods in Ireland and that no one could tell if it understood human speech or not.

The wild man was depicted in artwork throughout the later medieval period across Europe. The images all show a human with a thick pelt of hair and the figure appears in embroidery, carvings, paintings, statues, stained glass, illuminated manuscripts, and even on more obscure objects such as a bread mold.

Along with artwork, it is during the 14th century the term "woodwose" came into use as a way of describing a legendary wild man figure. The word is the origin of the modern surname "Woodhouse," but its etymology is somewhat unclear – although 'wood' definitely refers to woods or forests, the suffix wose has several potential meanings. The two most likely translations of wose are "being" and "forlorn or abandoned person."

For people in medieval Europe the descriptions of creatures like this, which had been exaggerated and passed on to people who had never seen them, must have been evidence that creatures like the woodwose really were roaming the forests, even if it was only in far off lands.

Rumored encounters with wild men have resulted in myths, legends, and artwork – and in one case, the founding of a town. According to local legend, the German town of Wildemann was founded by miners in 1592.

The miners claimed to have seen a gigantic wild man by the shore of the river Innerste. The wild man was swinging a fir tree as a club to defend his giant female companion from the strange men as they attempted to capture him and take him to show the local earl. They claim they were successful, but the wild man died on the journey to the earl.

When they returned to the spot, he had been, they found a rich deposit of ore and the town was founded and named in his honor. In a further tribute, the coat of arms for Wildemann bears the image of a wild man, which was also a symbol for miners in Renaissance Germany and appears on a number of other coats of arms.

Later, immigrants brought these traditions with them as they settled in the new world and the accounts of these creatures were passed down over time. It should be pointed out that the tales of "wildmen," especially in North America, aren't necessarily about

Bigfoot, but instead refer to actual humans that may be feral (wild) by birth or by choice.

Here are a few accounts of alleged encounters with wild people.

Wild Girl Captured in Local Woods, Liseaux Forest, Wisconsin, September 5, 1744

Shepherds recently found and captured a wild girl about sixteen or seventeen years old in this forest. She was taken to the hospital at Mauleon. She has not spoken or given any sign of recollecting the past. At some point, the girl let it be known that she had been left by some other little girls in the woods when she was about seven or eight, having been surprised by snow. The hospital people gave her grass and vegetables to eat, but she continued to droop, and in a very short time died of grief for the loss of her liberty.

Source: Scott McClean collection, from (same heading), the Wisconsin Argus, Madison, Wisconsin, USA, September 5, 1844 (The article recounts an event of about a century earlier).

Wild Man Seen in Local Woods, Liseaux, Wisconsin, 1764

A wild man has been reported in local woods. He is said to be very tall, strongly built, hairy like a bear, active as a lizard, and perfectly harmless. His delight is in coursing the sheep and dispensing them, uttering loud peals of laughter at the confusion he creates. Sometimes the shepherds sent their dogs after him, but he never suffered them to come up with him. Nothing is known or has been traced respecting his history. It is assumed he was some child left by accident or design in that savage solitude. About 20 years ago, a young wild girl was found in the same forest. She was captured and placed in a hospital where she died a short time later.

Source: Scott McClean collection, from (same heading), the Wisconsin Argus, Madison, September 5, 1844

New World Wild Man Arrives in France, January 4, 1784

There is lately arrived in France from America a wild man who was caught in the woods, 200 miles back from the Lake of the Woods, by a party of Indians; they had seen him several times, but he was so swift of foot that they could by no means get up with him. He is near seven feet high, covered with hair, but has little appearance of understanding and is remarkably sullen and subdued. When he was taken, half a bear was found lying by him, whom he had just killed. *Comment: It appears from this article that the reporter actually saw the creature when it arrived in France. No follow-up stories have come to light to my knowledge.*

Source: The London Times, London, England, January 4, 1784.

Another Wonder, Sacket's Harbor, New York, August 30, 1818

Report says that in the vicinity of Ellisburgh was seen on the 30th Ult., by a gentleman of unquestionable veracity, an animal resembling the Wild Man of the Woods. It is stated that he came from the woods within a few rods of this gentleman - that he stood and looked at him and then took his flight in a direction which gave a perfect view of him for some time. He is described as bending forward when running - hairy, and the heel of the foot narrow, spreading at the toes. Hundreds of persons have been in pursuit for several days, but nothing further is heard or seen of him. The frequent and positive manner in which this story comes induces us to believe it. We wish not to impeach the veracity of this highly favored gentleman – yet, it is proper that such naturally improbable accounts should be established by the mouth of at least two direct eyewitnesses to entitle them.

Source: Janet and Colin Bord, 1982. *The Bigfoot Casebook.* Granada Publishing Ltd., London, England, p. 17, from the Exeter Watchman, New York, New York, USA, September 6, 1818.

Mountain Monster Mystifies Huntsman Appalachian Mountains May 10, 1829

Meshach Browning, a huntsman, tells of a strange encounter with an unusual beast while out hunting in local mountains. Browning stated: "I saw a bear coming to his feeding place; and such a looking animal I had never in my life seen. He was long and tall, and his back bowed up like a fighting hog; his legs looked like a naked man's arms, and he walked along as if he scarcely felt the ground – in fact, he was the poorest looking beast I had ever seen. He came out until he reached the tracks which I had made in the forepart of the day, when off he broke. I sent two good dogs after him, and in a few minutes they were out of hearing; but in an hour or two the dogs returned, completely tired."

Browning recounted another incident that night or early morning, this time concerning an unusual forest sound. He tells us: "Sometime late in the night, I was awakened by the most frightful noise I ever heard in my life. It was as loud and harsh as the lowing of an ox, and seemed to echo from the other side of the hill on which I was camped, and the whole space above seemed to resound with the noise. It continued for twenty minutes, as near as I could judge, and seemed to die away by degrees, until all was again quiet. I supposed then, and yet think, that it was caused by two old male panthers, which had met and got into a fight; and being of the cat species, they make a similar noise, only much stronger and coarser. But I cannot say for certain what animal made the noise."

Source: Meshach Browning, 1829. *Forty-Four Years of the Life of a Hunter, The Autobiography of Meshach Browning.* Appalachian Background, Oakland, Maryland, USA, 1999, pp. 224-225, 228,229.

Wild Child Fish Lake, Indiana, December 4, 1839

Strange as it may appear, it is currently reported and very generally believed that a wild child, or lad, is now running at large among the sand hills round and in the vicinity of Fish Lake. It is reported to be about four feet high, and covered with a light coat of chestnut-colored hair. It runs with great velocity, and when pursued, as has often been the case, it sets up the most frightful and hideous yells, and seems to make efforts at speaking. It has been seen during the summer months running along the lake shore, apparently in search of fish and frogs, and appears to be very fond of the water, for it will plunge into Fish Lake and swim with great velocity, all the time whining most piteously.

Source: Jerome Clark, 2005. *Unnatural Phenomena.* ABC-CLIO (publisher), from 14 Adams Sentinel, Pennsylvania, December 30, 1839, reprinted from the Michigan City Gazette, Indiana, December 4, 1839

Wild Man Seen Near Dover. He Frightened Women and Killed a Dog, but Cannot be Caught. Dover, New Jersey, January 6, 1894

The residents of this vicinity are excited over the sudden appearance of a wild man near the town. He has taken up his abode in the vacant Mellon homestead, and first made his appearance to a number of women who were passing near the place. He uttered threatening sounds and started toward them, causing the women to run away. A searching party was sent out, but the man could not be found. A few days later he was seen running wild through the woods, wearing no clothing. Another party was sent out, and dogs were used. When the man was surrounded, he grabbed one of the dogs and killed it with a club, and then made his escape. He is still at large.

Source: Scott McClean, 2005. *Big News Prints* (self-published), p. 154, from (same heading) The New York Times, New York, January 7, 1894.

We'll finish this with a couple of more recent stories where some eyewitnesses claim to have seen or heard these feral people roaming the Smoky Mountains of Appalachia.

One North Carolinian writes on Reddit, "Since the 30s or 40s, there have been feral wild men living in these mountains. They are fast. They will snatch livestock and snatch children...And I'm not talking about some end of days extremist who took to the woods...I mean feral...completely wild men with their own language and possibly living underground. At night you'll hear them hollering and locals say the wild men are supposedly inbred."

Another Reddit user was hunting one night when he encountered one of these feral people. He explains, "I remember jolting a little when I saw that it wasn't really a bear, it was a man. Because he was so low and hunched over I thought I was looking at a young bear...I was about to call out when I adjusted my sights and noticed he was naked. No shoes, pants or anything. I remember being disturbed by his movements, like a squirrel or something. Twitchy and grabbing at the foliage, sniffing around and palming the tree."

Red River Gorge, near Slade, KY, in Powell County - Spring 1990. The witness encountered, face to face in the wilderness near Cloudsplitter Rock, an adult (thirties) Caucasian male, walking in the woods naked but covered with mud, leaves, and vines, which were matted into his hair and beard as well, giving him an almost absurd "Swamp Thing" appearance. He walked with a hunched, apelike gait.

He spotted the witness moments after it spotted him, and they stared at each other for what at the time felt like an eternity; finally he turned and fled. His eyes seemed to show some intelligence but he was still extremely animal-like and seemingly unable to speak. The witness made no effort to follow him.

Source: Phantoms & Monsters - phantomsandmonsters.com/2021/07/feral-human-sightings-encounters.html

Folklore experts now refer to these eerie tales as "contemporary legends," also known as "urban legends." While authorities dismiss any stories about wild people, longtime residents of places like Appalachia say these tales have been around for generations.

So, is there hard evidence like videos and photos of feral people in the Smoky Mountains or elsewhere? No, but there are plenty of accounts from those who have heard, seen, or encountered these wild people. For whatever the reasons, birth or choice, these people have allegedly tossed aside the shackles of civilization to live as nature intended.

MIB - ZOMBIE LOVE FEST

Timothy Green Beckley

Whenever I am on a talk show discussing the dreaded Men in Black, inevitably I am asked the hundred thousand dollar question: Who are the Men in Black? Are they government agents or radical ETs looking to cause chaos and confusion in an attempt to silence an individual who may have seen or found out too much about the UFO situation at hand?

For many years I stumbled and stuttered out any kind of answer, even if it was an illogical one, not knowing really what to say or how to hedge my bet as to who – or what – were behind the dozens of MIB capers that were being called to my attention. The MIB cases that I was hearing about seemed to come in "waves," followed by prolonged dry periods when these denizens of darkness seem to have gone back underground.

Recently the reports started to heat up again!

They were centering on the state of Iowa and were initially bought to my attention by my friends and colleagues, Brad and Sherry Steiger.

Addressing me as "Brother Tim," the missive went something like this: "Facebook and YouTube are crowing over MIBs. The first sighting apparently was made by an R.J. Strong of Port Louisa on or around June 13 (2016) at 2 AM as he was driving near Ogilvie Avenue in Muscatine County. He told the local TV station, KWQC, that some 'weirdo was walking down the center of the paved road in a long, black trench coat.'"

The local Sheriff's office said they had received maybe about six reports of similarly clad individuals either walking down the road or standing perched at the shoulder as if ready to pounce on their prey (passing motorists?).

"My son has experienced this and it's no joke," posted Beatrice Wilson Strong. "It was really a frightening experience to him."

Likewise, Cassie Pameticky posted on Facebook, "It's happened to a few friends of mine out on [Highway] 22."

In 1967, UFO investigator Timothy Green Beckley captured what could be the only known photo of a Man-in-Black in Jersey City, New Jersey.

This comes on the heels of West Quincy, Iowa, resident Jordan Law, who saw what she thought were two human bodies lying on the side of the road. She pulled over right away and called the police. Then the two "bodies" got up and started running after her.

This incident has been put down as a teenagers' prank, but the Muscatine County Sheriff's Office has taken notice, posting Monday on its Facebook page, "We have had several reports of 'men dressed in black' entering the roadway in rural Muscatine County."

Chicago's Channel 5 News added this report from an eyewitness. "My wife, mother in-law, and I were headed home on Highway 22 at 10:30 PM on June 15th, headed towards Muscatine from Quad Cities, and just past the big hill past Fairport. As we got just past the cabins, there was someone all in white with either white makeup on or a thin white mask lying in the ditch right by the road, and he sat up with his thumb up." The witness said he figured it was a mannequin at first, but when he returned later, it was gone.

It has also been noted that these same individuals have been spotted walking across homeowners' yards, on private property.

The MCSO is now asking anyone who encounters the individuals to "call 911 immediately."

The sheriff's Facebook post has generated several jokes and speculation that harmless pranksters are behind the sightings.

However, the MCSO says on its Facebook page, "We do take this seriously," and investigators are "hoping the public can assist."

ON PHANTOMS AND MONSTERS

Unfortunately, it is almost unprecedented for any local media to carry MIB reports, save for the Mothman flap in Point Pleasant, West Virginia, way back in the 1960s, so in order to get additional details one has to depend upon the Internet or one's own independent sources.

Hardly a day goes by when "On Phantoms and Monsters" doesn't add a substantial amount of new material pertaining to whatever is trending at the time. The recent MIB reports out of Iowa weren't any different than, say, the Dogman cases that were updated on their site a few days previously. As an example, this is what Craig C. posted:

"I got an email from a friend about a happening south of Iowa City around Muscatin, Iowa.

"The occurrence is from last Thursday: June 17th, 2016. Not sure if it's just pranksters or something else, but the following is what I got:

"Last night, around 10:50 PM, 'George' was driving home and experienced something really creepy. He was driving along Highway 22, just before Hon Geneva, when he saw a strange, tall man, dressed all in black step out from the ditch on to the side of the highway. As George passed him, the man stepped out from behind his car, into the middle of his lane, and stopped and watched him drive off. (As George described, the man cocked his head to the side while he watched him drive away and his arms weren't down against his sides, more curved, as if he were holding basketballs under his wrists against his hips, maybe to appear stronger in stature.) He said his face was also black...possibly painted or a mask, but he could not make out facial features. A bit shaken, he continued driving towards home when a second man (clothed the same way and with the same demeanor) stepped out from the ditch just before Sweetland Road. At this point, George floored the gas and sped home. When he came in the door he was distraught. Listening to him tell me about his encounter scared me. I reported the men to the sheriff. Alan took George back out to look for the men but never saw them again. The sheriff called and asked to meet with George about this in the last month. There have been sightings of the same thing near Fairport. I am posting this because I want to warn all of you that live along the highway or drive along 22 at night to keep a lookout. Not sure what they are up to, but it's creepy!"

To my way of thinking, it's kind of a crazy, somewhat confusing timeline of the MIB activity. Unless there were a group of them, they seem to have spread out over the landscape pretty far and wide – and for what purpose?

Tim Swartz told me that, in his preparation to appear on Clyde Lewis' "Ground Zero" program, he discovered that there had been some limited UFO activity in Iowa just before the appearance of the MIBs. A report filed with the Mutual UFO Network lists a sighting of a UFO complete with a row of windows. Several "fireballs" were also seen, though no details are displayed on the UFO Hunters site.

WHAT OF THEIR ORIGINS?

But getting back to square one – previewed before the MIB update – what are we to make of the origins for the MIB? Are they from Earth, extraterrestrial...or somewhere "in-between"? As astute researcher/author Nick Redfern has pointed out, we have considered what would seem like all the various possibilities, "including aliens, government agents, time-travelers, and dimension-hoppers." There is, however, at least one other possible theory that is scarcely considered. And it just so happens to be a theory I purposed to Nick some months previous to his public statement on the subject.

"What if the MIB are not extraterrestrials, time-surfers from the distant future, agents of officialdom, or inter-dimensional creatures? What if, incredibly, they are normal, everyday people, just like me and you? Or, to put it more precisely, what if they are everyday people most of the time? Could it be the case that the MIB are regular individuals who, now and again, become possessed by a paranormal force – a demonic force, some might even suggest – that uses those poor souls as vessels to perform tasks of the terrifying kind?

"To some, it may sound not just controversial, but beyond controversial. But, don't be so quick to write-off just such a possibility. One case in particular suggests that that may be exactly what is going on. And, for the answers to that case we have to turn our attentions to a longtime researcher of the UFO mystery: Timothy Green Beckley. Beckley's research suggests that the Men in Black may actually be regular individuals who have been placed under a form of mind-control, very much akin (in slave-like behavior, at least) to the kind of zombification that appears within Haitian lore."

Thinking back, I had apparently spoken to Nick about a highly frightening, ongoing series of threats by someone I had met at the office of an individual who was at the time publishing a nationally distributed newsstand magazine on UFOs. The magazine had printed several narratives detailing close encounters with the MIB.

I wrote for this publication in the 1970s; it was called "*Official UFO.*" They always published their address in the magazine, so they did get a few crank visitors to their offices. They also published dozens of other, non-UFO type magazines. One day, while I was there on other publishing business, there was this gentleman who showed up claiming he was being stalked by the Men in Black. The fellow was disheveled in appearance, rambling wildly, and kept scratching as if he were being repeatedly bitten by insects. I tried my best to ignore him as I knew that something was "just not right" about him.

Unfortunately, not too long afterward, I actually encountered the man in the street. He seemed to block my path. There was a glazed look in his eyes as if he could go ballistic at any moment. I excused myself as quickly as possible, and thus began a disturbing series of events that lasted across the late 1970s and early 1980s – during which time I received a series of disturbing and chilling phone calls from the man.

They were so chilling and disturbing – never mind threatening, too – that I finally chose to contact the police. It didn't take the NYC police long to find the man; he was living on the streets and sleeping somewhere in Grand Central Terminal, around Times Square.

I explained that this creepy character must have called fifty times and left crazy, threatening messages that would go on and on – and not only had he threatened me, but also several local politicians and a female DJ who he was stalking on the side. I told the police I had even spoken with his parents (he was a grown man in his forties) – who were in Florida – and they said that although he wasn't always like this, something came over him "now and again." On one occasion he had even held a knife at his brother's throat.

I began to notice this pattern over and over again, how these individuals – usually on the margins of society – were going into trance-like states, only to find their already surly disposition becoming far worse, to the point of hostility. This individual kept saying that he knew the astronomer Dr. Morris K. Jessup who had, of course, committed apparent suicide years before. From what I could see, he was taking on the character of a MIB. He was lock-jawed and zombie-like, repeating his threats over and over.

There is no doubt that he was possessed, under "someone's" spell. Some paranormal force takes hold of the person and they become a literal Man in Black, doing what the "outside force" wants them to do, but without their knowledge of their own behavior in most instances. Afterwards, they might not even remember any of what had occurred. These folks are living on the fringe of our society as it is; they are usually very simple-minded people who can very easily be manipulated and influenced. Someone, say, who might be living in some rundown apartment, is taken over in a sort of enchantment, and then becomes one of the Men in Black for a period of time. They threaten someone and then they go back to their normal life after the possession ends, unable to recall this schizophrenic episode. But while they are under the control of whatever is doing this, they're not "quite right." It's like being a full-blown zombie, which is the best way I can describe this state or mental condition.

Putting his stretchable, woolen thinking cap on, Nick Redfern sort of reinforces my position, taking a few elements from the theory I have developed.

"Beckley's description is certainly a highly apt one: George Romero's cannibalistic zombies in "Night of the Living Dead" – and, indeed in all of Romero's subsequent movies in the still-ongoing "Dead" series – are utterly driven by two issues: the desire for self-preservation and an unrelenting need to feed. The MIB are equally and similarly driven; however, their whole goal is to instill fear rather than feed upon flesh and bone. But, just like the reanimated dead of the big-screen, the Men in Black, too, appear to lack anything more than a basic awareness of why, precisely, they are carrying out the actions they dutifully and never-endingly perform. Might that be due to paranormal possession? Demonic possession, perhaps? It may not be wise to dismiss either scenario..."

* Originally published in *"Project Alien Mind Control,"* 2016, Inner Light/Global Communications

CONCLUSIONS

Tim R. Swartz

Even though this chapter is called "Conclusions," is it a reach to even suggest that we could be capable or even worthy to try and set down any sort of definitive conclusions? Considering that encounters with the "others" go back for centuries and entire mythologies have been created about these beings and their relationships with humans, do we really know anything about them?

Some people have called the others "friends," "co-workers," "lovers." They have forged relationships that lasted years, yet, in the end, they ended up knowing nothing about the mysterious "person" they had allowed into their lives.

While appearing on Hercules Invictus's YouTube show, "The UFO Entity Enigma: Mythic Gods," it occurred to me that our mimic friends can be hard to distinguish from normal people by sight, but can our other senses tell the difference between a human and a mimic? (www.youtube.com/@HerculesInvictus)

The sense of smell is extremely important to animals such as dogs, who, it has been estimated, can smell anywhere from 1,000 to 10,000 times better than people. But the human nose shouldn't be underestimated, especially when it comes to close human interactions. Pheromones are chemical compounds, excreted from the skin, which can trigger sexual attraction - at least that's how it works in the animal kingdom.

Scientists are still debating whether or not humans can actually sense pheromones. Humans don't have a functioning vomeronasal organ, which is what other animals use to detect pheromones from their own species. Instead, we sense smells via the olfactory system. So we may not be able to detect pheromones, but we can smell the difference between a human and an animal such as a dog or cat.

An unusual sense of foreboding or unexplained danger is often reported with mimic encounters. This could actually be a physical reaction to a smell that isn't registered consciously, but instead is an unconscious response from the amygdala, a part of the brain that is commonly thought to form the core of a neural system for processing fearful and threatening stimuli. This includes threat detection and activation of appropriate fear-related behaviors in response to threatening or dangerous stimuli.

The unreasonable terror that often grips someone who is having a paranormal encounter with unexplainable entities could actually be scent driven. Considering some of the reactions to David Daniels (chapter 18), where many people had an unreasonable and instant feeling of fear and hatred when first meeting him, it is obvious that the mimics may look like us, but possibly, they don't SMELL like us.

A bartender who wrote Nick Redfern about a strange encounter with a "couple-in-black," said that he noticed a stench coming from the woman. "Not only did she smell like she hadn't bathed in a month," he said, "she also smelled like chemicals. I used to apprentice as an embalmer, and I swear that woman smelled just like formalin."

Others have said their unearthly visitors smelled like "rotten eggs" or "dank and musty." Others have noted that not only did their visitor look like he had "crawled out of the grave," but he also smelled like "fresh dirt."

So, this could be one way to distinguish one of the others from a normal human being. That is for those of us who have had closer than usual encounters.

The majority of these encounters are not so intimate, nor do they last as long. Most encounters with the others are terrifying at their worst and at their least profoundly disturbing.

As I have noted before, Nick Redfern, in several of his books about the Men-In-Black (and Women-In-Black), postulates that these weird individuals can be broken down into two different types. Type one are real humans, possibly intelligence agents with the government or military. Type two appears to be non-humans trying (badly at times) to pass themselves off as humans.

Nick says that he has on record a large number of reports that strongly suggest entities from elsewhere are using camouflage to move among us. These creatures don't look entirely human; they wear hats, wigs, and large sunglasses to mask their true identities. The "alien tourists" wearing badly fitting wigs mentioned earlier in this book come to mind.

My good friend, the late Brad Steiger, had his own theories on who or what the "others" are. Brad had worked for years researching and writing about paranormal phenomena, including UFOs and their occupants. He was an early proponent of the theory that UFOs are physical spaceships from other planets. However, as time went by, he realized that there was an aspect of some UFO cases that seemed to show a relationship with the paranormal and other intelligences that were not human, but also not interplanetary.

"After more than 50 years of research in the UFO and paranormal fields, I have come to the conclusion that many of the mysteries that bedevil us are products of a reflexive phenomenon. This reflexive action does not usually occur in the more mundane pursuits of architecture, industry, mining, agriculture and the like, but once one begins actively to pursue Ufology or psychical research, one runs the risk of entering a surreal world in which the usual physical laws do not apply.

"In the case of the mythos of the Men in Black, I suggest that that eerie enigma may have begun with the machinations of a human agency assigned to investigate the actions of the more high profile investigators of the phenomenon and the more convincing witnesses of UFO activity with the goal of learning more about the growing interest in a worldwide phenomena. Somehow along the way, this activity of the human surveillance of other humans caught the interest of a nonhuman, paraphysical agency that has for centuries pursued goals that remain elusive, even sinister, to the individuals whom they visit. Whether motivated by a bizarre sense of humor, an essentially malicious nature, or a desire to learn how much some humans know about their eternal secrets, the 'others' began knocking on the doors of those who had witnessed or who had investigated UFO activity.

"Some of my experiences with the MIB seem most certainly the product of human surveillance that in most instances was conducted with awkward fallibility. The Men in Black we've just been talking about are, without doubt, human. But, they still wear the fedora hats and the old-time black suits. Now, let's have a look at the other group of Men in Black. There's no doubt about them: that group is not human. Those types of MIB don't even look human. For example, their skin looks like a shiny plastic and is the color of a sheet of paper. Their eyes bulge like someone with thyroid problems. They're skinny to the point of looking malnourished. They wear wigs, and it's obvious that under the wigs there is no hair at all. Not even stubble. They have trouble eating and drinking. Even stranger, it seems they only eat food to make them look more normal."

Steiger also offers a classic case from MIB investigator Gareth Midway where the individual seemed a little too perfect. Gareth wrote: "1961, September: W. D. Clendenon, who was corresponding with George Adamski, was visited by 'a short man in a tan topcoat,' who said he was engaged in a political survey to see whether people in the area had voted Republican, and 'he felt the strong impulse to invite the man in.'

"His skin was smooth as though he had never shaved in his life. His skin reminded me of a baby's skin. When he smiled, his teeth were prefect and very white. The color of his skin was brown, like an Indian; his hair was dark and trimmed in a business-like manner. He looked almost too good, and it bothered me."

THE RANCHER

Another good example along these lines comes to us from Lon Strickler's blog "Phantoms & Monsters." Titled "The Rancher," Lon writes that the following bizarre account was submitted to "Humanoid Encounters" at Reddit by user HYSTheRancher:

"Hi. I've never posted here. I'm not sure where to begin, but I feel I need to relay this story in a public place in case something happens to me. I am southern and almost 30 now, the incident related to this man who I call The Rancher happened when I was 18 working my first real job. It was the fall of 2007 when I met this guy, but it all started when I was 10 years old.

"I lived in Tennessee for the first part of my childhood; there is a very small town outside of Knoxville a couple of hours where my Grandfather had a farm. We'd visit semi-regularly and I would get to go and see the cows and chickens he raised. The first incident in question was during the summer of 1998 on this farm, I was actually out playing with one of their border collies, named Sweetie, while my Granddad was out in the field feeding

317

the cattle. The farm is in the hills as this area is part of the Smoky Mountains, and the farm was quite large.

"I was alone except for Sweetie when this occurred and I was so young at the time that the memory was and still is to some extent a bit fuzzy. But the important part is still very clear. During this particular excursion into those woods Sweetie and I came across what I can only describe as a large tree with a hole beneath it. As we came up on this hole I looked down into it and I couldn't see the bottom, and it was pitch black. My head started almost buzzing and I felt my hair stand on end. I started shaking but I couldn't look away from it, I felt like if I started to run I would die. It's really hard to describe the sensation but I would call it an impending sense of dread.

"There were eyes looking back at me from this hole, but I couldn't see the body at first. Then I saw what looked like a smile and a very small body of this humanoid looking thing. Its body was entirely black...it was unnaturally black; I mean it was like looking into the absence of light. The only light portions were the eyes and eventually the mouth; it kind of smiled at me. And I felt like I was going to die looking at it, but I couldn't run away. After that it's like I can't remember exactly what happened and my next memory is me walking back for dinner. I should also tell you that we could not find Sweetie after that. I felt so bad because I really loved that dog.

"I didn't tell anyone what I saw because I didn't want them to think I was crazy, or demon possessed or something. Over time this memory kind of faded and I ended up thinking I either dreamed this or I was simply remembering wrong.

"Fast forward to 2007 and I was 18 almost 19. It was the fall of that year, I was working at my first real job while attending college for computer science. Keep in mind by this time I did not believe in anything supernatural, extraterrestrial, or anything remotely paranormal. I was an avid reader of prominent atheists such as Richard Dawkins. My job was at a book store in Alabama.

"I had actually just gotten a promotion to work at the store's joint coffee shop as a Barista, but I also still sometimes worked the register or did stocking. The first time I encountered this man that I refer to as The Rancher I was actually working the front cash register. I often worked the late shift there, which was from 4 PM to midnight.

"It was around 11:00PM, and this guy comes in, and I immediately got this strange feeling about this guy. The reason I call this guy The Rancher is that he was dressed like a cowboy straight out of a western film. This guy was just very strange to be walking into a bookstore at 11:00 PM decked out in snakeskin cowboy boots, a cowboy hat and western looking clothes. I thought at first he was just a tourist or something and went back to reading.

"This guy walked to the back at some point for about a good 20 minutes, eventually he came up to the counter to buy a few books. I got the feeling that something about this guy's body was fake. His skin was extremely pale, not out of the realm of possibility but very unusual; he was the whitest man I've ever seen without being an obvious albino or something. The other thing was his eyes, they were beady-like, they almost looked like glass eyeballs, like maybe he was wearing contacts, but it was really hard to tell exactly why they looked that way.

"He smiled at me as well the entire time, and it was more than just a friendly grin, it almost felt like a sexual flirtation or something. At the end when I had finished ringing him up, I realized he hadn't said anything to me and I had been making my usual niceties I liked to think of as customer service. But at the

319

end, he stopped for a minute and stared at me before leaving, and asked 'What did you say your name was?'

"I thought this was really bizarre at the time, because I had a name tag on. I told him my name and he said 'Oh what a nice name that is, I'll have to ask for you if I return here.' At this point I just thought this guy was hitting on me or something. He was really creepy, and I just wanted him to leave as soon as possible. Thankfully he did leave.

"Unfortunately I would see him one more time about three weeks later. It was late again, a little after 10 PM, and this time I was actually working in the coffee shop. I was making coffee drinks for a group of students when I realized The Rancher guy was back, standing behind them. He was in the same cowboy-like attire, and he was standing very still and just looking up in my direction with that same weird, forced smile. I felt this weird sense of dread, the same feeling from my childhood encounter on the farm.

"The students left and he came up and ordered a bottle of milk. I got it for him and he left to go into the store where the book racks are. Around 11 PM I took a break and went to sit at one of the tables on our adjoined patio area. I was sitting there reading my book when I heard our patio door open and it was The Rancher guy again. He sat down at my table directly across from me with that same weird smile. When he took off his hat I realized he was also bald, and his scalp looked strange, like he had never had hair at all. It almost looked like rubber, it was very odd.

"I asked if I could help him find something, but he said my name rather calmly, and then the conversation got very strange and specific. He said 'I am actually here because you are one of my tasked individuals. I don't really know why you're on my list for this area but you are. And I like you so I'm going to be frank with you. I am not entirely human.'

"Upon hearing this I actually panicked and got up, and as I did, he said my address and I froze and realized this guy knew where I lived. He said, 'Sit down, you're making this difficult.'

"Then he told me, 'I'm not going to hurt you, that's not my job. My job is to simply keep track of individuals that I've been tasked with...that's all. I need to ask you a few questions to make sure there aren't going to be any problems.'

"He started smiling again and it was like a forced smile. It looked fake and he looked so strange but I sat down because this guy had threatened me at my home and I didn't know what else to do other than see what he wanted with me.

"He said, 'I'm actually from a certain organization that manages many things here on this planet, and I am what you would call a liaison between your kind and them. I am partially them, but mostly one of you and so I am tasked with direct prolonged communications with your type.'

"He proceeded to ask me some questions about whether or not I had ever seen anything out of the ordinary, and who I might have told about it. Obviously he meant other than him, because I remarked he's freaking me out and asked if this was some kind of prank. I finally told him about the strange black 'thing' I saw in the woods as a kid, including that I never told anyone about it. He remarked that would likely be the reason I was on his list.

"He also asked me a few other questions seemingly unrelated. He asked me what I was studying in school and where I thought I might work after I graduated. He seemed interested if I was considering military contractor work, and also asked about some of my family members' military service. In between each question he paused for like a good 20 or 30 seconds. I asked him what he was doing after the third time this happened, and he said he was scanning my possible timelines for confirmation. He told me his kind could actually see different spectrums than us and that he was having this conversation with multiple versions of myself. He was making sure none of them were going to become problematic for him because he hated having to return.

"After several questions he gave that smile and said all done. He got up and said, people weren't likely to believe me and I shouldn't talk about the small black creature. If I did, he said, I could meet with someone else from his organization with a different designation and it may not end as nicely for me.

"And that was it. He put on his hat and left the bookstore. I never saw the Rancher guy again. Since so much time has passed, I decided to post this story anonymously so there is a record. I am extremely afraid that I might be visited by that bizarre man or someone associated with him.

"Godspeed. I hope none of you have ever encountered this guy or any of his people."

After several questions/comments to the post, the user posted this follow-up:

"Honestly, meeting that guy was the worst thing that ever happened to me, and the reason I wanted to finally tell my story here is because I am so extremely terrified of him and whatever his people may be.

"I got the distinct sense that he was serious when he said he wasn't entirely human but mostly human. He said rather specifically he was more human than some others in his 'organization,' and that is why he had the job that he did. Mostly he seemed to be rather matter of fact about the whole thing, but wouldn't answer most of my questions.

"It seemed like the stuff he did tell me was to keep me calm until he was finished with whatever he needed from me. He asked me about three specific topics: What I had seen or experienced that was unusual. Which of my family members were in the military and what their military service had entailed. The last was the strangest to me: he asked me where did I think I will be working when I graduate and what did I hope to work on? And he specifically wanted to know if I was considering contractor work of any kind.

"During these periods he would stop for a good 30 or so seconds before continuing. He would shut his eyes, and I could see them moving under his eyelids, but it was really strange looking and they were moving rather fast in different directions.

"I was getting pretty unnerved during these periods because I kept looking at him and I couldn't shake the feeling that he looked fake...that he was something other than human. He was human looking enough so that most people wouldn't have given him a second glance. Nevertheless, when I was up close talking to him for that extended period of time, I felt like his face wasn't real and his scalp looked like rubber or plastic. When I asked him what he was doing, he explained that he was 'scanning my timelines' and 'speaking to different versions of myself,' and that his kind could see 'spectrums' that we could not. It was like a semi-explanation, it was not a normal conversation at all.

THE HITCHHIKER EFFECT

It does seem that witnessing a paranormal event, and this does include UFO sightings, can somehow attract the "others" like moths to a bright light. Does this mean that a person who has a paranormal experience somehow becomes "magnetized" (not literally), drawing in all sorts of otherworldly entities to feed and play trickster-type games with their unlucky victim?

This may play a huge role in what has been called "The Hitchhiker Effect," which has been defined as "bringing something home" and the subsequent person to person transmissibility of paranormal phenomena, some of which can last for years. This has been frequently noted with investigators involved with the infamous Skinwalker Ranch in Utah.

Dr. Travis Taylor, the lead investigator currently at Skinwalker Ranch, said during a live stream interview on "Den of Geek,""We don't like to talk about the hitchhiker too much because everybody's afraid it's going to trigger it or something."

The Skinwalker Ranch is not the only place where the hitchhiker effect has happened. It is a phenomenon that has occurred all over the world and under different circumstances when people seem to be "followed" by entities of various forms. Usually after having had encounters with ghosts and/or spirits, or creatures involved with UFO sightings.

Incredibly, not only do these entities and phenomena follow people who've had such encounters, but they often are reported to "spread" – almost like a virus of some sort – into the lives of people who simply know the person initially "afflicted." In other words, just knowing someone who's had an anomalous encounter like the ones described above is enough to trigger a similar experience of the paranormal – even when the matter was never actually discussed by either party.

The hitchhiker effect can present itself in all manner of different ways, including appearances of the "others." However, one doesn't need to be involved or a witness to paranormal activity to find themselves unexpectedly in the crosshairs of the others.

Historical researcher Colin Perks had long been fascinated with the legends behind the fabled King Arthur of Britain. His research led him to believe that Arthur was an actual, historical figure, and his grave must be somewhere near the old English town of Glastonbury.

In September of 2000, after spending the day digging in the woods around Glastonbury, Perks received a phone call from a woman who insisted that they discuss his Arthurian studies. Even though he was hesitant (after all, he hadn't discussed his ongoing research with anyone else), he agreed to meet with the woman several days later.

When the woman arrived, Perks said she was around 35 or 40 years old and clad in a "smart and expensive-looking black outfit. She had long black hair and pale, smooth skin and was very beautiful. The woman's face was completely devoid of emotion, and yet Perks could somehow sense an air of hostility or even hatred emanating from her.

She introduced herself as Sarah Key, and said that she and her poorly-defined "select group of people within the British ruling elite" had been watching Perks for a long time. She made it clear that the purpose of her visit was to order Perks stop his Arthurian studies immediately.

Naturally, Perks dismissed her order as well as scoffing at the idea that his every move was being observed. The woman responded by listing off everything he had done in recent memory – right down to which local pubs he would visit for dinner.

Sarah Key told Perks that Arthur's gravesite (or chamber) had been built atop some sort of portal or supernatural gateway, and claimed that the chamber had been constructed as a defense system to prevent the denizens of this alternate dimension from entering our reality and wreaking havoc. Apparently, Colin's research may have had innocent intentions, but it could potentially result in a paranormal catastrophe if he went any further with it. Key sternly told him that should he not stop his research immediately, he would receive another, less friendly visit (from who or what she didn't specify).

Roughly two months later, as Perks was driving down a small and winding road from the city of Bath back to Glastonbury, he approached an area of the road that was devoid of traffic or illumination. Suddenly, a bizarre figure appeared in the middle of the road in front of his car. This dark humanoid figure had bat-like wings and red eyes that seemed to be self-illuminated. Terrified, Perks hit the accelerator with the intention of running down the monstrous creature – but the creature vanished just as mysteriously as it had appeared.

However, Perks' ordeal was not over. About a week later he was woken up in the middle of the night by the visceral sensation of sheer terror. He was paralyzed in his bed, and monstrous hands were tightly gripping his wrists. Above him loomed what Perks could only describe as a gargoyle. It appeared to be around seven feet in height and pale-skinned. It had thin, almost emaciated limbs and large, leathery wings. But most horrific of all was the creature's head: bald and with two large and pointed ears. An evil grin crossed its hook-nosed face and appeared to mock him, while two large fangs extended down from a wide and black-tongued mouth.

A message appeared in his mind, once again warning him to stay away from the grave of King Arthur and to stop digging in the woods. Immediately after, the gargoyle vanished, leaving Perks unsure of if the visitation was just a horrific nightmare. Deep down he knew it wasn't.

Perks eventually concluded that Sarah Key and the gargoyle must've been one and the same—and that she was in fact a supernatural shapeshifter capable of taking on any form she desired. However, he couldn't figure out why the interest in his King Arthur research, unless the story about portals and ancient horrors actually had some validity. There is also the possibility that the area Perks was investigating had similarities to places like the Skinwalker Ranch. Once he started digging in this area, it activated the hitchhiker phenomenon, which manifested as a mysterious woman in black at first, and later a menacing red-eyed gargoyle.

Despite the paranormal onslaught, Colin continued on with his research. Unfortunately, he unexpectedly passed away in 2009 of a heart attack while walking around the border of Stonehenge. So far, King Arthur's gravesite, if it actually exists, remains to this day undiscovered. (*"The Monster Book: Creatures, Beasts and Fiends of Nature"* by Nick Redfern - 2016, Visible Ink Press)

HAIRY COUSINS

So many of the cases discussed in this book do seem to have a paranormal aspect to them...but not all. Could it be possible that some of the "others" are physical creatures just like us...in fact almost exactly like us? Rather than Homo sapiens, the mimics may be a closely related human cousin.

Most anthropologists are not exactly open to the idea that there could be other, surviving human species still hanging around. Nevertheless, a few scientists are willing to contemplate the idea that Homo sapiens are not alone. Jeffrey Meldrum at Idaho State University in Pocatello points out that other hominin species coexisted alongside our ancestors for most of human history. That's not all. Our family tree can still surprise us, as happened with the discovery of Homo floresiensis, aka the "Hobbit," on the eastern Indonesian island of Flores. This pint-sized hominin lived on the island until approximately 18,000 years ago.

Speaking of Homo floresiensis, retired anthropologist Gregory Forth, in his newly published book *"Between Ape and Human,"* speculates that Homo floresiensis may still be alive in the mountainous areas of Flores. Before the discovery of the Hobbit bones, Forth spent many years living among indigenous people known as the Lio on Flores. During his time there he heard stories about a rare and elusive species of ape-man, who were referred to as the Ebu Gogo, said to reside in deep forests on the island. Forth eventually concluded that these stories might be true, and that such a creature could exist largely hidden from view.

Forth sees a connection between the hominid bones that were found in a cave on Flores in 2004 and the stories told to him by the Lio. His conclusion is if these ape-men really do exist, they would most likely be the archaic human species Homo floresiensis.

Some of the people he spoke with in Lio villages told him that the small ape-men were no longer around. The last of the Ebu Gogo ("Ebu" means grandmother and "Gogo" means "he who eats anything") had been killed off by the Lio's neighbors, the Ua people, about 200 years ago. However, others swore to Forth that the Ebu Gogo still lived in nearby caves and forests. Gathering evidence to support this claim, Forth spoke to approximately 30 witnesses who said they'd actually seen the mysterious half-ape, half-man-like creature on at least one occasion.

In *"Between Ape and Human,"* Forth writes about the impact it had on him when the discovery of Homo floresiensis was announced in 2004. He realized right away that the descriptions provided by witnesses who'd seen the Ebu Gogo matched the physical characteristics ascribed to Homo floresiensis quite nicely.

The leader of the team that discovered Homo floresiensis, archaeologist Mike Morwood from the University of Wollongong in Australia, had also heard the stories about Ebu Gogo. Notably, he said the alleged creature "fitted floresiensis to a T."

It was said that the Ebu Gogo were fast runners, had very hairy bodies, broad faces, large noses, and could even mimic human words. Villagers were always cautious in the forests because it was thought the Ebu Gogo would kidnap children and eat human babies when given the chance.

All over the world there are other, similar looking creatures to the Ebu Gogo, like the short Homo Luzonensis discovered in the Philippines in 2007, and the Orang Pendek from Sumatra, the Nittaewo or Nittevo from Sri Lanka, the Menehune from Hawaii, the Maeroero from New Zealand, and the Nit-Nit, Nimbinj or Junjeri from Australia. All of these names identify types of small, hairy humanoids that are most likely related not only to each other, but to us as well.

This idea also extends to Sasquatch and others of the "big hairy cryptid hominids" group. If they actually exist, they are probably closely related to humans. However, we could write an entire book about beasties such as Sasquatch, Bigfoot, Yeti, Alma, and the rest that have been seen all across the world. For the sake of this book, such a creature would hardly be able to walk around a city street without being instantly noticed. That is, unless it got itself a good shave and a haircut, and then, looking past its huge size, it may pass as a human.

KISSING COUSINS

I'm not suggesting that some mimics are actually shaved Sasquatches, trying to get by in this cold, hard world just like the rest of us. What I am suggesting is that archaic human species such as Homo floresiensis and, whatever the hell a Bigfoot is, could still be with us. They didn't all go extinct and are living in the wild, desolate places scattered all across the world. And if these archaic human groups managed to stay alive, what about a human group that is much closer to us genetically?

Humans have the distinct ability to survive almost everywhere on the planet. I don't think it is a far stretch of the imagination to suggest that another species of humans, smart enough to realize that Homo sapiens is a formidable threat, decided their best line of defense would be to completely isolate themselves away from violent, crazy humans.

At first, like their more archaic, hairy cousins, the others moved into the deep forests, deserts and mountains to get away from humans. Eventually, they were forced to move into natural caves, which they later added onto with their own tunnels, until their civilization was entirely underground (with underwater enclaves as well).

Human societies have mythologies reaching back thousands of years that speak of the underground people – or demons, angels etc. – they've been given many names. Some of these ancient traditions claim that certain tribes are descendants of the mysterious underground people.

The underground people may have a technology that is slightly ahead of our own, but their greatest talent is subterfuge. This would make sense if you are a race of people who have spent the last 100,000 years steering clear of humans. You would have to develop some amazing abilities of trickery and deception to remain alive. Nevertheless, it is impossible to remain unseen all of the time. And this is where their ability to deceive and control us becomes useful.

What I am expounding here is not a new theory. It has been modernized to include some of the "new" mysteries like UFOs, but it has been around for a long time. In the 1940s you had Richard Shaver who claimed that there was a race of ancient underground deviants that he called "Deros." The Deros were an ancient human race (with some extraterrestrial giants thrown in for good measure) that were forced to go underground a million years ago. Since that time they have grown bored and cranky and use their ancient technology to bedevil those of us who live on the surface world.

The late Mac Tonnies helped resurrect the idea of another species hiding on Earth for the 21st century. He was in the finishing stages of his book *"The Cryptoterrestrials: A Meditation on Indigenous Humanoids and the Aliens Among Us,"* when he unexpectedly passed away. This was a great loss as Tonnies hadn't quite fleshed out his ideas when he died. However, his influence has continued with others carrying on with his research.

Using the UFO mystery as an example for this theory, we can see that modern accounts of human-looking extraterrestrials are as inconsistent as they are baffling. With the 1950s contactees, the "Space Brothers" said they were from Mars and Venus. Later it was distant star systems, and now galaxies and interdimensional realms. These accounts all seem to keep pace with our understanding of the universe.

A lack of consistency in these stories suggests some kind of deception. Could their actual origin be Earth, hence the misdirection? That would also explain their human-like appearance in many accounts. This could also explain their interest in us not blowing ourselves up with nuclear weapons. After all, this is their planet as well and they are obviously more rational than us and not intent on destroying our only home.

There was an interesting case that occurred in Sidney, Australia, in 1992. A man named Peter Khoury claimed to have had an encounter with two bizarre female beings that appeared in his bedroom early one morning. The two females were completely naked; one he described as having blonde hair and the other had dark skin and Asian features. The blonde seemed to be giving telepathic instructions to the other on sexual responses, but Khoury wasn't in the mood to cooperate and the two vanished just as mysteriously as they appeared.

Later that morning, Khoury discovered two strands of long, blonde hair wrapped tightly around his penis (both he and his wife were dark haired). Knowing this was something that he could offer as evidence to his weird encounter, he smartly saved the hairs in a zip-lock bag.

With help from UFO researcher Bill Chalker, the hair was taken to a laboratory and analyzed. The DNA results were startling.

Remarkably, the DNA showed a combination found among a small percentage of the British population and Basques of northern Spain, combined with a rare Chinese-Mongol type found in a very small population group in Taiwan. Due to a combination of genetic factors involving melanin, it is thought impossible that such a theoretical person could ever be blonde.

The hair DNA was extremely rare and it was highly unlikely that Khoury could have just discovered the hair by chance. When viewed in the context of Cryptoterrestrial theory, the DNA sample provides perhaps the first plausible evidence for the possibility that at least one group of our mimic friends is another branch of humanity living underground. (*"Hair of the Alien: DNA and Other Forensic Evidence of Alien Abductions"* – By Bill Chalker, 2005, Gallery Books)

BACK TO CONCLUSIONS

This brings us back to the beginning of this chapter... "conclusions," can any be made? I have often been cautious and avoided anyone who claims to have the definitive answers to anything from the world of the weird. One reason is that paranormal phenomena (and I'm including UFOs, cryptids, etc.) is subtly evasive. As soon as you think you are on to some profound truth, it changes course and takes on a new persona and characteristics.

The other problem is that the phenomena will actually lead you along by providing events that appear to confirm your favorite conclusions. John Keel once speculated that some UFO occupants appeared to be reptilian in nature. That same week, his "silent-contactees" started calling him, worried about their extraterrestrial friends who had suddenly starting acting snake-like and even asking to eat raw eggs from their refrigerator.

For those reading this book who love direct, to the point answers, you're going to be disappointed. We have mimics who appear to be physical creatures, which look human, but are not. We have mimics that appear to have paranormal characteristics, which also can look human, but are not. Then we have mimics that can act both ways and refuse to be pinned down one way or another.

Are we dealing with physical creatures...extraterrestrials, cryptoterrestrials, time travelers, etc.? Or are they paranormal...creatures from another realm of reality with the ability to interact with our physical world?

Maybe it's all of the above.

Maybe it's none of the above.

Maybe we should stop trying to be the first to find that elusive unified-field answer. And instead just continue to gather and investigate reports as they come in and not outright dismiss them because they seem "too weird to be true." I think that by introducing the fact that there are "others" with us on this planet, whatever their origins, we will come a long way toward coming to terms with how little we actually understand the universe we live in.

CONTRIBUTORS

Timothy Green Beckley

Tim Beckley was well deserving of the status of a true pioneer in the UFO/paranormal fields. In addition to having founded, as a teenager, his own niche publishing company, Inner Light/Global Communications (with over 300 volumes in print), Beckley said he must have been duly influenced by the strange goings on around him. His grandfather was frightened by a headless horseman; his life was saved by an invisible hand at age three; he lived in a house that was haunted; and has had three UFO encounters, the first at ten-years-old.

Beckley started his writing career early on. His published articles have appeared in "Fate," "Beyond Reality," "Saga," and "UFO Report." For many years he served as a stringer for "The Enquirer" and edited over 30 newsstand publications, including "UFO Universe," which lasted for over 11 years before almost everything became digital. He has appeared on a multitude of radio and TV shows, going back as far as the Long John Nebel program in the 1960s, and William Shatner's "Weird or What?" program.

Scott Corrales

Scott Corrales is a prolific writer and investigator of UFO and paranormal events in the Hispanic communities worldwide, he is one of the most respected names in the global world of UFOlogy, with contacts in South and Central America, Mexico, Spain and the Caribbean. The Institute of Hispanic Ufology was established in October of 1998 with the appearance of the first issue of "Inexplicata."The organization currently has representatives and contributing editors in over a dozen Spanish-speaking countries.

Scott has also authored and contributed to such books as: "*Alien Artifacts*," "*Chupacabras and Other Mysteries*," "*Alien Blood Lust*," "*UFO Repeaters*," "*Alien Lives Matter*."

Visit his website at: inexplicata.blogspot.com

Sean Casteel

Sean Casteel is a freelance journalist who has been writing about UFOs, alien abduction and many other paranormal subjects since 1989. Sean's writing appeared in many UFO and paranormal-related magazines, including "UFO Magazine," Tim Beckley's "UFO Universe," "Fate," "Mysteries Magazine," and "Open Minds Magazine," most of which are now defunct but were a major part of a thriving UFO press in their heyday. Magazines in the UK, Italy, Romania and Australia have also published Sean's work.

Sean has written or contributed to over 30 books for Global Communications and Inner Light Publications, all of which are available from Amazon.com. Sean's books include *"Alien Artifacts," "The Excluded Books of the Bible," "UFOs, Armageddon and Biblical Revelations: Signs, Symbols and Wonders - The Whole Truth!," "The Heretic's UFO Guidebook,"* which analyzes a selection of Gnostic Christian writings and their relationship to the UFO phenomenon, and *"Signs and Symbols of the Second Coming,"* in which he interviews several religious and paranormal experts about how prophecies of the Second Coming of Christ may be fulfilled.

Paul Eno

Now celebrating more than 50 years in paranormal research, Paul Eno is one of the world's most experienced and controversial supernatural adventurers. One of the first ghost investigators of the early 1970s, beginning while he was studying for the priesthood, his theories and methods are now shaking the paranormal world to its core. Paul's early mentors included parapsychology pioneer Dr. Louisa Rhine, Fr. John J. Nicola S.J. (technical advisor for the film The Exorcist) and legendary, first-generation ghost hunters Ed & Lorraine Warren (of The Conjuring fame).

Paul graduated from two seminaries but, in 1977, was expelled from a third because of his paranormal work with less than two years to go before ordination. He ended up as an award-winning New England journalist, including six years as a news editor at "The Providence Journal."

He is the author of eight books on the paranormal and two on history. Some of his books include: *"Behind The Paranormal: Everything You*

Know Is Wrong," "*Footsteps In The Attic,*" "*Faces At The Window,*" "*Dancing Past the Graveyard.*"

Along with his son, Ben, Paul has co-hosted the CBS Radio (2009-2014) and WOON 1240 AM/99.3 FM Boston/Worcester/Providence Sunday destination show "Behind the Paranormal with Paul & Ben Eno" for nearly 13 years. The show has an estimated three million listeners in 60 counties.

Chris Holly

Chris Holly spent a great deal of her life building different entrepreneur ventures, however her one true passion has always been writing. Chris found out long ago it was far easier to explain the paranormal by way of a true story told in an interesting form. She lived a life filled with extreme experiences and unique events involving that which we do not understand and felt it her destiny to tell these true events to the world by way of her short stories or articles based on true experiences of her own or reports told to her by those who read her work.

Chris is known to be a writer who will protect her sources understanding how difficult the world can be to those who come forward with experiences of the unknown. Chris learned how cold the world can be to those who have encountered the paranormal. She learned this lesson as a young woman after her own UFO event. Chris has been writing Chris Holly's Endless Journey with the Unknown for many years as well as hosting on many radio shows that cover the unknown.

You can read her articles on her site, "Chris Holly's Endless Journey With The Unknown" as well as other outlets, including "Phantoms & Monsters."

Hercules Invictus

Hercules Invictus is a Lemnian Greek, a proud descendant of Argonauts and Amazons. He is openly Olympian in his spirituality and worldview, dedicated to living the Mythic Life, and has been exploring the fringes of our reality throughout his entire earthly sojourn. For over four decades he has been sharing his Olympian Odyssey with others. Having relocated the heart of his Temenos to Northeastern New Jersey and the Greater New York Metropolitan Area, he is now establishing his unique niche locally and contributing to his community's overall quality of life. Hercules is also recruiting Argonauts to help him usher in a new Age of Heroes.

Hercules has published two e-books on Kindle *"Olympian Ice"* and *"The Antediluvial Scrolls"* and has contributing to such books as: *"Tim R. Swartz's Big Book of Incredible Alien Encounters,"* *"Alien Strongholds on Earth,"* *"Alien Artifacts."*

Visit Hercules YouTube channel:
www.youtube.com/@HerculesInvictus

Philip Kinsella

Philip Kinsella is both a clairvoyant medium and UFO investigator/author. Having had many bizarre UFO/paranormal experiences throughout his life, along with his identical twin brother, Ronald, he began to research the phenomenon on a serious level of investigations after an alien abduction in 1989. This led to him writing several books: *"Reaching for the Divine: How to Communicate effectively with your Spirit Guides and Loved Ones on the Other Side,"* *"Believe: Bridging the gap between the psychic and UFO phenomenon,"* "A Passage Through Eternity: The Enigma of the Dead, UFOs & Aliens," and *"SKY CRASH – Throughout Time: A Continued Investigation Into the Rendlesham UFO Mystery."*

Philip, along with his brother co-host a radio program for the Paranormal UK Radio called "Twin Souls" where they interview many authors/experiencers/investigators on all topics within the world of the bizarre. He is currently working on more books surrounding the UFO field of investigations. Philip Kinsella can be contacted on email at: philip.kinsella2@aol.co.uk

Brent Raynes

Brent Raynes has been researching and investigating the unexplained since January 1967, at age 14, and is the author of *"Visitors from Hidden Realms,"* *"On the Edge of Reality,"* and *"John A. Keel: The Man, The Myths, and the Ongoing Mysteries."*

Brent began "Alternate Perceptions" Magazine back in 1985 as simply a 4-page newsletter entitled "ParaUFOlogy Forum." It has come a long way since it's early beginning. In 1993, good friend and colleague Dr. Gregory Little, who had been contributing articles from the get-go, came onboard as a publisher and co-editor, and pretty soon it was a very professionally done color cover magazine of some 58 pages, with distributors from coast to coast and up into Canada. Then around 2000, we followed the growing trend and moved the magazine, which had become Alternate Perceptions, onto the internet.

www.apmagazine.info Email Brent at brentraynes@yahoo.com

Paul Dale Roberts

Paul Dale Roberts is a Fortean investigator who delves into ALL things paranormal – from Mothman, to the Chupacabra, UFOs, Crop Circles, Ghosts, Poltergeists, Demons and more. Roberts is the HPI (Hegelianism Paranormal Intelligence – International) Owner. www.facebook.com/groups/HPIinternational

Roberts writes community stories and is a former columnist for "The Sacramento Press," former columnist for "Haunted Times Magazine," and has written small blurbs for "Newsweek," "Time," "National Geographic Traveler" and "People Magazine."

Roberts was recently picked up by "Paranormal Magazine UK" and works for the online national news site "Before It's News." Roberts' articles are featured in some of the legendary Brad Steiger's books as well as books by Timothy Green Beckley. Roberts has now published four books in the HPI Chronicles series.

Gene Steinberg

Veteran UFO researcher Gene Steinberg is Host and Executive Producer of The Paracast (www.theparacast.com), considered since its 2006 debut as "the gold standard of paranormal radio." In his "other life," he is the author of numerous articles and over 30 books on personal technology, plus two sci-fi novels.

Lon Strickler

Lon Strickler is a Fortean researcher, author and publisher of the syndicated Phantoms & Monsters blog. He began the blog in 2005, which has steadily grown in popularity and is read daily by tens of thousands of paranormal enthusiasts, investigators and those seeking the truth.

His research and reports have been featured on hundreds of online media sources. Several of these published reports have been presented on various television segments, including; The History Channel's Ancient Aliens, SYFY's Paranormal Witness, Fact or Faked: Paranormal Files, and Destination America's Monsters and Mysteries in America. He has been interviewed on several radio broadcasts, including multiple guest appearances on Coast to Coast AM.

Lon is the author of such books as: *"The Meme Humanoids: Modern Myths or Real Monsters," "Alien Disclosure: Experiencers Expose Reality," "Winged Cryptids: Humanoids, Monsters & Anomalous Creatures Casebook," "Mothman Dynasty: Chicago's Winged Humanoids," "Phantoms & Monsters: Strange Encounters."*

Tim R. Swartz

Tim R. Swartz is an Indiana native and an Emmy-Award winning television producer and videographer. He is also the author of *"Gef The Talking Mongoose: The Eighth Wonder of the World," "Alien Artifacts," "The Lost Journals of Nikola Tesla," "Tim R. Swartz's Big Book of Incredible Alien Encounters," "Time Travel: Fact Not Fiction,"* and many others.

As a photojournalist, Tim has traveled extensively and investigated paranormal phenomena and other unusual mysteries in such diverse locations as the Great Pyramid in Egypt to the Great Wall in China. He has also appeared on the History Channel programs "The Tesla Files," "Ancient Aliens"; "Ancient Aliens: Declassified" and the History Channel Latin America series "Contacto Extraterrestre."

His articles have been published in magazines such as "Fate," "Strange," "Atlantis Rising," "UFO Universe," "Mysteries," "Renaissance," and "Unsolved UFO Reports."

Tim is also the co-host of the radio show The Paracast along with Gene Steinberg. - www.theparacast.com

Nigel Watson

Nigel Watson has researched and investigated historical and contemporary reports of UFO sightings since the 1970s. In the 1980s, he gained a BA degree in Psychology (Open University) and a BA (Hons) degree in Film and Literature (University of Warwick).

He is the author of *"Portraits of Alien Encounters"* (VALIS, 1990), *"Phantom Aerial Flaps and Waves"* (VALIS, 1990), *"Supernatural Spielberg"* (with Darren Slade, VALIS, 1992), editor/writer of *"The Scareship Mystery: A Survey of Phantom Airship Scares, 1909 – 1918"* (DOMRA, 2000), *"The UFO Investigations Manual"* (Haynes, 2013)," *"UFOs of the First World War"* (The History Press, 2015). For the UneXplained Rapid Reads e-book series he wrote; *"UFOs: The Nazi Connection," "Spontaneous Human Combustion," "UFO Government Secrets, The Great UFO Cover-Up,"* and *"Ghostships of the Skies"* (all 2015).

He has also written for numerous books including *"UFO Hostilities," "Area 51 – Keep Out!" "Alien Artifacts."*

John Weigle

John Weigle was born in 1941 and would live his life as a California native. After his mother had a UFO encounter in the 1950s, John would become a lifelong believer, in spite of having no sightings of his own. After a brief stint in the army, he completed a BA degree in journalism and began working as a reporter and editor for the Ventura County Star Press, the local daily newspaper. He was also the director of the Ventura County chapter of the Mutual UFO Network (MUFON) for a few years.

He was the coauthor, with Timothy Green Beckley and Sean Casteel, of a book called *"Disclosure! Breaking Through the Barrier of Global UFO Secrecy,"* as well as coauthoring with Sean Casteel articles for the now defunct newsstand publication "UFO Magazine" and the website "UFO Digest." John was also an avid stamp collector, presiding over various collector organizations and leading an annual youth stamp fair in Ventura. He died in 2020.

Brian Young

Brian Young is a researcher, writer, historian, lecturer and podcast host. He specializes in Boxing history, Victorian crime, with a focus on The Whitechapel Murders (Jack the Ripper) and has had a lifelong interest in the weird, the wild and the paranormal.

He is Co-author of the critically acclaimed *"The Wrestlers Wrestlers': Masters of the Craft of Professional Wrestling"* (2021 ECW Press) and is co-host of "Transatlantic History Ramblings," an international podcast hosted out of The United States and Wales UK.

INDEX

MIMICS – THE OTHERS AMONG US

If you have any questions or comments about this book, please email us at: commanderx12@hotmail.com

TIMOTHY GREEN BECKLEY'S

ALIEN ARTIFACTS

Incredible Evidence of Exotic Material From UFO Encounters

Sean Casteel And Tim R. Swartz

Additional Material By: Scott Corrales, Tom Hackney, Hercules Invictus, Mark Olly, Calvin Parker, Paul Dale Roberts, Alejandro Rojas, Gene Steinberg, Lon Strickler, Diane Tessman, Nigel Watson

www.ingramcontent.com/pod-product-compliance
Lightning Source LLC
Chambersburg PA
CBHW081412270326
41931CB00015B/3246